One Breath at a Time

One Breath at a Time

BUDDHISM

AND THE

TWELVE STEPS

KEVIN GRIFFIN

RODALE

The Twelve Steps and a brief excerpt from the book *Alcoholics Anonymous* are reprinted with permission of Alcoholics Anonymous World Services, Inc. (A.A.W.S.). Permission to reprint brief excerpts from the book *Alcoholics Anonymous* (pages 59, 60, 64, and 85) does not mean that A.A.W.S. has reviewed or approved the contents of this publication, or that A.A.W.S. necessarily agrees with the views expressed herein. A.A. is a program of recovery from alcoholism only; use of the Twelve Steps in connection with programs and activities which are patterned after A.A., but which address other problems, or in any other non-A.A. context, does not imply otherwise.

Excerpt from *After the Ecstasy, the Laundry* by Jack Kornfield reprinted with permission of Bantam Books/ Random House.

Excerpt from *The Kabir Book* by Robert Bly copyright © 1971, 1977 by Robert Bly; © 1977 by the Seventies Press; reprinted by permission of Beacon Press, Boston.

Excerpt from *The Life of the Buddha* by Bhikkhu Nanamoli used by permission of Buddhist Publication Society.

Excerpt from "Small Boat, Great Mountain" by Amaro Bhikkhu, Abhayagiri Monastic Foundation, used by permission of author.

Excerpt from "Christianity and Buddhism," unpublished manuscript by Buddhadasa Bhikkhu, translated by Santikaro Bhikkhu

Buddhadasa Bhikkhu, *Christ-Dharma, Buddha-Dharma* (original in Thai), unpublished translation by Santikaro Bhikkhu, to be published in 2005.

Printed in the United States of America
Rodale Inc. makes every effort to use acid-free ∞ , recycled paper ♻ .

Book design by Christopher Rhoads

Library of Congress Cataloging-in-Publication Data

Griffin, Kevin Edward, date.
    One breath at a time : Buddhism and the twelve steps / Kevin Griffin.
      p.   cm.
    ISBN 1–57954–905–5 paperback
    1. Twelve-step programs—Religious aspects—Buddhism. 2. Self-help techniques—Religious aspects—Buddhism. 3. Compulsive behavior—Moral and ethical aspects. 4. Wisdom—Religious aspects—Buddhism. 5. Spiritual life—Buddhism. I. Title.
    BQ4570.T85G74   2004
    294.3'4442—dc22   2004004016

Distributed to the book trade by St. Martin's Press

2   4   6   8   10   9   7   5   3   1   paperback

Visit us on the Web at www.rodalestore.com, or call us toll-free at (800) 848-4735.

To RG and GLG.

It's with the two of you that I find my deepest comfort.

I send you every bit of my love.

CONTENTS

PART THREE
FULFILLMENT

PREFACE

If you're an alcoholic or addict, you're probably too impatient to read a preface. "Get me to the important stuff, I don't have time for this." Still, there are a few things you should know about this book before you begin reading.

First of all, the title is wrong. Well, the subtitle. My background is mostly in one school of Buddhism, the Theravada, or Way of the Elders. Out of this tradition comes the very popular Vipassana, or insight, practice of meditation. But, if I'd called the book *One Breath at a Time: Theravada/Vipassana and the Twelve Steps* it just wouldn't have had the same ring. So, my apologies to the Mahayana, Vajrayana, and other schools of Buddhism.

When I talk about "alcoholics" or "addicts" in the book, I mean these terms in a general way. I include overeaters, sex addicts, compulsive gamblers, codependents, AlAnon members, debtors, adult children of alcoholics, and anyone else who might find benefit in using the Twelve Steps. People from all these groups, and more, have attended my workshops and benefited. Certain concepts will fit more specifically substance abusers, but my experience is that many similar feelings and behaviors appear in people who have all kinds of dysfunctional behavior.

Beyond this obvious audience, I believe the greater population of Buddhists and other meditation practitioners can benefit from applying Twelve Step principles. As I've probed the Steps deeper and deeper, I've seen how they illuminate my meditation practice; they are not just tools for recovery, but an archetypal spiritual path in and of themselves.

Many people when they hear I'm writing a book on Buddhism and the Twelve Steps think I'm going to rewrite the Steps from a Buddhist perspective. I'm not. I love the Steps, I honor and respect them; that's why I'm writing a book about them. I'm trying to translate the Steps and discover their relationship with Buddhism, but I'm not trying to change them.

Some people have asked if they could see my manuscript because they were having a hard time getting sober in Twelve Step meetings and they hoped my book would offer an alternative. I'm a meditation teacher and I've been sober for a while, but I'm not an addiction counselor or a therapist. I'm no expert on substance abuse—except my own. This book isn't really meant to get you sober but rather to deepen your spiritual life in sobriety.

What I think people are really saying when they don't like Twelve Step meetings or programs is, "I don't want to do this. I don't want to admit I'm powerless, find a Higher Power, write an inventory, make amends. Isn't there an easier way?" Maybe, but I haven't found one. The problem isn't really the Steps or the program or the meetings or "those people." The problem is that getting clean and sober and rebuilding your life is difficult and painful work. Whether you use the Twelve Steps or some other system, it's going to be hard. Choose your poison—or I guess I should say, choose your antidote.

The names of all Twelve Step members whose stories are used in the book have been changed, except for one who has published a memoir. A few of the people are composites, and most of the dialogue is from memory. I was fortunate to be able to interview Ajahn Amaro, whose quotations are transcribed from that interview.

May all beings be free from suffering.

INTRODUCTION

I knew when I started writing this book that I wanted it to follow the Twelve Steps, exploring them one by one in a linear way. As it unfolds, nothing else is linear about the book. I write about the distant past, the near past, and the present whenever they serve to illustrate the ideas I want to talk about. My driving questions were, How does this Step relate to Buddhism and its practices, and what practical use can be made of these connections? Some of the connections surprised even me; the book is a true exploration in this way—I didn't follow a map and I didn't know how I would get to my destination. So, for instance, I find myself talking about the first Twelve Step gathering I ever attended in Step Five because Step Five involves sharing.

One of the things that I explore is the language in the Steps. Most of the chapters do this in one way or another, trying to take apart the meaning of terms like *powerlessness* or *defects of character* and put them back together again from a Buddhist perspective.

Anticipating that many of my readers are new to Buddhism, I have tried to cover many of the foundation elements of the teachings as I understand them. Again, because I'm following the Steps and not the Buddhist teachings as a framework, this isn't linear either.

In the spirit of nonlinearity, I start near the end of the story . . .

* * *

TWO WEDDINGS

JULY 3, 1997

I'm rushing down the flagstone path, straightening my yellow-striped tie, when James comes out from behind the tall hedge to catch me.

"Are you okay?" he asks. He puts his hands on my shoulders and looks me in the eye.

"Fine," I say, although I'm actually in something of a daze.

"Okay, take a breath," he says.

I do as he suggests. My heart starts to slow, my shoulders un-hunch.

James leads me around the hedge onto the patio of the Brazil Building. We're in Tilden Park, in the wooded hills above Berkeley. We're here for a wedding. Mine.

And I'm late.

Beyond us is a lawn, which falls away down a hill to the botanical garden. I turn around to look at the crowd and smile broadly. There are the faces of my family, the old one and the new one: two of my brothers, their families, and my soon-to-be in-laws; a group of Buddhist friends who attend the local meditation group with me; and lots of friends from Twelve Step programs who have come to support me on this remarkable day.

James, who has been my meditation teacher and mentor and has fostered my own development as a teacher, is to my right, ready to perform the ceremony. My best man, to my left, is Stephen, my sponsor, who has seen me through the last twelve years of recovery, guiding me through the Steps and through the building of a new life, a life which, on this sunny early July afternoon, includes an event I'd doubted could ever happen.

The piano begins the Pachelbel *Canon*, and Rosemary and her father emerge. I remember James' admonition to breathe. This is a moment I want to be present for; I feel my heart beating rapidly, the glow of joy in my chest, the sun above the building warming my face. I see the crowd following Rosemary's steps toward me. She looks as giddy as I feel, and as beautiful as a bride could ever look.

With all the preparation for this day, I didn't expect the sheer happiness that's overtaken me. It's happening; it's happening *now*, this brave, crazy, inevitable, surprising moment.

We recite our vows— "To hold you dear and to be worthy of your love"—and James leads a Buddhist meditation on lovingkindness, asking everyone to focus kind thoughts on us. "May Rosemary and Kevin be joyful, filled with peace. May their joy touch all beings." And then he asks people to spread this joy outward to all beings, just as the Buddhist sutras suggest. He rings a small Tibetan cymbal and the sound vibrates in the stillness.

Everyone moves inside for the reception, a whirl of food and conversation. There's chicken, which I eat, and wine, which I don't drink. After dinner, a group of my musician friends start to play. Three songs into the set, I join them, changing from my blue suit coat to a shiny lamé jacket, strapping on my Stratocaster and launching into "Blue Suede Shoes." Rosemary twirls across the dance floor, laughing and glowing.

This is the happiest day of my life.

MAY 1982

Another wedding—that of the manager of a rehearsal studio in Cambridge, Massachusetts. The leader of the band I'm playing for owns the studio, so I'm invited partly as a guest and partly as free entertainment.

We're packed into a suburban banquet room, and the soup comes around.

"Does this have beef stock?" I ask the waiter.

"Yes, it does," he says.

"I'll pass," I say. I've been a vegetarian for five years, and it's important to me to maintain this purity. There's plenty of wine, so I pour myself a glass to keep from feeling too hungry while I wait for the next course.

I'm a bit uncomfortable here, since I know hardly anyone. I have another glass of wine, then go looking for a friend who usually has some pot. Without food, the wine is getting me pretty high, and some pot will take the edge off that and help me slow down drinking.

I find Joey out on the patio.

"Hey, man, have you got anything to smoke?" Two other guys are with him.

"I just finished my last joint," he says. "Sorry."

"Is there any more around?"

"I don't know," says Joey. "I'll check it out—hey, nice jacket."

"Thanks." He hasn't seen me in my tan sport coat, brown slacks, and peach tie before. They're left over from a disco band I played for.

I've never seen him dressed for a wedding before, either, and he looks a little odd, his long, straggly hair hanging over the collar of a blue undertaker's suit. Joey's father owns a funeral home, and his sons drive the hearses and help out around the place. Today they're lending some of the limos to the wedding party.

I go back to my table just as they bring around the main course: beef stroganoff. The noodles are drowned in the meat and the salad is all iceberg lettuce. Not even close to organic. I pour some more wine and slather some butter on a roll. I'm getting edgy, not eating anything substantial, being in this alien environment.

Just one season has passed since I left the fall retreat: three months of silent meditation, an intensive training based on the traditional monastic Rains Retreat held each year in Asia. By the end I felt I'd been washed clean, my meditation had become luminous, fluid, lighter than air. I still practice two hours every day and often get to that same place of vast stillness. Only, today I skipped my afternoon sitting to get here, so I'm not quite as serene as usual. I haven't been drinking much or smoking much dope since the retreat. I've always told myself that as my spiritual life deepened, drinking and drugs wouldn't be a problem anymore. Not that I ever admitted they *were* a problem.

The musicians are setting up, and I figure I better get my guitar in tune. I stagger up to the stage.

"Where do you want me to stand?" I ask Chris, the bandleader.

"Uh, I don't know," he says, as he runs a wire behind the drum set. He looks at me oddly. "There's a lot of guitar players here, so maybe you should take the night off."

"But I thought you needed me to play lead."

"Don't worry about it," he says.

I'm a little disappointed and surprised, but I go back to the table and have some more wine. The band plays through a set of old Beatles and Beach Boys songs while I continue to drink.

During the next set a conga line starts, and I slip behind the bride, who is quite attractive. I enjoy holding her hips as we slither around the room. I think I'm a little drunk now, but I can tell she likes me. Of course, I probably shouldn't hit on her right now. Things begin to get a little foggy, and the bar starts charging for drinks. I'm broke, so I sidle up, trying to find someone who'll spot me a five. There's a half-drunk cocktail no one's attending to on the end of the bar. I look around, then pick it up and guzzle it. It tastes like crap—it's got gin in it, which I hate—but it's pretty strong.

"Kev, whatcha doin'?" It's Joey beside me.

"Buy me a beer," I say.

"We gotta get going," he says.

"Come on," I say. "Just one beer."

He pays for the beer and I take a big gulp. The wine isn't mixing so well with the cocktail and the beer, but I manage to get it down.

Joey drags me down the steps where the bride and bridegroom are seeing people off.

"Hey," I say to them. "What sign are you guys?" I figure the bride as a water sign, compatible with me.

They laugh as though I've made some joke and Joey pulls me away. Everyone seems to be treating me as if I were wearing polka-dot pants.

We get in Joey's white limousine and head back toward Cambridge. My stomach's queasy as a squabble breaks out among the wine, beer, and gin.

"Where's my beer?" I ask Joey.

"You finished it," he says.

We come onto the bridge across the Charles going into Cambridge. I'm really nauseous now.

"Roll down my window!" I shout.

The window goes down and I lean out of the car. I vomit down the side of the sparkling white limousine.

Hours later I wake up, still dressed in the tan sport coat and brown slacks. My peach tie is still on, though loosened. I'm lying on my futon. I open my eyes. Something smells awful. Then I see it: I'm covered in vomit. I've thrown up in my sleep. Gingerly, I move to get up; then the shattering headache explodes. I want to fall back onto the bed but the pillow is also coated in puke. I roll over, trying not to touch anything. I go into the bathroom, strip, and turn on the shower. I choke down four aspirin and climb in the steaming water. Vague memories of the night pop up and I groan at the images, each one more humiliating than the last.

I think of Jimi Hendrix, who vomited in his sleep, choked, and died. That could have happened to me. Only I wouldn't be remembered as the greatest guitar player in the world, just some guy who never got it together.

If only they'd had a vegetarian option on the menu, I think, or if only Joey had had some pot.

Who, me?

It's amazing the lengths of convoluted thinking to which an alcoholic will go to avoid the truth. Getting drunk, hitting on the bride, blacking out, and waking up in your own vomit is not "normal" drinking. But on that day I wrote it all off as a small glitch.

Although I'd been practicing meditation for four years, and Buddhist meditation for two, I was still far from the serenity that Buddhism promised. The blind spots in my spiritual development were glaring—or at least should have been. Something wasn't falling into place for me, and I couldn't see what it was.

Over the next three years I would fall back, ending up lost in a fog of booze and drugs, barely hanging on to the semblance of a meditation practice, much less a spiritual life. I would flounder in my career, bumble through relationships, and finally lose all sense of integrity and morality.

Still, the idea that I was an alcoholic and addict was unfathomable to me. My associations with those words—a drunk collapsed in an alley, a junkie with a needle hanging out of his arm—seemed much more extreme than my case. I kept telling myself I was going to get it together in my own way, that some magical event like rock stardom or enlightenment would save me. Of course, it didn't.

Putting it together

It may be more common that people come to meditation and Buddhism after working with the Twelve Steps, rather than, like me, practicing Buddhism first. The Eleventh Step encourages people to make meditation a regular part of their lives, and Buddhism is known for its effective meditation techniques. Also, Buddhism offers an alternative to the Judeo-Christian slant found in the Twelve Step literature. Issues of God and faith, of prayer and powerlessness can alienate people who have never had a religious training, or who have rejected their religious upbringing.

As I began a life without drugs and booze, I joined a support group where I had to make sense of the Steps for myself. At first I tried to suspend my discomfort with the Christian tenor of the literature. I saw that the authors of the Twelve Steps used their Protestant background very skillfully in building a spiritual program, at times touching the deepest meanings of this tradition. But, finally, that wasn't a tradition that touched my heart, and I had to bring an authentic understanding of the Steps into alignment with my Buddhist training and beliefs.

At first it seemed that admitting my alcoholism didn't fit with my search for the perfection of nirvana. Digging around in my past by doing the Fourth Step inventory seemed opposed to the idea of living fully in the present. Going to meetings and talking about my pain and the difficulties of sobriety seemed negative and self-indulgent.

Over time, though, I found that the ideas behind the Steps have parallels in the Buddhist tradition, and that using the two together brought a deeper experience to my Buddhist meditation and a more satisfying, integrated understanding to the Steps.

What makes Buddhism and the Twelve Steps so compatible? The Buddha said that the cause of suffering is desire, and the Twelve Steps try to heal people from desire gone mad: addiction. This connection is the gateway into integrating the two systems. Both ask you to look at the painful realities of life, to understand them, and to use this understanding as the foundation for developing peace, wisdom, faith, and compassion. Both systems culminate in an "awakening" or "enlightenment."

Their respective means may seem very different at times: for the Twelve Steps, support groups, dependence on a higher power, writing inventory; for Buddhism, sitting meditation, developing mindfulness and lovingkindness, following the precepts. But I have found that as I learned more about both traditions, the deeper means and purposes of each came into harmony: understanding powerlessness helps me let go in my meditation practice; investigating my mind in meditation helps me do inventory work; listening to the suffering of others in self-help groups develops my heart of compassion. This book begins an exploration of the many connections between these two traditions, and I hope it will help you to develop the understanding and tools to harmonize them for yourself.

I believe that even if you are not an alcoholic or addict, these tools can serve your meditation practice. The stories of alcoholism and drug addiction can even be thought of as dramatizations of common, subtler behaviors and mind states which meditators often see in their practice. The integration of the Steps with Buddhism can still be applied skillfully to these behaviors and states.

WHO NEEDS IT?

Although my writing is often directed toward the person in recovery or the Buddhist practitioner, the heart of this book is the timeless truth that speaks to every spiritual seeker. Beyond the needs of recovery, the Twelve Steps can be seen as an archetypal journey, just as the Buddhist teachings seek to solve the human dilemma of suffering.

Not everyone will feel the need to combine these traditions. As a practitioner and teacher of Buddhist meditation I've met many people who didn't need anything more than those teachings to fulfill their spiritual lives. In my years of recovery, I've also met many people whose spiritual aspirations were completely fulfilled by the Steps. I admire and respect these people. But I needed a strong dose of both remedies to find fulfillment. I need the discipline and depth of concentration and mindfulness which Buddhist practice has brought me; I need the honest self-appraisal and practical tools for living that I learned in recovery. I need the wisdom of the Buddha to absorb the realities and mysteries of life; and I need the voices of a thousand alcoholics and addicts to keep me on track today.

One Breath at a Time

Part One

SURRENDER

Steps One through Three can be characterized as the Surrender Steps. First, a surrender to the truth of our disease and our inability to control it; then surrendering to a Higher Power, seeing that we will have to depend on something besides our own will and knowledge to stay sober and develop spiritually.

No one wants to surrender. The word itself implies failure and vanquishment on the field of battle. But as we enter the process, we often find that it's the battle itself—with drugs and alcohol, with the world, with ourselves—that has crippled us in many ways. In this case, surrender becomes preferable to going on fighting.

Surrender is a traditional element of every spiritual journey. Before we can begin to realize our potential, we must break out of limiting concepts of who and what we are and what we think is possible. This may mean giving up long-held beliefs and comfortable behavior patterns. Cynicism or fantasy, fear or control, anger or grief—many of us cling to these patterns and others. As we begin to surrender, we see that we will have to let go of these destructive habits of mind before we can move toward freedom.

The Twelve Steps are a great tool in this movement. While many people tend to think of spirituality as looking up, toward the heights of perfection or saintliness, the Steps remind us that we must first look down, into the darkness of our souls, and see and accept our shadow before we attain an honest and authentic spiritual life. Until we explore the difficult side of our nature, our spiritual work will always lack depth and integrity. Our hearts and minds are complex and mysterious; they can only be known through the heroic work that begins with surrender.

STEP ONE

"We admitted we were powerless over alcohol;
that our lives had become unmanageable."

In Twelve Step parlance, we "work" the Steps. There's effort involved, action—we're not just thinking about them or meditating on them—and the work of Step One is quitting drinking—or drugging, overeating, gambling, or whatever activity brought us to this point. We don't just "admit" we've got a problem, we do something about it. Often what precedes that action is what's called a "moment of clarity," that brief flash where we suddenly see the truth of our situation. In that moment we can no longer hide from the suffering we are experiencing—and causing. The light of awareness shines, sometimes blindingly, on our devastated lives.

In Buddhism, this moment of clarity is called "Right View," and is the first stage of the Eightfold Path—the Buddha's practical blueprint for spiritual development. With Right View we more generally see the truth of suffering—our own and that of others, and we also start to develop a vision of the possibility of freedom.

For me, a "moment of clarity" and "Right View" both are pointing to a kind of seeing, something visual. To bring this metaphor together, the type of meditation that I practice and teach is called *Vipassana*, usually translated as "insight meditation." Vipassana means to "see clearly."

Rather than understanding wisdom as an intellectual process, this language points to the senses, grounding our understanding of the truth in the body, rather than the mind. Right View means the blinders are taken away and we see the truth clearly; a moment of clarity is when the lies we've lived with fall away and the stark reality of our disease is revealed to us. This vision is the beginning of recovery and the beginning of the path of awakening.

A BOTTOM

June 6, 1985

Every alcoholic or addict reaches a bottom, a moment when the misery of addiction becomes so overwhelming that it's impossible to ignore any longer. Unfortunately, for me it took another three years after the Cambridge wedding to reach that point. My bottom didn't come in one of my many blackouts or incidents of driving drunk; it didn't come during the violent fights with my girlfriend in my twenties, or when I was arrested for possession of methadrine at nineteen. It came quietly in my own moment of clarity at age thirty-five.

I was standing in the doorway of the Red Robin, a restaurant in a suburban L.A. mini-mall. My friend Steve was making a final trip out to his car after packing up his drums. The last-call lights in the bar shone brightly as the waitress cleaned the semicircular red leatherette booths and blew out the teardrop candles.

"Now I remember why I don't like playing in bars," said Steve. He carried his snare drum case in one hand, his stick bag in the other. "I hate drunks." He waved his sticks toward three stragglers hanging on their barstools. The one on the end was arguing with the bartender about getting one more drink. The other two were squabbling about a spilled beer, which one of them was wiping off with the other's sweater.

I tried to conceal my own state of inebriation, shamefully aware of the cold, green bottle of Heineken I was holding in my hand. I had no idea this would be my last drink of alcohol.

We had just been fired from the gig because I'd tried to throw an un-rehearsed band together on a moment's notice out of desperation. Steve, a drummer good enough to do studio work in L.A.'s highly competitive recording scene, had only been playing with me as a favor.

When Steve said he hated drunks, he wasn't talking about me, but I still heard it that way.

For a long time I'd been telling myself that drinking wasn't my problem. Neither was smoking pot, which I did as often as I drank. No, my problems were women, money, depression; my lack of spiritual at-tainment; my failure as a musician. If only I could solve these issues, I thought, the drinking and drugs wouldn't be a problem.

But I couldn't solve these problems, and they'd only increased over the past three years. After the wedding in Cambridge I ran off with a New Age guru who promised instant enlightenment. After three months of "living on faith" with him in a mad crisscrossing of North America, I bailed out—losing faith not only in him, but in myself. He had insisted I stop practicing Buddhism, so even that support was lost for a time. While living on the streets of Venice Beach, I fell back more and more into drinking and taking drugs.

Finally I found a job, and then another band. I moved in with a new girlfriend, Margaret. But soon she was accusing me of being an alco-holic. One day I promised her I would stop. That night the drummer in the band got me stoned in the parking lot of the club we were playing. I wasn't drinking, so I thought it was okay. Before long, though, with a beer here and a shot there, I was back to daily drinking, along with the pot.

Margaret persisted in her accusations. Angry with her, I began an af-fair with the waitress at the Red Robin, and after a few months my life had lost all semblance of sanity: every night I drove Margaret's car for an hour to the Red Robin where I drank beer, smoked pot, snorted cocaine, and made out with the waitress in her blue Corvette on my breaks. Oh yeah, I also played old rock 'n' roll songs for a bored audience.

And all the while I was thinking that I was a spiritual person.

When the band wanted to go on the road, I quit and tried to hold the same gig with Steve on drums and some pickup musicians. We went in without rehearsing and quickly got fired.

Although I was still unconvinced that drugs and drinking were my real problem, it seemed like my whole life had become too much of a mess. I had to stop.

I was lucky. When I woke up the morning after the Red Robin, my hangover was slight but my resolve was strong. That first surrender—the first of many—seemed effortless. I'd finally given up fighting the idea that I was an alcoholic. I felt the great burden of addiction and compulsion lifted and a confidence in my decision. Somehow I knew it would stick. This was one of those mysterious moments of grace that come to so many recovering alcoholics. I had no idea where my life was headed, but I knew instinctively that I was going in the right direction, that I'd be okay.

I was wary of joining a Twelve Step program—I wasn't much of a joiner—but I felt that it would be unlucky at least, dangerous at worst, to refuse to at least check it out. While I felt confident in my commitment to stop drinking and using, I'd seen myself through enough binge cycles to know that there's always the possibility of falling back.

Still, a couple of weeks passed before I went to my first Twelve Step gathering, and then only because Margaret was going. I shook no one's hand and didn't raise my own hand; I took no phone numbers and spoke to no one but Margaret. I was there; that was going to have to be enough for now. A banner with the Steps printed on it hung by the podium where the speakers stood. I read through them, trying to figure out if the program made any sense. I saw Step Eleven: "Sought through prayer and meditation to improve our conscious contact with God *as we understood Him.*" So, these people were into meditation, too. Maybe this wouldn't be so bad. Meditation was something I trusted. I first heard about it when the Beatles got involved with Hinduism in the 1960s, and anything the Beatles did was good enough for me. I didn't get around to actually learning to meditate for years, but when I did my addictive impulses served me well for once, as I stuck religiously to the twice-daily routine. Soon I discovered Buddhism and embarked on a series of meditation retreats, culminating in the three-month silent intensive. The irony of my arrival at the retreat with a terrific hangover was lost on me at the time.

In the years since, things had slipped a little, what with the drinking, drugs, and general disaster of my life. But now I got back to meditating more regularly. These Twelve Step people didn't seem very spiritual, really; for one thing, they couldn't sit still during the meetings. And they were always talking. Buddhists are very good at stillness and silence, and that's what I thought of as spiritual. But the alcoholics did seem kind of happy, and they knew how to stay sober. I decided to take the helpful information and try to integrate it into what I thought was my more sophisticated Buddhist practice.

POWERLESSNESS OVER ALCOHOL AND DRUGS

At that first gathering I bought a copy of *Alcoholics Anonymous* (known as the Big Book) and began to study the Steps. Step One, "We admitted we were powerless over alcohol; that our lives had become unmanageable," took time to sink in.

I'd always worked at controlling my drinking and drugging, often counting drinks, even counting hits of weed. In one band I was known as "Mr. Toke" because of my habit of stopping rehearsal to take a single drag off my little pipe. It always seemed to me that if I was able to moderate and (usually) control how I smoked dope and drank, it meant I didn't have a real problem.

Because I was often working at night and didn't have the constitution to drink constantly, I rarely drank during the day. But, right after breakfast I would smoke pot to get myself ready to write songs. Writing and practicing the guitar, I would maintain my high until dinnertime, then stop. I wouldn't smoke again until after the first set of my band's gig. That way I'd have the energy to get through the night. After the second or third set I'd start drinking beer, keeping close track of how many I'd had and timing it so that I wouldn't be too drunk to play the last set. After the gig, if there were any kind of party, I'd drink Tequila with my beer or snort cocaine if it was around, always punctuating everything with more pot.

After getting sober I began to see that the very need to try to control showed my powerlessness. If I didn't have a problem, I wouldn't have to think about controlling—counting, pacing, mixing proper proportions. And then there were the times when I didn't control myself, nights when a feeling came over me like a tidal wave, a craving so strong there seemed no choice but to drown myself in drink. And I would, going wild in a kind of hysteria until I'd blacked out, like the night at the wedding in Cambridge. This happened many times over my twenty year drinking career. Afterward I'd be wiped out and need days to recover. Then I'd start the cycle of control, pacing, mixing again.

One friend went through a similar cycle. A bright, stylish woman in her late fifties, Paulette's son had died in a drunk-driving accident some years ago. While she'd been a serious meditator and worked with her grief in various groups and workshops, she'd never dealt with her own alcoholism. Recently she wrote me an e-mail about her struggle. "Most of the time I have no trouble with alcohol. Occasionally, something happens and I drink with a feeling of omnipotence and abandon. Such was last evening."

"Omnipotence and abandon," that's just how it feels—until you do something you regret. She goes on. "At a party last night, under the influence of too much champagne, I revealed someone's secret to those who should not have heard it. So a huge can of worms is open at my doing . . . Over my life, there have been far too many mornings filled with remorse and no memory. Even of last night, there are things I don't recall, but I completely recall this inappropriate secret revelation—and the tone and attitude with which it was done—and I just ache with self-loathing and guilt and shame. I realize I must not drink."

This note captures so well the darkness and despair of a bottom. When Paulette shared this with me, I felt strangely happy because I could see what she couldn't: that rather than a terrible failure, what she was experiencing was the beginning of a new life. With grace and luck, things would only get better from here.

DENIAL AND PURIFICATION

Denial is what keeps us from taking the First Step. Until we acknowledge that we have a problem—that indeed we are powerless—we can't even begin to recover.

Clearly many people with addictive behaviors find ways to deny for years—sometimes for a lifetime. My own denial came out of being raised in a family of heavy drinkers so that my drinking seemed relatively moderate and controlled compared to theirs. One of my brothers used to drink a fifth of vodka every day. When drugs became popular, my friends and I pointed to the lies of our parents' generation to show that they didn't know anything about drugs: marijuana wasn't addictive, we knew that. So maybe heroin wasn't so bad either. Of course, after smoking "nonaddictive" marijuana every day for nine years, as well as having long runs with amphetamines, barbituates, and hallucinogens, I might have considered whether my beliefs were accurate.

As I got into my thirties, denial only deepened with my increasing involvement in a spiritual life. Having practiced meditation since I was twenty-eight, gone on a three-month retreat, lived on faith, and attended every talk by every famous spiritual leader I could for years, I thought I qualified as almost enlightened, and an enlightened person couldn't be an alcoholic. Could they?

In fact, until I was willing to address my addiction and the many ways it crippled me, my spiritual life never became fully integrated; it remained only a sort of pleasant compartment in my life. While *something* was happening to me—I won't discount the powerful effects of meditation even before sobriety—it wasn't until I faced up to my shadow side that life began to radically change.

The Steps force you to face the seamiest side of your life—your failure to control or manage your drinking and drug use; your sexual addiction; your compulsive eating; your failures at intimacy; or your crippling emotions—and furthermore, the Steps seem to imply that you don't have control over a lot of other things in your life. This can seem like a depressing and negative way to go about developing a spiritual life. But this material, which one teacher calls "the manure for enlightenment," becomes the fertilizer for spiritual growth. Starting at the bottom means you build a solid foundation so that the earth won't suddenly shift beneath your feet.

When I started meditation, even before practicing Buddhism, I did TM, or transcendental meditation. Transcending—that's what I wanted to do with life; get over, get out, avoid. This is sometimes called a "spiritual by-pass," using a spiritual practice to try to get around more earthly problems. I'd struggled with depression through my teen years and beyond; I couldn't make a relationship last; my musical career was forever stalled in second rate gigs. I wanted something that would take me beyond all that, some kind of enlightenment that would fix everything: my emotions, my love life, my career. In other words, I wanted magic.

What I got was a little more calm in my life and a new self-image, a new hobby. The regular meditation, which I followed strictly, twenty minutes twice a day, seemed to lower my stress level. And it let me think of myself as a spiritual person, no matter what I was doing with the other twenty-three hours and twenty minutes a day.

THE STEPS AS *SILA*

In Buddhism the initial, purifying stage of spiritual development is called *sila*, usually translated as morality or virtue—what one teacher calls "cleaning up your act." This involves living an ethical life; treating others *and ourselves* with kindness; and letting go of destructive behaviors. In Buddhist teachings, sila is formalized in the Five Lay Precepts—and number five is "I take the training to abstain from alcohol and drugs which make me heedless." So, guess what? The Buddha didn't think getting loaded was that good an idea either—the Twelve Steps are, in fact, sila.

Sila is one of the three classic stages of practice. The other two are concentration and wisdom. When I began to practice, I didn't put much emphasis on sila, figuring that concentration and wisdom were where the action was. None of my teachers talked much about the Fifth Precept, and I certainly wasn't going to worry about it. In fact, psychedelic drug experiences were the inspiration for much of the sixties movement toward Eastern religions. In the Beatles song "Strawberry Fields," for example, we're told, "nothing is real, and nothing to get hung about"—

sounds a lot like being stoned, but it also sounds like the stuff of certain Buddhist teachings. With this blurring of drugs and religion, no wonder some teachers felt ambivalent about the Fifth Precept. For most of them, drugs and alcohol weren't a problem, and they probably didn't want the teachings to come off as puritanical or moralistic.

Unfortunately for me, LSD, mescaline, and mushrooms were all just another high, just another way to get loaded. They never had much of a spiritual effect on me. Even though there were times I wanted to explore them as a gateway to some higher states, my trips always devolved into drug fests, often concluding with alcohol to ease the crash. That's the trouble with being an addict: it takes all the fun out of drugs. I always admired and envied people who could make their trip a spiritual one, but for me tripping was not much different from drinking beer.

The purifying aspects of sila work on more levels than just the physical. It's not just following a set of Precepts—just as real sobriety is more than putting down the bottle or joint. Buddhist teachings are said to "reveal what was hidden," and to "hold up a lamp in the dark." And meditation practice itself tends to uncover the repressed aspects of our psyche.

Even before I got sober, the dharma was working to reveal what was hidden, though I didn't know it. One image the Buddha uses is of a goldsmith who heats gold in a crucible, burning off the dross. So, as my inner gold began to shine more brightly, the dross of my destructive behavior stood out more distinctly.

I saw this unfold with Dan, a beginning meditation student who impressed me with the intensity with which he approached his practice. He reported putting in great effort, sitting as long as he could through knee pain, restlessness, and sleepiness. His commitment reminded me of my own at his stage of practice.

One day he called and said, with a quaver in his voice, "I won't be at class for the next few weeks."

"Are you okay?" I asked. "What's happening?"

"Last week I was arrested for drunk driving . . . again."

Dan told me that even though he had known he had a problem with drinking and had been arrested before for drunk driving, he still thought he could control it. After he and his wife, Karen, started meditation, he tried to hide his drinking because he was feeling shame and a sense of disconnection from his growing spiritual life.

"In retrospect, it doesn't really seem accurate to say that I had a meditation practice because I wasn't really practicing in the strict sense of the word. I spent time on my cushion, but there was no consistency and the sittings felt fragmented and unfocused."

Finally, he said, his last arrest was almost a relief; there was no need to pretend anymore, and he could begin the work of recovery. Dan's been sober for more than two years now, and still attends my group. Here's what he says about the change:

"When I committed myself to sobriety, I regained a sense of openness, honesty, and a feeling of actually living with the ethics that I accepted. Instead of sitting around my garage smoking cigarettes and thinking about the dharma, I was putting it in motion within my day-to-day life. I felt that I was taking the right action, and in doing so my integrity was awakened."

The Buddha talks about "the bliss of blamelessness." When there are no secrets in your life and you're living cleanly, a sense of safety arises. You're not looking over your shoulder all the time. For a recovering addict or alcoholic, this delight can arise at odd times, like when you get pulled over for a traffic violation and realize that the worst you can get is a ticket—no fear of a drunk driving charge or drug bust.

Dan's experience of meditation has changed as well. "My meditation often has a feeling of lightness and ease that I seldom felt before. When intently focused, it's at a depth that is new for me. When it's tough and I'm feeling some type of existential distress, I've got the awareness to be attentive and accepting instead of simply giving in to a habitual desire for escape."

POWERLESS, NOT HELPLESS

People sometimes hear the word *powerless* and think it means "passive," that people who work with the Twelve Steps think they are victims, that life is just happening to them. While it's true that there are lots of things you can't control in the world—the weather, the economy, your parents—chances are no one is shoving booze down your throat or a line up your nose or a supersized fast-food meal into your mouth. We are powerless over the disease of alcoholism and the effects of alcohol, but we are not powerless over whether we pick up a drink or not. The Buddha was emphatic on the point that we are responsible moment to moment for our words and actions, not just victims of destiny or hidden forces; we have an element of free will.

Noah Levine, a recovering addict, meditation teacher, and author of the moving spiritual memoir *Dharma Punx*, puts it this way: "I don't have power over what desires I have, but I do have power over what actions I take." Noah recognizes, though, that his sense of powerlessness can become corrupted. "I can see a tendency towards nihilism both in my spiritual practice and in my recovery. At times I use the First Step and my meditation practice as excuses to avoid the suffering in the world, feeling that I can't do anything about it or that it is just everyone's karma unfolding." This is a distortion of the concept of powerlessness. It's an excuse to give up and bail out on life and responsibility.

The Buddhist term *near enemies* can shed light on the difference between powerlessness and helplessness. For example, the near enemy of compassion is pity; the near enemy of equanimity is indifference. I think helplessness or, as Noah puts it, nihilism is the near enemy of powerlessness. This tendency to turn spiritual ideas upside down and inside out is very dangerous for an alcoholic, or anyone who has negative habits of mind. It can be the beginning of a slide into depression, despair, and eventually drinking again—or worse.

Noah brings the First Step and Buddhism together when he says, "Yes, I am powerless, but I also have the ability to purify my actions of speech, body, and mind through the practice of spiritual principles."

Buddhists are sometimes accused of being passive as well. In fact, meditation lays the groundwork for acting skillfully in the world. The Buddha was as concerned about the way we live in the world—as shown by his emphasis on qualities like generosity, non-harming, and compassion—as he was about meditation itself. But the Buddha was intensely practical—and very clear about the truth that we can't control certain things: the fact that we are going to grow older, and all the difficulties inherent in aging; the fact that we are going to get sick; the fact that we are going to die; the fact that everything around us is going to keep changing and will eventually disappear.

So, no matter how much exercise I get, or how much organic food I eat, I'll die. All the vitamins and supplements in the world can't keep me from sometimes catching cold or the flu, getting cancer or heart disease (or even the disease of alcoholism!). Plastic surgery, herbal elixirs, and skin creams can't stop the fact of my aging; my car will eventually wear out, my roof will leak, my children will grow up and leave me, and my parents will die. I'm powerless over all these things. The Buddha saw how much suffering we create fighting with these facts, resisting and trying to circumvent aging, illness, death, and loss, and he realized that clear understanding and acceptance was the key to letting go of that suffering.

After the Buddha tells us all of this, essentially pointing out what we are powerless over in this world—everyone, not just addicts or alcoholics—he says that there is one thing that we do have power over: our karma. This means that we are responsible for our own situation—up to a point. The Buddha said that people do have free will, and that this is what karma is, the energy of our will. The way I express this will, whether skillfully or unskillfully, determines the results of my life—a simple cause-and-effect formula.

Karma, like powerlessness, is often misunderstood. People commonly think it means destiny or fate. But both the Twelve Steps and Buddhist teaching point to the ways in which we shape our own destiny. The Buddha said everything starts with thoughts; that we speak and act based on thoughts; that our words and actions turn into habits—or addictions; and that those habits shape our character into something inflexible. So, he says, "Watch the thought and its ways with care, and let it spring from love born out of concern for all beings. . . . As the shadow follows the body, as we think, so we become." This underscores a strong argument for the value of meditation practice. Meditation makes it possible to see your thoughts more clearly, and when you see your thoughts clearly, you can consciously decide how to respond to them.

This idea can be taken too far, though, and we can blame ourselves for things we have no power over. The Buddha points out that because there are so many causes and effects happening simultaneously, our own will can have only a limited impact. It's up to us to find the balance between responsibility and powerlessness.

Sorting this out is what the Serenity Prayer, often recited at Twelve Step gatherings, tries to help you do, with its plea to "grant me the serenity to accept the things I cannot change, courage to change the things I can, and wisdom to know the difference." Though this prayer calls on God for help, the Buddhist teachings and the inherent wisdom that comes through the practices can bring the same acceptance, strength, and clarity. Meditation develops in us the power to sit through all kinds of experiences without flinching, with a willingness to see what is true. This non-flinching willingness can be called courage. So, the courage, wisdom, and acceptance of the prayer come from the same place, from the inner strength that grows through continuously opening the heart and mind.

LEARNING BALANCE: THE MIDDLE WAY

Some people think of the Buddha as a god or a mythic figure and believe that trying to emulate him would be impossible. However, the Buddha himself made clear that he was just a man, a man who had perfected his human consciousness. Before he reached this perfection, he lived a life of extremes, not unlike what many alcoholics and addicts do. Viewed in this way, as a journey toward balance, the Buddha's life offers the alcoholic and addict a great example.

As the story goes, when Siddhartha Gotama was born, a seer prophesied that he would be either a great king or a great religious leader. His father, the king, was obviously biased toward the first choice and tried to make his life extra comfortable so he'd have no desire to seek anything beyond the castle walls. Siddhartha was surrounded by music, beautiful women, the best food and drink—essentially, sex, drugs, and rock 'n' roll. Being the prince, he got to play out the materialist fantasy to the limit. Then one day he found out the truth: that everyone gets sick, gets old, and dies. This shattered his world, destroying the illusion that his paradisiacal life would never end.

Out of the despair he felt on learning the bitter truth of life's struggles grew a new obsession. If the external world wasn't going to be perfect, maybe he could find perfection in the inner world. To get there, though, he took another extreme route, following ascetic practices so harsh he nearly killed himself. Over six years he tried every spiritual exercise that was available to him, including eating only one grain of rice a day. Finally, his awakening came after he realized that both extremes—of pleasure and of renunciation—are futile, he could neither live in perfect comfort nor wrest liberation from an emaciated body.

Neither heroic effort nor complete self-indulgence brought freedom. He was powerless. What was needed was something in between: enough comfort to practice meditative awareness, but not so much as to be a distraction. After he took nourishment and regained his strength, he was able to complete his spiritual search. When the Buddha began to teach, he expressed this insight as the Middle Way. This way meant not clinging to a single answer but responding to what was happening right now. Just as you can't tell someone who is learning to walk a tightrope, "Just lean to the left," there's no schema for attaining a Middle Way. Life—and spiritual practice—is more like a tightrope than a highway.

The idea of a Middle Way was a problem for an alcoholic like me. The last place I wanted to be was the middle. Extremes of behavior and thinking are typical of alcoholics, and I always romanticized the party life. I played it out by being a musician, thinking I was a rebel, an outsider, living on the edge—driving down the freeway at 3 A.M., half drunk, the radio blasting, rolling a joint while I steered the van with my knees— that's who I *wanted* to be. When I came to the spiritual life, I brought along these same attitudes, trying to make meditation into a glamorous thrill ride.

In sobriety I began to understand the Middle Way. It meant living a simpler, less dramatic life, seeking peace instead of a spiritual fix. This is where Buddhist meditation guides us, to letting go of grasping after transitory pleasures and finding the happiness of equanimity. This quality of equanimity is prized in Buddhism as one of the purest states of mind, and a quality that leads toward complete freedom, or enlightenment. With the Middle Way, free from the painful push and pull of craving and rejecting, we find transcendence.

PATIENCE, ONE BREATH AT A TIME

Alcoholics want it now—whatever *it* is: thrills, satisfaction, pleasure, the end of unpleasantness. This demand for instant gratification, this driving impatience is one of the marks of the addict/alcoholic, and unlearning that habitual craving is one of the toughest jobs of sobriety. One of the ways we do it is by counting the days, rewarding ourselves as we go along for our continuity, for our longevity. Meditation formalizes this practice of patience, one breath at a time.

In meditation you learn to be nonreactive. There's a thought, you let it pass without jumping on board; there's an itch, you let it be without moving; there's a sound, you notice it and come back to the breath; there's an emotion, you just feel it fully without turning it into a story. Learning this nonreactivity in meditation practice gives a formal structure to the nonreactivity you have to learn in order to stay sober: I have the urge to drink, I go to a support group instead or make a phone call; I want to quit my job this minute, I wait and try to stick it out until the end of the day; I want to leave my wife, I remind myself that I spent twenty years trying to find a partner so maybe I can live through a bad day or two.

In Buddhism, this nonreactivity is called *mindfulness*: the first step in Buddhist meditation. This simple—not easy—practice helps you to see the difference between what's actually happening and what the mind is making up. Mindfulness means trying to keep the mind focused on what you are experiencing in the present moment without commentary, analysis, or judgment; without reference to past experiences or plans for the future; without expectations or fear. Typically you try to follow the breath in this way, but mindfulness can be applied to anything: sensations in the body, sounds, emotions, even thoughts. Finding the clarity of mindfulness, letting go of all the distractions that carry us away from the present moment, only happens with time, commitment, and a surrender to the process.

The beginning of this process can be as scary as beginning the Twelve Steps, as we start to see that we can't control our own minds. When people sit down to meditate for the first time they often say, "I'm no good at this. You tell me to follow my breath but I can't shut off my thoughts long enough to do that." The typical alcoholic or addict may find this phase even more difficult than the ordinary person because impatience, self-criticism, and perfectionism are such common traits for us.

Ultimately, though, meditation isn't some contest to see who can stop thought. Thought happens. What we learn in meditation isn't so much to *stop* thoughts, but to change our relationship to them. We learn to be less reactive, less ruled by our thoughts, and to see that they aren't all true. "You don't have to believe your thoughts," one of my teachers says. What a revelation! When I see my thoughts more clearly, I'm able to make choices to act or not act based on what I see; I can exercise Right Intention to steer my life in the direction I want to go.

Sometimes thoughts and emotions seem overwhelming, even in the context of mindfulness. At these times you might fall back on compassion—not pity—for yourself, for the great task you are attempting: facing down the demons of the heart and mind. Perhaps then you can begin to forgive yourself and your failures.

THE FOUR NOBLE TRUTHS

The Four Noble Truths are at the core of all Buddhist teachings. Laid out by the Buddha in his very first discourse, they encapsulate his view of the difficulties of life, their cause, and their solution. These Four Truths relate directly to the struggles of alcoholics, addicts, and other Twelve Step participants.

In the First Noble Truth, the Buddha said that life has an inherently unsatisfying quality, which he called *dukkha* (usually translated as suffering), and his goal in his own search was to find a way to free himself from this suffering. When we take Step One—admitting our powerlessness and the unmanageability of our lives—we are recognizing the First Noble Truth. The Buddha said we should respond to this Truth by seeing it clearly, not shying away from the pain, not living in denial, by *understanding* this suffering.

We see the First Noble Truth in large ways—the hunger and poverty in the world, the wars and violence—and in small—the subtle movements of the mind in meditation toward or away from an object. Before we can engage this Truth skillfully, before we can let go of the suffering, we must be willing to look directly at it in all its forms. In the same way, only when we admit to our disease can we begin the process of recovery.

Some people rebel against the First Noble Truth. "Everything's not suffering! That's a negative view of the world." And, of course, it's true that the world is filled with delights. But the Buddha saw that even in our moments of triumph and joy there remains a grasping toward more. My favorite example of this is the traditional commercial at the end of the Super Bowl, where the newly chosen MVP is asked, "What are you going to do now?" And this man, who has just reached the pinnacle of his profession, turns to the camera and says, "I'm going to Disneyland." For me, this sums up dukkha: you've got it all but you want more, and since you've got everything possible in the *real* world, the only place left to go is to a fantasy world, a place where dreams are made.

Once the Buddha recognized the inherent unsatisfactoriness in life, he wanted to understand where it came from. The Second Noble Truth was his answer: the ceaseless desire for pleasure and self-centered gratification. Here's where we addicts can relate. If anyone knows about "cease-less desire," it's an alcoholic or addict or overeater. When we take Step One we are acknowledging that we're powerless over this desire—and that following every desire doesn't bring satisfaction but, in fact, just creates more and stronger desire, the very definition of addiction. We see that this effort to satisfy our desires by taking drugs or drinks or food only reinforces our desire.

The Buddha said that the appropriate way to respond to the Second Noble Truth is to stop following every impulse and develop restraint around our cravings—sobriety itself. The abandonment of desire forms the core value of Buddhist practice. Letting go, dropping the tendency to chase after external—and even internal—gratification brings the greatest joy. This teaching is counterintuitive: if you stop chasing after the things you want, you will find the thing you want. If you stop struggling for satisfaction and happiness, you will become satisfied and happy. What causes our suffering isn't a *lack* of material things or emotional experiences, but rather the craving, the desire itself, the energy that keeps driving us to engage in the chase.

In the Third Noble Truth, the Buddha sees that when desire ends, suffering ends; when we let go of craving, the pain dissolves. He sees in this letting go the possibility of freedom. This inspiring vision is the awakening of faith that happens in Step Two.

The Fourth Noble Truth is the way to the end of suffering: the Eightfold Path. Here the Buddha tells us how to live and attain freedom—he shows us what we need to do to learn how to let go. He says we need to develop our hearts and minds, as well as live ethically and with kindness. Like the Twelve Steps, the Eightfold Path is practical and profound. As we examine the Steps, we'll look at many of these elements in detail: Right View, Right Intention, Right Livelihood, Right Action, Right Speech, Right Effort, Right Mindfulness, and Right Concentration.

M EDITATION AS ADDICTION

Although meditation can be difficult at first, after some practice it becomes pleasant. It can even become another kind of high. And, while the Buddhist texts warn the meditator away from getting attached to the pleasure of meditation, when one slips into a place of great peace, of rapture, of connectedness, it's easy to think this is what it's all about. Sometimes you feel like you've got it, like you've figured out how to make meditation work, and for a while you might be able to maintain a blissful state in your practice. When this inevitably ends, it's not unlike withdrawal, a feeling of loss, frustration, and grief.

In another way, the very structure of the meditative experience can help us to stay in denial about our dysfunction. We can use meditation as a place to hide. Here's how.

You go on a retreat. All your "stuff" comes up the first couple days—anxiety, depression, self-hatred—but you know it will pass because you're a good meditator. So you sit through it without any real self-examination and in a couple days you're settled in, just following your breath, being mindful through the day, feeling calm and peaceful. You see that all those problems, your poverty, your loneliness, your binging, are all just passing phenomena, they aren't "you." You go into interviews with your teachers and you don't bother to mention these problems because you know they are just an illusion, so your teacher never hears about them or gets a chance to comment or give direction.

When the retreat ends, you go home refreshed. You aren't acting out your dysfunctional habits because you feel so mellow and happy. Your poverty, loneliness, and binging just aren't a problem.

Then, after a few days/weeks/months, things start back up again. Your dead-end job is not satisfying and doesn't pay enough; your relationship ends; you're drinking/drugging/eating/sleeping around, whatever, a little too much—or maybe a lot too much.

How about another retreat?

This isn't to say that retreats can't have a healthy, healing role in spiritual life. They can certainly help us through difficult times in life, as well as giving us powerful experiences of mindfulness, concentration, and other precious qualities. But, when our practice becomes a palliative, covering over our real problems, then we're using it unskillfully.

Before she got sober, Paulette spent months practicing meditation in an Asian monastery. "In Burma," she says, "I would watch all these desires coming up. And away they'd go. All while I just sat there. I would not act on desire. That's the joy of the meditation pillow." Of course, it's easy to stay clean and sober when you're living in a monastery.

It's important to talk about our practice. There's nobody in there watching you as you meditate, so, unless you share with a teacher or friend how your practice is going—how it's *really* going—it's easy to get stuck in nonproductive patterns. Twelve Step meetings provide this forum for people working the Steps, but many meditators lack a feedback system. One helpful tool is a small meditation group. Joining or starting such a group can give you a safe place to discuss your meditation practice and provide support during the different stages of spiritual development.

ALWAYS BEGINNING

The entryway into both Buddhism and addiction recovery is to look at our own pain and admit our own difficulties or failures in life. This isn't easy. Both traditions require us to give something up right away: when we begin to practice meditation we close our eyes and take time away from the outer world; when we take the First Step, we stop using our drug of choice. In these ways, the beginning of the journey into Buddhism and the Steps can be difficult and often requires a strong motivation, whether an alcoholic bottom or a gut-level sense that there is something more to life, that something is missing.

The great irony of beginning the process of recovery is that only in surrender do we begin to grow. It's hard to see how powerlessness and pain could be a blessing, yet it's through the recognition of the problem that we begin to find the solution.

While this is the beginning of the path, powerlessness is also a touchstone that you may return to over and over on your spiritual journey. The Zen Master Suzuki Roshi said, "In the beginner's mind there are many possibilities, but in the expert's there are few." Once you think you know it all, you stop learning and growing. Especially for the alcoholic, this is dangerous. You will find, too, that as you delve into Buddhism, if you remain open, the levels of insight seem endless.

In another way, too, you are always a beginner: every time the mind drifts in meditation, you start again, coming back to the breath, back to the beginning.

In the Korean Zen tradition, there is an attitude called Don't Know Mind that recognizes that each moment is completely unique, completely unpredictable. Who knows what the next breath, the next sound, the next thought will bring? If I'm an "expert," I think I've seen it all, and I lose interest in what's happening right now. If I "don't know," I'm always on the edge of my experience, opening to, investigating, welcoming, the next miraculous moment. When you approach your life and practice with this attitude, there's a joy, a freshness, and a mystery that reveals itself in the richness of each moment.

MEDITATION EXERCISE: VIPASSANA

Vipassana, or insight meditation, uses the tool of mindfulness to focus the mind in our present moment experience. As we watch what appears and disappears in our body and mind, over time, insights arise, psychological, intellectual, and most important, spiritual.

Begin by finding a comfortable place to sit. If you choose a chair, sit with both feet on the floor. If you are sitting on the floor or on a bed, be careful that you don't cross your legs in a way that cuts off your circulation. (You might want to look for one of the books that show pictures of meditation postures.) Sit with your back straight, but not rigid. Make sure that you are able to breathe easily. It's important to be still when meditating, to not fidget. If you need to shift posture while meditating, do so slowly and mindfully, then return to stillness.

Now take a few minutes to move the attention through the body, from head to toe, relaxing each part of the body, the muscles in the face and jaw; the shoulders; the back; the arms and hands; softening the chest and belly; relaxing through the hips and down through the legs and feet.

Now just feel your whole body sitting.

Notice if there are any sounds. Don't concern yourself with them, just allow them to be there.

Notice if there is any strong emotional or physical energy present. Try to aware of what that feels like in the body.

Now begin to focus your attention on the breath. Feel the breath either at the nostrils where the air enters and leaves the body, or at the chest or belly as they rise and fall with each breath. Don't try to breathe in any special way, just allow the breath to be as it is and notice the sensations that occur with it.

If a thought takes your attention away, as soon as you are aware of that thought, let it go and come back to your breath. Keep coming back to the breath.

If sounds appear, try to hear them without thinking about what they are, just allowing them to wash over you. Then bring your attention back to the sensations of breath.

Start to examine the breath in detail, the beginning, middle, and end. Feel the temperature of the inhalation and exhalation. Watch how the breath changes, long breath, short breath, smooth breath, jagged breath; deep breath, shallow breath, gross breath, subtle breath.

You can make a soft mental note as you breathe of "In breath; out breath," guiding and anchoring the attention. The noting should be very soft and in the background of the mind; the awareness of the sensations of the breath should be in the foreground.

As your attention becomes more subtle, notice the quality of each thought. You might make a soft mental note "thinking, thinking." And if you can see what kind of thought it is you can note "wanting, wanting;" or "aversion, aversion." Any kind of thought can be noted: planning, judging, remembering; anger, sadness, joy. You can note music in the mind or images. Whatever the contents of the mind, try putting a soft mental note on it.

Keep coming back to the breath, letting the body relax, the mind be clear, the attention precise.

At some point in your practice, as you become calm and focused, you may want to drop the noting, or it may fall away on its own. Keep the mind focused on the flow of present moment experience, opening to the range of physical and mental objects, breath, sounds, sensations, thoughts, and emotions. Don't push anything away, and don't grasp after anything. Just watch the passing show with clarity and equanimity.

STEP TWO

"Came to believe that a power greater than ourselves
could restore us to sanity."

After admitting our own powerlessness over our disease in Step One, Step Two offers us an alternative source of power and healing. Instead of depending on our own willpower or virtue to protect us from alcohol or drugs, we are asked to turn to a "power greater than ourselves," or at least consider the possibility of such a power helping us. Gently, we are encouraged to begin developing a spiritual life, to "come to believe." We don't have to wholeheartedly embrace this possibility right now, but simply look around—with our new clarity—and see if we can envision a life not controlled by our desires and will, a life in tune with something other than our own drives and master plan.

Step Two is a process, a growing into understanding. Many of us have struggled with this growth process; but no one can work the Step for us. We each must "come to believe" in our own way and find our own Higher Power. As we move toward the development of a meditation practice, we may be faced with the same kind of difficulties. While we may want the serenity and intuitive wisdom that Buddhism seems to promise, we may not be sure that all this sitting around with our eyes closed is really the way to achieve it. As we are guided to "let go" of desires, judgments, resentments, and opinions—at least during the period of meditation—it may seem that this is a dangerous surrender of what we trust most: our rational intellect. In the interest of spiritual advancement are we being asked to become mindless drones?

These kinds of fears attack many people who get sober or pursue some other spiritual practice. They aren't necessarily unskillful; there's a certain wisdom in being skeptical. But we need to hold our skepticism lightly, with a willingness to explore before dismissing outright the value of spiritual work. Step Two acts as an entryway into this work: a place where we can consider faith and its practical application; a place where we recognize the need for some other resource than our own will; and a place to nurture hope for our own healing.

Now what?

When I first got sober, I had a great feeling of relief, that this burden of controlling my drinking and using had been lifted. My life seemed simpler, and the feeling of clarity was gratifying. The First Step was working. But soon, physical sobriety alone wasn't enough.

A few weeks after getting fired from the Red Robin I hooked up with some former bandmates and went on the road, playing a series of one-nighters across the Southwest. The band called itself the Hollywood Argyles, the name of an early-sixties one-hit wonder whose tune "Alley Oop," based on a comic strip character of the time, was a classic novelty song. None of the original members of the Hollywood Argyles were in the band, but that didn't deter the booking agent from sending us on tour. In fact, we often traveled with other bogus acts: the "Shirelles," the "Boxtops," the "Coasters." Apparently if you avoided the large urban centers and didn't get too much publicity, you could get away with this kind of larceny. For me, it was just a gig, a way to make a living at my craft, if not an ideal one.

We traveled in discomfort, the four of us and all our gear packed into an old station wagon. For weeks we played one-nighters, often traveling hundreds of miles between dates. The leaders of the Argyles, a husband and wife team, squabbled endlessly in the front seat about bookings, money, whether the agent was ripping us off, and what material we should play. Apparently, she believed that her experience as a legal secretary qualified her to initiate lawsuits against anyone who crossed her path. But he thought that suing a club owner for not providing a make-up mirror in the dressing room would not be helpful to our careers. The drummer and I sat in the backseat staring out the window like two oppressed kids.

While I appreciated my newfound sobriety, I had a feeling of raw-nerved nakedness, being stripped of the protective fog of pot and booze. Going between the station wagon, the clubs, and the motels, I sometimes wanted to run off into the desert and hide under a rock. The bickering in the band wore on me, the tackiness of the music humiliated me, and the audiences who seemed to actually believe we were the Hollywood Argyles embarrassed me. (We were way too young for the part.) In the past, getting loaded every night had given me a refuge, however bleak and destructive, from the stresses of a musician's life. But now there was just me and the world.

Drinking and getting stoned had helped me avoid facing the larger problems in my life. Instead of being present for life's challenges, I had done a shadow dance with reality, never really moving forward. When I went on the road with the Argyles, I had an alternative escape—a geographic escape—without drugs and alcohol, leaving behind my girlfriend, my failed ambition, and my poverty.

Back in Venice, my relationship with Margaret had become frustrating and painful, but I didn't know how to even start a conversation about it, much less begin to make changes. I was writing songs and recording them in a home studio, but never doing the footwork to get them published or performed by anyone. I didn't own a house or a car, have health insurance, a savings account, or a credit card. If I wanted to go on a meditation retreat, I had to depend upon the generosity of a teacher who I had known for several years who let me come along for free.

After some time on the road in New Mexico, Colorado, and Texas, all these realities began to sink in. Sobriety not only brought the benefit of clarity, but the pain of seeing my life in its stark limitations. I needed something more than physical sobriety, than admitting powerlessness and putting down the drink and drugs.

I needed Step Two.

I needed the hope and the sense of possibility that Step Two offers. When we admit powerlessness in Step One it opens us to letting go of our addictions, but it also makes us vulnerable. Step Two shows us a new, more reliable, and more healthy form of protection.

From a Buddhist perspective, Step One can be used to address our addiction to thought and self and our need to try to control an uncontrollable world. When we begin to let go of these addictions and this control, Step Two gives us some comfort, a sense that we'll be okay if we let go. In Buddhist terms, we begin to trust in the dharma or in our own Buddha Nature, which is beyond our small self.

Buddhism teaches that the self is an illusion made up of thoughts, emotions, memories that have no center, no abiding core. To rely on this illusory amalgam is to live in delusion, to mistake the movie of our minds for Truth. Step Two leads us toward a less self-centered view of the world, toward seeing ourselves as part of a system: I do my part, not picking up a drink or drug, and my Higher Power (God, Buddha, nature, the dharma . . .) does its part.

During my time on the road in my first year of sobriety, I didn't get to many Twelve Step gatherings. But I did begin reading the literature and trying to understand the Steps. Over and over I fell back on the Serenity Prayer, especially the words "grant me the serenity to accept the things I cannot change." I needed this prayer, particularly because it helped me let go of the need to control everything in my life. This was my way of beginning to work Step Two. Again and again I would realize that the things causing me pain or difficulty fell into the category of "things I cannot change." Over time I saw how those things tended to work themselves out in one way or another, that I needn't worry about many of these things. And faith began to grow.

To cease fighting

Step Two is a stumbling block for many addicts and alcoholics who are atheist, agnostic, or fighting a battle with the Higher Power idea. Many describe praying out of desperation when doubled over a toilet bowl or scraping through shag carpet for a trace of cocaine—and receiving no answer. The idea that there is a loving presence or being that might help them at these times seems unlikely at best and silly at worst.

Some people come to the Twelve Steps with painful personal history around religion. In elementary school I was a devout Catholic, serving as an altar boy at our church. However, when my mother took me out of Catholic school in sixth grade, the Church wouldn't allow me to be an altar boy any more—defrocked at age eleven. Here I was, a devoted kid who wanted to serve and be involved in the ceremonies of the Church, but because I wasn't in the right school I couldn't. This was the beginning of my growing away from Catholicism.

Other people have much more serious memories of betrayal. And some people simply can't buy the logic of religion, of a God up in the sky who's running things.

Bill Wilson in *The Twelve Steps and Twelve Traditions* (commonly called *The Twelve and Twelve*), talks a great deal about this attitude in Step Two. Many people who come to the Twelve Steps think God is unscientific, illogical. Danielle, an artist who has been sober for many years now, told me that the "God stuff" kept her out of the program for a long time. "I was proud of being an atheist," she said. "I thought God was a crutch for weak or stupid people." When Danielle finally went to AA, her husband discouraged her, saying she'd be hanging out with "a bunch of Jesus freaks." Danielle found that, indeed, some meetings and literature had a Christian flavor. But she also saw that the Steps gave her permission to find her own understanding of a Higher Power. Eventually, "I decided to let my Higher Power be a mystery that I couldn't understand."

Danielle's struggle is a common one. This Step helps us to stop fighting the Higher Power idea. Maybe we're not clear on who or what that Power is, but we see that the battle itself is counterproductive. In the Big Book it says, "we have ceased fighting anything or anyone." It's more important that we cease this fight than it is that we adopt a particular idea of what a Higher Power is, because, as long as we are fighting with ourselves, with our Higher Power, and with the world, we can't let in the peace and joy of spiritual connection. As Jack Kornfield says in his classic *A Path with Heart*, if we want to develop a spiritual practice, we need to "stop the war"—whatever war we are fighting. When we stop the war with a Higher Power, it's part of letting the spiritual life take us over, and beginning to live from a place of love and awareness.

The fight with the Higher Power idea is just one of the many battles addicts and alcoholics wage. This war stems from a core negative state, called in Buddhism "aversion." The very attempt to intoxicate ourselves is an act of aversion to life. When we dull or blot out our consciousness with drugs and alcohol, we are cutting ourselves off from life itself. The Steps and the practices of Buddhism give us a way to gently "stop the war," "step out of the battle," to "cease fighting," to surrender. This surrender, which begins in Step One, means, in Step Two, that we are giving up our own attempt at incessant control and opening to what life offers.

Before we can fully take this Step, we have to see the battle clearly. Meditation helps us in this process. When we watch our minds in a meditative way, the warfare becomes evident in the mental, physical, and emotional turmoil that appears. Danielle told me that when she started to practice meditation, she was shocked to discover that her mind spent most of its time judging other people's behavior, looks, and lifestyle. "What a revelation," she said. "Meditating on the sensations of my body, I realized how uncomfortable I was while judging. My shoulders hunched up, I was tense and really gripped my opinions. No wonder I had to drink."

Initially this look into our hearts and minds as battlefields is quite disturbing; with time, though, we are able to step back and see it impersonally, as a process, and to learn to let go. This letting go means, first of all, not judging ourselves for the inner war; then, opening ourselves to the possibility that our "likes and dislikes" are just that—conditioned preferences, not facts. We are conditioned by parents, teachers, and friends; we are conditioned by our culture, our genes, and by evolution itself. Once we see the habitual, relative, and conditioned nature of our opinions, it becomes easier to open to new ideas, such as how a Higher Power might restore us to sanity.

All of this takes time—and practice. What is required is our own patience and willingness to continue to look honestly at our experience and question our own belief system. First we must acknowledge that *we* are not a Higher Power, and then open to what a Higher Power might be. Again, this is something that usually happens through a process, not a revelation, and our understanding of Higher Power often changes over time, as I will talk about later in this chapter.

For now, just putting down our fists and climbing out of the ring is enough to start us on the way to "coming to believe."

COMING TO BELIEVE IN THE PATH

JANUARY 2, 1993

Three of us were sitting in front of Ruth Denison, the grande dame of Western Buddhism, as she's known. We'd been part of her annual holiday retreat at her center, Dhamma Dena. The rough buildings sit on a flat, barren mesa above Joshua Tree, California, sandy paths connecting the meditation hall, bunkhouses, and outhouses. The eponymous cactus spots the landscape, while prickly creosote bushes, rabbit holes, and anthills cover the ground. In silence we'd been doing sitting meditation, walking meditation, eating meditation, and, with Ruth's special flare, dancing meditation. Because we were leaving that day, she had asked us to meet her after the morning sitting period. The other retreatants were outside walking in the cold, high-desert morning.

I was over seven years sober then, seven years when I'd rebuilt my life. I was a senior at U.C. Berkeley, and the other two people with me, Jennifer and Dave, were also students there—only twenty years younger than I was. They were also both sober; we'd met at Twelve Step meetings on campus. Each of them had been involved with the Twelve Steps since they were teenagers. I was forty-two, and my recovery was allowing me to go back and live the experiences I had missed twenty years earlier—and to get them right this time.

Ruth asked each of us about our retreat.

"Amazing," said Jennifer. I looked over and saw her face lit by a ray of morning sunlight coming in the meditation hall. Her golden hair glowed. "It changed my whole idea of what meditation is."

"Very good," said Ruth in her German-accented English. "Now you must continue to go deeper, yes? Just because you have one experience doesn't mean you can stop, you know?"

Jennifer nodded and smiled.

"And you," said Ruth to Dave. "How was your retreat?"

"Very interesting," said Dave. "But I could have done without the 'Little Drummer Boy.'" One night Ruth had played a twenty-minute version of the Christmas song while we danced in circles around the hall. Her unconventional teaching style wasn't for everyone.

"And did you note 'aversion' when you were listening to the music?" she asked.

"For a while," said Dave. "But then I got tired of it."

"You must keep being aware, even when you get terribly bored. This is how you learn about your mind."

She turned to me.

"And what about you?" she asked. "What did you learn this week?"

I smiled because I was hesitant to claim I'd "learned" anything at all. Sometimes it seemed I just kept getting the same lesson over and over. But something *had* happened on that retreat.

"I really see that this is the path for me," I said. "I've never had such confidence in these teachings before. I'm ready to commit myself to my practice."

"Good. You're at the Third Noble Truth," she said.

Wow, the Third Noble Truth. Wait a minute. What is the Third Noble Truth? I'd been practicing Buddhist meditation for twelve years, but all these lists still eluded me. *Let's see: First, the Truth of Suffering; Second, the Cause of Suffering; Third, the End of Suffering.*

The three of us bowed to Ruth and left the hall. We crowded into my ten-year-old baby blue Datsun 210 and began the drive back to Berkeley. To avoid the freeways around Los Angeles we cut through the mountains.

"What did she mean about the Third Noble Truth?" asked Jennifer as we swept down a broad valley. The surrounding hills were tipped in white.

"It's about faith," I said. "The Third Noble Truth is when you recognize that you're on the path, that this practice can work, that you can get enlightened."

"It's like 'coming to believe,'" said Dave. "Like the Second Step."

Dave was right. Much like the Second Step, the Third Noble Truth is a sort of staging ground from which we will leap into the work of meditation. Arriving at the Third Noble Truth is like seeing a path stretching out before you, knowing that the way is clear, that all that's required is that you continue to move forward.

The Second Step is also about trust and confidence. After making the surrender of Step One, Step Two opens the door to a new approach to life—to sobriety and a spiritual path. Step Two reorients the alcoholic or addict toward a less self-centered life. By looking to a "power greater than ourselves" we open to new possibilities, possibilities we couldn't even imagine while living in the seemingly endless cycle of addiction.

It keeps changing

As you work with the Steps, your understanding of a Higher Power may change many times. It can be helpful to know that you don't have to commit yourself to one concept for life. In fact, oftentimes the change in understanding is a developmental process that moves from a more external Higher Power to an inner power.

Noah Levine, the punk meditation teacher told me that as his sense of self got healthier, so did his idea of a Higher Power.

"In my early sobriety it was difficult for me to grasp the Higher Power stuff. Other people were trying to point inward toward an inner-power/true-nature, but I was unable to grasp that. I felt like everything inside my mind and body wanted me dead." Not finding anything inside, he looked for an external Higher Power, something to pray to.

Although sober, Noah had been arrested for vandalism and graffiti."Looking at going back to jail at almost two years clean, I was finally ready to admit the insanity, and I tried to accept that a power greater than myself could restore me to sanity." He began by "acting as if" he believed, and found that by praying to a Higher Power outside himself he began to get some relief.

This "acting as if" and using an external Higher Power, carried Noah for some time. As he became more involved in Buddhist meditation practice, gradually things changed.

Now, after many years of recovery and Buddhist practice, Noah finds the Higher Power has become more internal. "It is still a power greater than myself, but, understanding that the self is an illusion, the Higher Power is more like the potential for awakening or the Buddha Nature that is at the very core of all things."

My own experience was similar. By the time I got sober, my Buddhist practice had slipped and, through my time with the New Age guru who taught me to "live on faith," I had reverted to an externalized vision of God, much like my childhood understanding from the Catholic Church. I didn't let this trouble me early in my sobriety. What was most important to me at that time, besides not drinking or using, was getting my life together on practical terms. Traveling with the Hollywood Argyles and relying on the Serenity Prayer, I didn't worry too much about how I defined God. I just "acted as if" I really believed.

Back in L.A. I left the band and made the painful decision to break up with Margaret. I continued to rebuild my life, until, at three years sober, I decided to go back to school. I was thirty-eight years old. Twenty years before I'd dropped out of high school thinking rock stars don't need degrees but now had finally come around to the possible value of education. On a sunny afternoon I walked across the campus at Santa Monica College toward the registrar's office for the first time. Would they accept my Pennsylvania GED? What would the English and Math entrance tests be like? Would I be able to handle school at all? I said the Serenity Prayer over and over. It was clear that I could try to get into college, but I couldn't control the results of that, and seeing that did bring serenity. Amidst all my fears, somehow I felt taken care of by my Higher Power and completely willing to trust. The Higher Power was becoming a part of me, not just something to pray to. I stepped into the registrar's office and got in line.

Many people have strong experiences of faith early in sobriety, when they are able to surmount obstacles that seemed impassable before they got sober, and when everything good that happens seems miraculous. What can be more difficult is dealing with faith later on, as life becomes more complicated and the novelty of sobriety wears off.

Six months before the holiday retreat with Ruth Denison, I went on a solo retreat for a week at a Buddhist monastery in the hills above Santa Cruz. The first couple days of sitting I continued my usual prayer rituals, morning and evening. But, as I got deeper into practice, I found praying to something or someone outside myself started to feel false and artificial. I asked myself what "God" felt like. As I meditated day after day, the idea of a being called God faded and was replaced by a sense of spirit that was in me and in everything. The name Great Spirit sprang to mind. This sounded almost silly, as if I were adopting a Native American belief system, and yet, these words fit best my sense of a Higher Power: a vast, subtle energy pervading all things—a Great Spirit.

So, for some years, I adopted these words when I prayed. My Higher Power was both inside and outside. Today, verbal prayer sometimes falls away entirely, replaced simply by the effort to be aware and awake, to be mindful in each moment. At other times I use Buddhist forms of prayer (which I'll explore in Step Eleven).

I don't mean to say that I've got the Higher Power thing all figured out and I'm on the right side. Rather, this is where I've come to. Buddhist practice, in one way, strips everything away, so it's hard to hold on to concepts like "God." On the other hand, the practice gives you such powerful inner resources that another kind of trust may supplant the formal faith in God.

The idea of a Higher Power changes; like everything, it's impermanent. We learn to trust our own understanding, and to let it evolve. Sometimes our inner landscape is so parched, there's no sense of power or life; at other times we feel a gentle hand guiding us. Mindfulness, developed in meditation, helps us to see our relationship to our Higher Power in this moment and to work with that relationship in the most helpful way. In fact, mindfulness itself can be used as a Higher Power, as we shall see in Step Three.

WHO YOU CALLIN' CRAZY?

Step Two doesn't just talk about a "power greater than ourselves," it tells us that this power can "restore us to sanity." For an alcoholic or addict, being "restored to sanity" refers to the insanity of using, of destroying your life with alcohol and drugs—and all the other extreme behaviors that come along with addiction. In Buddhism, insanity, or "delusion" as it's called, is not following the dharma, not living in accordance with the Truth. The two are closely related.

One way that alcoholics deny the dharma is not recognizing the cause-and-effect relationship between their drinking and the problems in their lives. This is a denial of the workings of karma.

When I was living in this denial, I tried everything but sobriety to solve my problems. I changed my diet, becoming a vegetarian; I started exercising, jogging every day; I followed my horoscope closely, hoping to see good fortune in my future; I traded in one relationship for another, over and over; I got into psychotherapy; and, finally, I tried to meditate my problems away. One day after getting drunk and fighting with my girl-friend, I sought out a Buddhist meditation class, thinking that would solve my problems with my girlfriend, who was already practicing Buddhist meditation. All of this was a denial of actual cause and effect. The cause: I smoked dope and drank every day. The effect: My life was going nowhere. Not seeing this was a form of delusion.

Another kind of insane denial of the truth, of the dharma, relates to the Buddhist teaching called the Three Characteristics of Existence. These Characteristics are said to be in every element of life and reality.

The first of these is Suffering, or unsatisfactoriness, called *dukkha* in Buddhism. Dukkha is the aspect of life that keeps us restlessly searching for comfort. Suffering is apparent in large ways, in the hunger and poverty of many of the world's people; in the misery of war and political oppression; in the destruction of the planet and its species. Suffering appears in our daily lives as well, through depression, anxiety, and stress; through boredom, alienation, and frustration; through sickness, old age, and death. In meditation, one begins to see more and more subtle forms of suffering: the moment-to-moment grasping of the mind for pleasant thoughts; the physical twinges that keep us shifting our posture; the habitual emotions that drive our behaviors. The Buddha said that all these forms of suffering, from the grossest to the most subtle, are caused by desire and attachment, and that we had to find a way to let go of desire and attachment if we wanted true happiness and peace. The insanity of the addict is, instead of learning to let go, we hold on even tighter. We act as if becoming *completely* attached to our drug will bring happiness and peace, turning the Buddha's teachings upside down.

The Second Characteristic of Existence is Impermanence, or *anicca*. As with dukkha, anicca can be seen operating on the gross level, as civilizations come and go; people are born, live their lives, and die; we buy a new car, and in ten years time it's a junker. On the subtle level of meditation, we can see our own bodies and minds in constant movement, energy coursing through us in an amazing display of life's dynamism. This insight shows us quite clearly that there's *nothing to hold on to*, because, quite simply, nothing is standing still. And yet what does the addict want but to retain, *permanently*, the high. Oftentimes people spend years trying to recreate one moment. Maybe it was that perfect combination of drugs and alcohol that you hit at the lake when you were seventeen. Now you're forty and you still haven't gotten back there. Insanity.

In 1967, two powerful forces came together for me one night in Philadelphia: marijuana and Jimi Hendrix. My band had played a frat party at the University of Pennsylvania, and I was staying overnight at a friend's place. He was an artist and had painted the walls of his loft in psychedelic patterns of red and yellow and purple. His couch faced a big stereo system on the wall, and we all sat down and smoked a few joints. Then he put on Hendrix's *Are You Experienced?* album. I'd been high before, and I'd heard Jimi, but I'd never experienced both at the same time. As the magical music swirled around my head with the pot, I felt I'd arrived at my own, personal bliss. Jimi's guitar dived and danced, sang and cried, aroused and soothed. I'd never heard anything like it, and I'd never felt this way before. "I want to feel like this all the time," I said to no one in particular. And that's what I set out to do. Every day for years I stayed high, or tried to. I was trying to make something permanent out of a passing experience. That moment could happen only once, but in my delusion, my insanity, I thought I could hold on to it forever.

Many people run into this same problem in meditation. They're on a retreat and a great stillness, or peace, or bliss, or vision comes over them. They think, "This is it, I've got it," and then spend years trying to re-capture that illusory moment. They keep telling themselves (and others) that their practice isn't going well, because they are comparing what's happening now to what happened in the past. The truth is, the pleasures of meditation are as impermanent (and sometimes seductive) as those of drugs and alcohol.

The Third Characteristic is called No-Self, or *anatta*. When we don't see the ways that our lives are interrelated to everyone else—to every-

thing else—we are living in what Einstein called "an optical delusion of consciousness." Although No-Self can become a heady, esoteric concept, when it comes to the behavior of alcoholics (and others), it may be enough to point out how lost we often are in our own dream—our wants and dislikes, our fears and opinions, in what we call "my life." Our bodies are born of another; language is learned from those around us; our way of understanding the world is largely conditioned by family, friends, teachers; the atmosphere provides us with oxygen; food, water, and for most of us clothing and shelter are dependent on nature and other people. How can we think of ourselves as independent when our very life, moment to moment, depends upon all this and more?

If we apply the concept of No-Self to a gross level, we might ask, What is a nation? Is it the people in the country? But they are always being born and dying—always changing. Is it the land? But that's going through constant geological and sometimes geographical change as well. Is it the national constitution? But a constitution can always be modified. There is, in fact, no one thing we can call a nation.

When looking at the question of personal existence, the Buddha used the example of a chariot: Is it the wheels? the axle? the seat? In the same way, we might ask ourselves: Am I my body? my thoughts? my emotions? my name? my possessions? my past? my job? None of these things is permanent, none of them holds any essence of "me." I am just made up of these ever-changing processes.

Later chapters will explore this idea further, but in the context of alcoholic insanity it can be related to what's called in the Twelve Step tradition "self-will run riot." This is the quality many addicts and alcoholics have which makes them act as if they are the center of the world. Since Buddhism sees the idea of self as delusion, this typical alcoholic tendency is another element of insanity—running around trying to satisfy the demands of an illusory "self" makes no sense. All the Steps work toward dismantling this illusion. Step Two continues this process, which begins

45

with the humility required in the First Step by both looking for help from a Higher Power and admitting that, up to now, we've been insane in our behavior.

The Second Noble Truth tells us that the cause of our suffering is desire and the attachment that forms from desire. This is the very definition of addiction: first the craving for the drug or drink, then a constant desire for it. So, addiction means being buried in suffering, living entirely in desire and attachment. Why would anyone want to suffer, to make their life a veritable realm of suffering? This is surely insane.

We can find another way of understanding being "restored to sanity," in the root of the words themselves. "Sanity" has the same route as "sanitize," to clean or purify. This is the meaning of the Buddhist term sila, mentioned in Step One. When we embark on any spiritual path, there is this process, called in Buddhism the Path of Purification. Buddhism and the Twelve Steps can work together to "sanitize" our hearts and minds, to return us to sanity or purity.

HOW CAN I BELIEVE?

Buddhism offers a safe way to approach faith. The Buddha invited people to "come and see," *ehi-passiko*—to come and see for yourself. In the same way, Twelve Step programs don't recruit members but use their members' success in dealing with addiction to speak for itself, a policy called "attraction rather than promotion." Nobody's trying to sell you something with Buddhism or the Twelve Steps—quite literally, since both are primarily supported by donation—but rather they invite you to see how they work for others and yourself before making a commitment.

The Buddha understood the challenge of faith. In the India of his time, many competing teachers claimed to be the repositories of Truth. One community of eager spiritual seekers, the Kalamas, were confused, and asked his advice. In his famous and fundamental teaching, "The Dilemma of the Kalamas," the Buddha explains how to decide whether a teacher or teaching is useful.

The Buddha starts by sweeping away the past as the container of wisdom. It doesn't matter what people tell you or what's been written down; you don't have to believe something just because it's got the weight of history and tradition behind it, he says.

He goes on to assert that it's not enough that a teaching appeals to our intellect, our logic. While the ideas behind a teaching may be appealing, that doesn't mean they work in real life. What's also implied here is that, just because a teaching "feels right" doesn't mean it is right—a critical point, since we are often drawn to ideas that fit with our own preferences, whether accurate or not.

Finally, he warns against accepting an opinion just because your teacher holds it.

The Buddha takes away many of the standard routes to faith: scripture, tradition, logic, authority. And what he says then is that if you want to know the value of a teacher's offering, you have to try it out and see what the results are. If the results are good, keep it up; if not, drop it. But, to guard against bias in your own interpretation of the results, you should also check with the wise. One way to determine if someone is wise is to see if they are living a skillful life. In Twelve Step terms, "Do you want what they have?" To check with the wise means to listen to the advice of those we trust: a sponsor, mentor, therapist, sibling, parent, friend, or teacher. (Although we don't do something automatically because someone else said we should, we do not dismiss out of hand the suggestions of those who are close to us.)

For those of us skeptics who need proof of the value of a practice or belief, this is a helpful invitation. You can try out the practice, study the teachings, sit with a teacher, and see what happens. If your life gets better and if "wise" people approve, you know you're on the right track. For those whose faith has been damaged, this is also a gentle approach that can rebuild trust and help to gradually open to the possibility of a renewed spiritual life.

FAITH, THE SPIRITUAL FACULTY

Alcoholism is a disease of faith. Alcoholics often develop a cynical attitude toward life, not seeing anything to believe in. When you persistently feel the need to change your consciousness through drugs or booze, you are expressing a lack of trust in life itself. And, in some ways, you are expressing a lack of trust in yourself, in your ability to tolerate life undiluted, to find value in your own, unadulterated experience.

This same difficulty confronts the beginning meditator. Meditation is even more unadulterated than sobriety. Intentionally stopping activity and any diversion can be intimidating. Many people say, "I could never sit still for that long—twenty minutes!" Even without drugs or booze, many of us are trying to control our consciousness with food, TV, music, reading, and other daily habits. Stopping *all* activity as we do in meditation is like a new layer of sobriety: ultimate abstinence (a new X Game?). Trusting this process is frightening, whether you are an alcoholic or not.

Nick, an independent filmmaker, went through a remarkable process with faith. When he began meditation practice he told me that he'd never been able to sit still. Even as a kid he'd always gotten in trouble in school because he was always squirming in his seat. As an adult he'd been treated for anxiety and panic attacks. He was nervous about the idea of meditating for even twenty minutes. We talked about different ways to work with this, and he decided to try an unusual approach.

Each day he would go to a park on the UCLA campus near his house. He found a beautiful glen that was usually quiet. There he did walking meditation for twenty minutes. After developing some calm through walking, he then sat on a bench. In the beginning he would just try to sit for five minutes. After some time, he began to stretch the sitting period, first to ten minutes, fifteen, and up to twenty.

He was beginning to develop confidence in his own ability to sit still and be with his anxiety. He continued to practice in this way until he was able to skip the walking altogether. He bought a meditation cushion and began sitting at home, eventually taking daylong and weekend retreats that required longer and longer periods of stillness. Although in times of stress he still has feelings of anxiety, he's learned to work with these feelings by opening to them and developing calm. In this simple, step-by-step way, he has developed faith in himself and faith in the power of the practice as well.

Although Buddhism and the Twelve Steps both require us to develop faith, thankfully neither requires that we swallow a dogma or belief system whole. Both allow us to take on the amount of faith we can handle, little by little. Step Two says we "came to believe that a power greater than ourselves could restore us to sanity," not that this power could fix everything in our lives. Restoring us to sanity in this case, means helping us get clean and sober.

This isn't a huge Step, and it is often initially made by accepting the group of sober people who you practice the Steps with as a kind of Higher Power. Seeing how the Steps have allowed these people to stay sober—sometimes for unimaginably long times, like six months—can give you the confidence to venture into the process yourself.

In the same way, when we begin meditation, like Nick, we may not feel much calm or insight ourselves, but joining a room full of peaceful meditators often convinces us that there's some value to practice. Once we have this seed of faith, we're on the way to developing our program and our practice.

We all need this seed of faith to weather the difficult early stages of practice when the mind seems to wander endlessly, alternating periods of restlessness and sleepiness leave us frustrated, and sensations we've never felt before appear in the body. And we all need faith to weather early sobriety, with its roller-coaster ride of emotions, awkward first stabs at living more ethically, and unfamiliar, deer-in-the-headlights clarity.

As you practice more, the meditative experience grows deeper and richer. At the same time, you may want to read and hear more of the Buddhist teachings or make a connection with a Buddhist teacher who seems to be living the teachings. In the Twelve Step process, as sobriety takes effect, things improve in your life. You begin to read the literature and gather with others who help you learn how to live without booze or drugs. Finally, when you find a sponsor, you begin to have regular support and inspiration from someone who has truly benefited from and fulfills the promise of sobriety.

These are three of the foundations of faith: practice, study, and contact with a teacher, guide, or spiritual friend. As you practice, you see for yourself the results; as you study, your own experience gets put in perspective of the dharma and the Steps; and, as you sit with a teacher or spend time with a sponsor, you are guided and inspired. In this way, faith develops organically, not based on threats from a punishing God or the mysterious, inscrutable teachings of a foggy past, but through direct experience.

STEP THREE

"Made a decision to turn our will and our lives over to the care of God as we understood Him."

In Step Two we began to break down the resistance to the Higher Power and to build faith. In Step Three we "turn our will and our lives over" to this power. There's nothing mysterious about this process; it's not a magical ritual and doesn't require special grace to accomplish. What it requires is commitment.

When we "make a decision" we are committing ourselves to our spiritual life, committing to placing that at the center of our lives, as the guiding principle. For me, this happened in stages. First, I committed to sobriety itself; then I committed to the program and the Steps; finally, as I was healed from my addictions, I committed more deeply to my Buddhist practice. This commitment, this "decision," is what I think is most important about Step Three. It may not matter what we use as a Higher Power, but our commitment to follow a higher purpose does.

Of course, I can't ignore the Higher Power question we began to explore in Step Two. I often get phone calls from people who are having trouble getting sober and, having heard that I work with combining Buddhism and the Twelve Steps, hope that I'm going to tell them that they don't need a Higher Power to get sober. People hope that Buddhism, a nontheistic religion (or at least not monotheistic), will give them an out, that they'll be able to skip over Step Three. That is neither my intention nor my conclusion about Buddhism and the Steps. In fact, I think that Buddhism offers a more profound understanding of Higher Power than the one I got as a Catholic boy. (That's not to say Catholicism, or any other religion, doesn't offer a profound vision of God, only that I never went beyond the childish understanding.)

For some, Step Three is simple, a turning toward something they're already comfortable with. For these people, working the Step means reconnecting with an existing faith and trying to bring that faith more fully into their lives.

For others, the Step is a giant obstacle. Some may have been raised with no religious beliefs; others feel betrayed or disillusioned by their faith; and many are accustomed to denying the existence of anything that can't be proved scientifically. Some people have turned entirely away from the Twelve Steps as a potential path to recovery solely because of their resistance to this Step. Using Buddhist principles and teachings can make it easier to work this Step, particularly for those with skeptical habits of mind.

Step Three completes the surrender initiated in Step One. In that Step we acknowledge the ways we are powerless over *substances*; in this Step we seek out and commit ourselves to accepting a *spiritual* power. We move from trying to cope with the world through manipulating our consciousness with gross physical intoxication to attuning ourselves to a subtler realm wherein acceptance and alignment with truth brings a deeper and truer transformation.

In a sense, alcoholism, drug addiction, and other dysfunctional behaviors are the act of turning our will, unconsciously, over to a *de*structive higher power. In Step Three we consciously turn our will over to a *con*structive power, or at least turn our focus toward our spiritual growth and away from our spiritual destruction.

Making a decision

The Third Step says we should "turn our will and our lives over," to learn to trust and have faith. Where in Step Two we recognized the possibility of faith and recovery, in Step Three we try to figure out how to act on that faith. It was only when I became willing to get a sponsor after a year's sobriety that I fully took this Step. For that to happen, I had to hit another kind of bottom in sobriety.

When I got sober in the summer of 1985, it was a grudging act. As though with gritted teeth, I said to myself, "Okay, this isn't working, I'll give it up." But I wasn't ready to be a full member of a Twelve Step program. Instead, I would drop in to meetings occasionally and stand in the back, then leave without a word to anyone, much less sharing with the group. Although I wasn't willing to commit myself, I was afraid to go it alone, since I'd never been able to stay sober that way.

During this time I worked the First Step, recognizing my powerlessness over alcohol and how unmanageable my life was. As the sober days added up, a trust in my own ability not to drink grew into a greater trust, that I was going to be able to handle life, that I would be okay.

As I traveled with the Hollywood Argyles, I would meditate and read the Twelve Step literature in my motel room, trying to understand this sobriety work and deepen my spiritual connection; onstage and at rehearsal I'd pray to get through the difficult band situations; and through it all I tried to trust that my life would get better.

So much of that first sober year was spent on the road, in Odessa, Texas; Tulsa, Oklahoma; Jackson Hole, Wyoming; Huron, South Dakota; Quesnel, British Columbia; Yellow Knife, Northwest Territories. Playing in bars and hotel lounges across North America, I somehow kept my commitment to sobriety. Through band fights and agent screwups; through driving into a ditch in a blizzard in Wyoming and fighting our way through blinding thunderstorms in West Texas; through crossing the Great Plains of the Midwest and the Ice Bridge of the Great Slave Lake.

One night, in Yellow Knife, in the middle of "Gimme Some Lovin'," the old, wooden stage began shaking under us as we rocked harder and harder. I danced past the drummer, smiling and ripping off licks, when I saw a look of terror on his face. I turned just in time to see the PA speaker, which was perched precariously on a small, round bar table, tip off, coming down as though in slow motion on the center of my second guitar, which lay on the floor at the side of the stage. Strings popped, wood cracked, metal bent. The sickening sound of a guitar neck shattering was drowned out by the roaring notes of Stevie Winwood and the Spencer Davis Group; I felt oddly disconnected, as though I were watching a movie with a blaring soundtrack. As we ended the song and I walked over to the beautiful guitar that lay like a corpse on the side of the shabby stage, the reality of the loss hit me. My heart sank; I was a "Buddhist," so I wasn't supposed to care about material things. But it was like a child, this instrument, fragile and magical, full of unrealized notes. I wanted to blame someone, yell at someone, somehow change what had happened. I picked up the instrument and a splinter of wood from the neck stabbed my hand. I wanted a drink. But instead of losing it—my temper or my sobriety—the words of the Serenity Prayer came to me: "God, grant me the serenity to accept the things I cannot change. . . ."

Like a mantra, I repeated this prayer: when we were fired from the club in Odessa; when we got shorted our pay in British Columbia; when the truck broke down in Tahoe. Accept, accept, accept. I'd never known what that meant. I'd raged my whole life at things I couldn't change. Some years before when I'd been a strict vegetarian, I discovered meat in a burrito I'd brought home. I screamed, "There's meat in my burrito!" going on and on about how terrible it was that the taco stand had made a mistake, how unforgivable it was, how terrible it was for me. My girlfriend laughed—even more galling—in disbelief that I could be so hypersensitive and rigid: "It happened, it's over, deal with it." All I could do was focus on my perceived agony and slam down a six-pack, drinking myself into oblivion.

Now, on the road, I at least had this tool of acceptance, which helped me to keep from drinking. But, in terms of my sobriety, I had little else.

Finally, around the time of my first anniversary of sobriety, I began to see that I had another problem besides booze and drugs: waitresses.

When you're on the road with a band, the easiest women to meet are the waitresses in the clubs you're playing. You're working with them, so you have something in common, and they're always at the club at closing time. Road life ain't all that exciting: wake up in a strange motel room; eat crappy food in a diner; rehearse in a dark and smelly bar; perform to an often disinterested and sometimes downright hostile audience. Take away the pot and booze, and there's not much to recommend it. Except the waitresses. So, from one town to the next I would sidle up to the waitress station after the first set on the first night and strike up a conversation. Oftentimes this at least provided some friendly talk; occasionally it led to a date; rarely sex was involved; and once that year I "fell in love." Meaning, I developed an addictive craving for a waitress I met in British Columbia. A beautiful redhead with penetrating blue eyes and a wild streak, she dumped me when I came back to visit her in Vancouver at the end of our trip.

I headed back to L.A. with the sense of deep craving, the feeling that I needed sex to survive. Over those long, lonely months on the road, the habit of filling my time with women had grown into an obsession. Back in L.A., I sought out the waitress I'd known at the last bar I played before getting sober. Afterward I felt shame and completely unsatisfied. Not only was sleeping with women not satisfying my desire, it was making it stronger.

Finally, I came to see that this was an insatiable desire; in fact, the more

I sought out sexual comfort, the less satisfied I was. A classic example of the Second Noble Truth: Desire is the cause of suffering. Knowing a little about Buddhism, about how acting on craving creates more craving, not less, I saw that I needed to stop.

As I tried to understand what was happening to me, I realized that what was at the root of this obsession was loneliness: my hunger for sexual contact was fundamentally a desire to connect. Further it occurred to me that if loneliness was my problem, maybe I should try participating more in the Twelve Step program I'd watched from afar.

It was then, in August of 1986, at a year sober, that I "turned my will and my life over"—perhaps not to God yet, but at least to the Program.

The first thing I committed to was a dictum I'd heard suggested for newcomers: ninety meetings in ninety days. I'd also heard that you should get a sponsor, so I began looking around.

I remember seeing Stephen at one or two meetings before the day I heard him speak at a Friday morning meeting in Santa Monica. He was celebrating eleven years of sobriety, and as he spoke, he told how over the last year he'd almost gotten drunk. Everything had gone wrong—his business, his relationship, even his car had died. He'd been suicidal. His friends in the program had helped him get through it all, and now he felt reinspired and recommitted to his program and the Steps.

Many times, the people who had been sober for a long time seemed superficial to me; everything was great and they seemed to think that if it wasn't, that was because you were doing something wrong. But Stephen seemed real. Even though he'd been sober so long, he still had problems—and he dealt with them and got through them. He was a survivor, and that's how I saw myself.

As the meeting broke up, I walked over to him. He was laughing with a friend, but when I asked him to be my sponsor, his demeanor changed immediately.

"Well, let's talk," he said. "How long have you been sober?"

"A year."

"And you haven't had a sponsor?"

"No."

"You're lucky to be alive."

At the time I thought he was exaggerating in the way that I'd heard from people trying to scare you in meetings. Only years later would I come to appreciate the accuracy of this statement, after seeing so many people die of alcoholism and drug addiction. People who can't stay sober are people who can't "turn it over," who can't, in the words of the Big Book, "completely give themselves to this simple program." It's this giving ourselves over that happens in Step Three, letting go, at least to some significant degree, of our own control. Just being willing to take the advice of a trusted friend, mentor, teacher, or sponsor is a huge movement away from acting out of our own ego-driven impulses. For an addict or alcoholic, so often these impulses, over years of drinking and using, have become so destructive as to no longer be trustworthy. So, before we can begin to trust our own inner direction, it's best to allow another, more sane voice to guide us.

Stephen and I went out for coffee after that meeting and he told me to start writing a Fourth Step. He said that if I got through a year, I must have already worked the first three Steps to some degree. When I look back now, I think maybe I really worked the Third Step for the first time when I asked him to be my sponsor. I finally committed myself to sobriety and all that it means. I'd always been afraid to get a sponsor because I didn't want someone to tell me what to do. Now I was willingly offering myself to him, stepping into the unknown of spiritual work. I had "made a decision," and there was no turning back.

In Buddhism, the "decision" to commit ourselves to our spiritual growth is called Right Intention. This means "making a decision" to try to live a life based on the principles of compassion, awareness, and openness. As with Step Three, we try to keep our purpose in mind in all our activities, bringing our spiritual commitment to bear in all things. The Buddha said, "Intention, I tell you, is karma," which means that the motivation behind actions determines whether the action is skillful or not. A little girl runs into the street; you scream and grab her, ripping her out of the way just before a car speeds by: good karma. A little boy walks in front of the TV just as the winning field goal is kicked; you scream and grab him, ripping him out of the way as the ball splits the goal posts: bad karma. One was an unselfish act based on compassion and protecting the child's life; the other was a selfish act based on your own craving for mindless entertainment with no regard for the child.

Developing Right Intention means paying closer attention to ourselves, to seeing what's really behind our words and actions. Meditation itself trains us to watch in this way, to see, moment to moment, what's going on in our minds in a clear, nonjudgmental way. When we apply this kind of attention to ourselves in daily life, we can catch when we're about to do or say something destructive; and, we can notice opportunities to act more helpfully.

In meditation we set the intention to be present to our experience and kind to ourselves. Then, when our mind wanders or we become uncomfortable, we can remind ourselves why we are practicing and bring ourselves back to our present experience. This returning, over and over, is the way we subvert the mind's habits of clinging to thoughts and feelings. Intention acts as the driving force behind our spiritual growth, a constant reminder of what to let go of and where to point our minds.

UNDERSTANDING GOD

Of course, the decision or commitment or intention that we make in Step Three isn't the whole of the Step. There's also the question of "God *as we understood Him.*"

In some sense, I think it's impossible for me to "understand" God—God is beyond understanding. Like Right View, I can have some intimation of God when I begin my spiritual search, but only when I'm "fully enlightened" can I have perfect Right View and a true understanding of God. Who knows? In fact, just holding this "Who knows?" can be a powerful way to work with the God idea. I'll explore that later, but I think it can be of value to explore how Buddhist teachings parallel those of the Western ideas of God.

As I described in Step Two, my first understanding of God came with my Catholic upbringing. God was apparently a man—or looked like a man—and was kind of like a combination between Santa Claus and a punishing parent: he'd give you great stuff sometimes if you asked for it, and smack you down if you broke one of his Commandments. He seemed a little irrational. He was supposed to be loving, and yet could really make people suffer; sometimes he punished little kids for no apparent reason. Buddhadasa, the great twentieth-century Thai Buddhist master, calls this, "the God of people language," and equates it with a childish understanding.

He goes on to say that people who have this misunderstanding of God "do not yet know God in the true sense of the word, the God that is neither person, nor mind, nor spirit, but is the naturally self-existent Dhamma, or the Power of Dhamma."

God doesn't have emotions, he says. God isn't angry or loving, joyful, or funny. This is what humans do, not God. God doesn't favor one people over another. God doesn't care what people think about "Him." God isn't a human or anything like a human (and definitely not a guy). God isn't a being. God is a power.

When I was a child I was taught that God is everywhere and God knows everything. This confused me. Like Santa Claus—"He sees you when you're sleeping, he knows when you're awake," and worse yet, "He knows if you've been bad or good"—God somehow was all over the place. How could one person be everywhere? He couldn't. But something could: the Law of Karma.

The Law of Karma says that everything operates under the rules of cause and effect. Every time you do something, there is a reaction. If you go in the closet with a bag of Cheetos, no human being will know. However, you'll still gain weight and feel sick afterward: you will experience the karmic results. As Ruth Denison puts it, "You don't get away with nothing, dahling." The Laws of the Universe, the dharma, is inescapable. We are all, always, governed by these rules.

The Law of Impermanence can't be wished away, either. Everything is constantly changing. This is a law, an impersonal fact that is equally true for everyone and everything. It is part of the dharma.

So, we could say that "God" is the way things are and the underlying rules that govern the way things are. God includes all of nature and the laws of nature. (Nature is too limiting a word, unless we recognize humans as part of nature and therefore anything we create is also part of nature.)

Buddhadasa says there are two other components to God besides "nature" and the laws of nature: the responsibilities of humans in relation to the laws, and the fruits of fulfilling those responsibilities. This means that if we make certain choices, we will get certain results. If we align ourselves skillfully with the Law of Karma, we will have pleasant results—the fruits. In the Steps, this is what is meant by "the care of God." This is not a God who takes care of us just because he's a nice guy. It's far more impersonal than that. Instead, we fulfill our karmic responsibilities, and we receive the karmic results. Every religion provides a map for these responsibilities. This is how the Ten Commandments can be seen: as models for creating positive karma. And this is what the Eightfold Path is. The Buddha gave a clear map of skillful behavior that will lead to happiness and freedom. The map is his gift to us, but we have to work it for ourselves if we want to realize the gift.

So, when we "made a decision to turn our will and our lives over to the care of God *as we understood Him*" from a Buddhist perspective, we were deciding to try to follow this map, trusting that there was value in living skillfully, of making the sacrifices this path requires, and of committing ourselves to our spiritual growth. The alternative is to believe that there is no cause and effect, that the universe is random, that our actions have no effect, and that therefore it doesn't matter what we do.

Certainly, for an addict or alcoholic cause and effect is pretty clear: when we stop using our drug of choice, things change for the better. For a meditator, it's equally clear that when we follow the Eightfold Path, our practice deepens and becomes more rich. This is how the Law of Karma comes alive for us, as we see it operating for ourselves.

Buddhadasa opens up an understanding of God that fits with Buddhist and Twelve Step principles. This Higher Power of the dharma guides us, protects us, and inspires us. Turning our will and our lives over to this power means living in accordance with what is true; it means acting out of compassion and kindness; pursuing our noblest goals; seeking truth in all things; it means striving for perfection of heart and mind while bowing to the truth of who we are, with all our imperfections and failings.

THE REFUGES

I think it's easier for us to understand a God who is somehow like us. Seeing God as simply a power or set of laws, while perhaps accurate, is not particularly warm and fuzzy. The Buddhist teachings on the Three Refuges—Buddha, dharma, and sangha—offer us a more embodied form of Higher Power. On the most literal level, the Refuges refer to the historical Buddha, his teachings, and his monastic followers. Taking refuge is making a commitment to live by and to trust in these "Three Jewels."

The idea of "refuge" is the same as "turning our will and our lives over to the care" of a Higher Power. But, before these teachings could become meaningful for me, I had to study them more deeply.

Several years ago I was on retreat with some Theravadan monks and nuns in Northern California. The retreat was put on at a Catholic retreat center built in a Mediterranean style around a central courtyard. A big conference room had been cleared of chairs and tables so we could sit on the floor. Tall, eastward-facing windows let streams of morning light into the room; in the evening, the sounds of crickets outside laid a carpet of sound. Each morning, before dawn, we gathered to begin the day with the traditional Theravadan morning chants. In the evening we chanted as well, long, tritonal verses that we intoned first in Pali, the Theravadan ecclesiastic language, then in English. Many of the chants centered around praising Buddha, dharma, sangha.

Along with the monastics, we would bow each time we entered the hall, kneeling with hands held in prayer, touching the forehead to the floor three times, to symbolize respect for the Refuges.

I found myself resisting these words, the formality and ritualism reminding me of the Catholic Church; the constant praising reminding me of praising Jesus or God in the Christian tradition I had left as a teenager. Even though I had great respect for the monastics, the tradition, and the Refuges, I found my meditation becoming more and more agitated as I struggled with these old feelings. I rebelled at the idea of supplication, of obsequious pleading to something, hoping that by saying nice things about God, Buddha, whatever, that I'd be taken care of. This behavior always seemed so false to me, as though by kissing up to God I could get "Him" to fix things up for me, keep me safe, take care of my job, family, soul. I didn't want my Buddhist practice to deteriorate into this kind of falseness and superficiality.

A week into the retreat, I decided I had to confront this problem. I began a contemplation of the Refuges. It made no sense to me to ask the

Buddha to take care of me: he was a person, not a God, and he's dead; the dharma, his teachings, are a bunch of words in a book; the monastics are people too, no more capable of solving my problems than the long-dead Buddha. There had to be a deeper meaning.

I went for an interview with the lead teacher, Ajahn Amaro, an Englishman who had ordained in his early twenties in Thailand. Now about forty, he was an "elder" in the tradition, the abbot of a new monastery nearby. His wry sense of humor and clear, natural teaching style made him accessible and, for me, trustworthy.

Interviews took place in a room next to the meditation hall with the same morning light shining in. The furniture from the larger room next door had been moved in here, long tables pressed up against the wall, and chairs bunched together in the corner. A small area had been cleared where we sat on broad, leather couches with a coffee table between us.

"I've been struggling with the whole ritualistic thing around the Refuges," I said. "It reminds me of the Catholic Church."

"Yes," said Ajahn Amaro. "It does get a bit sort of baroque. But you have to look at the underlying meaning." He was sitting cross-legged on the couch and adjusted his orange robe. In the warm November weather, he wore it in the traditional way, with one shoulder bare. His shaved head made his prominent nose seem even larger; his broad forehead looked to contain an unusually large brain. "As you know, the word 'Buddha' means 'one who is awake,' or 'the one who knows'; so taking refuge in the Buddha is taking refuge in that awake part of you, it means making the effort to bring mindfulness into each moment."

"So you're saying mindfulness itself is the protection, the refuge?"

"Exactly. It's not something outside yourself, but your own, innate ability to engage in each moment fully." His shaved right eyebrow rose archly. "Mindfulness itself—the Buddha—keeps you safe by letting you see clearly the results of your actions."

"And dharma?"

"Dharma is the truth of the way things are—it's what you see when you are awake. In being mindful, you start to see things more clearly. Then you have to live by those things you see. The only dharma you can really take refuge in, that you can fully live inside, is your own insight into the truth."

I took a deep breath and smiled. A week's meditation had grounded me so that my body sitting here, the sunlight crawling up my leg, the monk before me, everything had a strong feeling of immediacy, of fullness, of aliveness.

"And sangha," I said. "What is the interior sangha?"

"Well, when 'the one who knows' sees 'the ways things are,' what comes forth from that is unselfishness and benevolent activity. Refuge in sangha is this capacity to harmonize with other beings and situations: spiritual communion. If we choose unselfishness, we realize our connectedness and harmony is the result."

I look at him. This is a surprising conclusion for me. I thought sangha was supposed to be people—monks or other Buddhists. I have to take in this new idea. "So you mean that when we get clear—awake—and see what's really true, we tend to be more kind, generous, and all that?"

"Yes."

"But for me, I was practicing pretty seriously and still using drugs and alcohol—still in denial, and it doesn't seem like meditation helped."

"It's well acknowledged that delusion—the Pali word is moha—is the trickiest of the fires to extinguish. Sometimes there is not even a whiff of smoke yet it's still burning. Still, although the capacity to be unselfish might be severely obstructed by circumstance or habit or whatever, the fact is that the refuge is there. Even when you still drank, there must have been a part of you that at least *wanted* something different. There you were, going on retreat or whatever, trying to find something more meaningful, trying to develop the qualities of compassion and lovingkindness."

It's true. I tend to devalue my spiritual work before I got sober, but it must have meant something; it wasn't all an attempt to escape. There was some sincere desire to grow and develop all the positive qualities that Buddhism fosters.

"What about the more literal aspect of sangha—being part of the community?" I ask.

"It's very difficult to practice alone. The Buddha set things up so that the monastics would be dependent on the lay community. That way, if they don't do their job, they get immediate negative feedback: no lunch." He smiles, his eyebrow again rising. "For you to be on this retreat, there's all the volunteers, the manager, the cooks; then there's your family at home who support your being here—hopefully. Then there's your boss, who presumably let you take time off, and on and on. And, of course, there's this whole history, all the people who have practiced before you who kept the teachings alive for more than twenty-five hundred years."

"So sangha is a web," I say. "I mean, you could say the earth and sky, the water and all of nature were somehow supporting me."

"Yes, in a very real way they are. Without that 'web,' there's no possibility of practice."

I come away from the interview, and from the retreat, with a new appreciation of the Refuges, not as ritualistic totems to which you bow down, but as the very essence of spiritual life, the nourishment that makes that journey possible.

"I take refuge in the Buddha." I commit myself to being mindful, to being conscious in every aspect of my life. I won't shut out parts of myself: when I'm cheering my favorite baseball team, I'll try to feel the energy in my body; when I'm fighting my way through traffic, I'll try to open my heart to the other drivers and to my own suffering in this moment; when I'm craving an escape, a drink, a drug, another life, I'll try to be gentle but firm with myself, to show compassion for my own desire and resolve to stay with my sobriety. And, finally, I will practice meditation daily and find ways to strengthen my practice through retreats, study, and self-examination.

"I take refuge in the dharma." I commit myself to looking for the truth of the way things are and fulfilling those insights, to living by the principles that I have come to understand: impermanence, karma, suffering, that all things are without an independent self. I can't hang on to anything, because it is impermanent; I will try to practice letting go. I am responsible for my own karma; I will try to practice skillful living in words and actions. I recognize that life is inherently difficult; I will try to help others who suffer and be gentle with my own pain. My sense of self is a delusion; I will try to act less self-centered and to find ways to serve others.

"I take refuge in the sangha." I commit myself to compassion, lovingkindness, generosity, and a moral life; I commit myself to supporting and being supported by the community of the spirit. I will regularly attend gatherings to fulfill this commitment. I will work toward the development of a greater and more diverse community. I will remember to be grateful to all that makes this life and this practice possible, to the bounty of nature, the bounty of this tradition, and the bounty of my own life.

DON'T KNOW

Some people may feel I'm trying too hard to describe God. All of my ideas may just be attempts to find words to explain what is, ultimately, unexplainable. As the opening lines of the Tao Te Ching say, "The Way that can be spoken is not the true Way." This calls into question any verbal teaching, and reminds me of the great twentieth-century Indian sage Ramana Maharshi. After his awakening, he rarely spoke. He lived in a cave on a sacred mountain in Southern India where his followers came to be in his presence. Sometimes just being with someone of this level of realization can be more powerful than hearing him speak. The main practice he taught was a continuous asking, "Who am I?" By probing deeper and deeper into this simple question, many people have had profound openings. The point isn't to find an answer to the question so much as it is to keep shedding limiting concepts until nothing remains.

Another contemporary Zen Buddhist teacher from Korea teaches "Don't Know." In this practice we recognize that we really don't have answers to many of life's basic questions. What happens after death? Don't know. How exactly does karma work? Don't know. Is there a God who created everything? Don't know. What's going to happen next? Don't know.

Life is full of surprises. Much of our time is spent trying to control what happens and to understand how things work. When we practice "Don't Know," instead of thinking—or hoping—that we have the answers, we stay alert to each unfolding moment as a unique experience. In this way we bring a freshness to each moment—Beginner's Mind, Zen master Suzuki Roshi called it—which helps us to stay awake to the magic of life.

Recently I was coteaching a workshop on Buddhism and the Steps and I gave what I thought was a profound and cogent talk on Buddhism and God, using many of the ideas I've just told you about. When I was finished, my teaching partner added that, in fact, "God" is a mystery. We don't know if there is a God or what he/she/it is like. He said that any ideas about God were just thoughts, and that ultimately God was a mystery, and that's the way he liked to hold the God idea.

After I'd tried so hard to encapsulate God with words and concepts, I felt somewhat deflated to be followed up in this way. But I also felt relieved. On some level, all the ideas and concepts about God might be helpful, but my partner was right: I can't know what God is. I can't define God. And, ultimately, I think we have to let this truth in. As the saying goes, we need to "Let Go and Let God." We need to let God be, just fall into a trust that this mystery can't be solved. When we do this, we may be able to be with God, to live in that immanence without words and without questions—or answers.

So, when I look at this Step, I realize that I don't have to understand God. I can live in the mystery, stay awake in the Don't Know.

I'm grateful to the authors of the Steps who put in the critical phrase, "*as we understood Him.*" God can certainly be understood in many different ways. It's not important how we understand God, but rather that we have a sense of that which is greater than us, the wonder of creation, of consciousness; the miracle of the loving heart, of the innocent child; the joy of exploring the inner life; the marvel of engaging the world. It's these connections that grow as we place ourselves in the stream of spiritual life through our commitment to Step Three.

GROWING ON THE PATH

Like the moment when I asked Stephen to sponsor me and fully committed myself to the Steps and sobriety, a moment came when I dove into Buddhist practice as well. It was shortly after the retreat with Ruth Denison when she told me I was at the Third Noble Truth. I'd met with my teacher, James, after that retreat to talk about what had happened. Shortly after our meeting he asked me to take more of a leadership role in our local Buddhist community as a co-facilitator of a Kalyanna Mitta group. I had heard about these small groups of meditators who would meet regularly to discuss their practice and support one another's spiritual growth. In fact, it sounded kind of like a Buddhist Twelve Step meeting. However, I was hesitant at first to take on this responsibility. I wasn't sure I was ready.

We met in his back garden amidst lush, overgrown California coastal plants, live oak, jasmine, jacaranda, and ivy. James introduced me to Sheridan, the person he wanted me to lead the group with.

First he told us about how the groups were organized and that we had a lot of latitude in structuring our gatherings. Then he assured us that we didn't have to be teachers, that we just had to keep things harmonious and focused on Buddhist teachings. Eventually, despite our reluctance, the two of us agreed.

At that point, I'd been sober for more than seven years and practicing meditation for longer than that. Through my Twelve Step work, I'd tried to live with faith, to trust that if I stayed sober and did my best that things would work out. And they had: I'd found my way back to school, where I was on the verge of my B.A. from Berkeley and ready to go off to graduate school. The possibility of escaping the poverty I'd lived in since leaving home to become a musician was now very real. And, while I still hadn't made a relationship work long-term, it did seem like the ones I'd been in lately had been healthier and less messy.

I felt I'd been living a "spiritual" life, and yet I knew that my commitment to my meditation practice had been less than total. When I got sober, I thought that somehow Buddhism had failed me. If it was so great, then why did I hit this bottom on alcohol and drugs? Why wasn't my meditation enough to cure me of alcoholism? In the first few years of my sobriety I continued to practice and go on short retreats, usually once a year, but I didn't feel that Buddhism was my main practice; I felt that the Steps were the center of my spiritual life.

But after the retreat with Ruth and then the opportunity with Sheridan, I saw there was a shift happening. I wanted to deepen my involvement in meditation and Buddhism. Although I didn't quite see how the Steps and Buddhism went together, I sensed that they could complement each other, and that, just maybe, my spiritual life could become even deeper through their integration.

Sheridan and I went on to form the Kalyanna Mitta group. A big surprise for me was that most of the people who joined were also in Twelve Step programs. Maybe I wasn't the only one who was seeing a connection between Buddhism and the Steps.

At that point I began to make the commitment to Buddhism that I'd earlier made to the Steps. I began to bring the two together in my life instead of keeping them isolated from each other. And once I did that, my spiritual life became more integrated, and my commitment to growth became more total. I was "turning my will and my life over" in a new way.

TOTALLY UNDER CONTROL

Before any of this happened, before Step Three, before sobriety, before Buddhism, my attempts at growth lacked something essential—a true surrender. Like many alcoholics, I spent years trying to "control and enjoy" my drinking. For almost an entire year, when I was twenty-six, I didn't drink at all.

SPRING 1976, BETHLEHEM, PENNSYLVANIA

I walk into my parent's kitchen and see my father pouring some strange looking brown powdery stuff into a glass of tomato juice. He stirs it in, then knocks it back—the whole scene reminiscent of the times I'd seen him downing a shot of crème de menthe in the pantry of our old house. Only this time he's drinking for health.

He's been retired for five years now, and he and my mother have moved into an apartment in a converted mansion, a building that was once owned by one of my mother's uncles. If my grandfather hadn't drunk himself out of the family business, we might have owned one of these giants, too.

"What are you drinking?" I ask my father.

"Bran," he says. He points to a book on the kitchen table: *The Save Your Life Diet*. "Take a look."

The book was one of the first mainstream publications to come out of the health food movement begun by hippies in the sixties. It explains how our diets don't have enough fiber, and that fiber is important to digestion. It says that a lack of fiber causes colon cancer. I decide I should try the diet.

I've just turned twenty-six and I'm worrying about colon cancer. What's going on here? I've been trying to find a way to change how I feel for years. Pot and booze have not been that effective in curing what I've diagnosed as depression. So, maybe diet will do it. That week, during a brief stay with my parents between gigs, I start washing down bran with my father. I like the results. I continue reading the book, and near the end it says, "As with any healthy diet, no alcohol should be consumed." Huh? Who says alcohol shouldn't be part of a healthy diet? Oh, well, if that's what the man says, I better do it. There and then I decide to stop drinking. No big deal. I can control my drinking; I've been doing it for years—well, sort of controlling it. I mean, most of the time I don't get drunk, just occasionally, and there's nothing wrong with getting drunk once in a while, right?

When I stop drinking I feel as if I'm confirming once more that I'm not an alcoholic. "See, I can quit anytime I want." (Of course I continued to smoke pot every day, but that's an "herb.") What happens over those months that I'm not drinking? Well, a lot.

I start jogging every day—my first adult exercise routine. One day when my band is playing at a Ramada Inn in North Carolina during the Bicentennial celebration, I take a book on meditation by Alan Watts to the red dirt track I've been running every morning. After my run, I open the side doors of my van and sit. I read the instructions and close my eyes. Nothing happens. Oh, well. I guess I can't meditate.

Meanwhile, my struggles with my girlfriend, the lead singer and coleader of the band, go on. She's still drinking, which gives me something to be self-righteous about. One night she locks me out of our apartment. I put my foot through the door.

The band's not doing so well, either. We get fired from a hotel gig in Mt. Kisko, New York, and I smash up our room. (The agent sends me the bill.)

There's a name for this kind of behavior: dry drunk. I'm not drinking, but the underlying causes of my problems are still there.

Eventually the band breaks up, I break up with my girlfriend, and in January of 1977, I move back in with my parents while I record a demo tape to take to New York. One night I go out to a bar to see a local band. It's uncomfortable standing there with my hands empty; I'm used to being on stage, not in the audience. I'm thirsty, and I barely remember why I stopped drinking. I order a tall Rolling Rock. When I drink it I feel as if I've been poisoned. The alcohol feels awful in my system, alien and toxic. I know what the cure for that feeling is—I order another one. I start to relax, leaning back against the wall. When the band takes a break I introduce myself. Soon I'm sitting with the women who came with the band. Everything is normal in my life.

Nothing really happens that night—no doom descends, no arrests or crises. But I've opened the door again, and it won't be closed for another nine years.

So ends my experiment with sobriety.

Why didn't things work out when I stopped drinking? Why was my behavior just as bad, if not worse, during that time? Why was I able to go back so easily to drinking? The answer, at least part of it, is that I was trying to stop drinking on my own. I was acting purely on my own will, not turning the process over to a Higher Power or seeking any support or help. I had a vague desire to get more healthy, with some idea that happiness or less depression would result. Nothing had really changed, and I didn't see any particular benefit to not drinking. The Big Book tells lots of similar stories.

It was soon after I started drinking again that I became a vegetarian, once again thinking that I could fix myself through some external means. Fiber diets, vegetarianism, jogging, even quitting drinking altogether without a spiritual program are simply end runs, attempts to solve problems without the real surrender required. I hadn't "made a decision," either, to turn my life over, or, in fact, to truly change. I was hoping I could tweak a few things without giving up control. I hadn't recognized or acknowledged either that I was an alcoholic or that I couldn't control my own drinking. I hadn't recognized my powerlessness, my insanity, or my need to get help from something greater than my own stubborn will.

FINDING OUR OWN WORDS

In Step Two I talk about the evolution of my own understanding of God or a Higher Power. The short phrase at the end of Step Three, "as we understood Him," is what has allowed many people to work this Step. Without this escape clause, a large percentage of the people who have gone through Twelve Step programs would have stopped at this point. In fact, some people still have trouble with the Step because of the word "Him."

Language is always an issue in spiritual teachings. First of all, as I've talked about, these teachings are trying to explain something that goes beyond language; words are only an attempt to represent reality, they are not reality itself. But still we must speak, we must try to find a way to communicate our understanding. Language always comes out of a particular time and place, a particular culture. Inevitably it becomes dated.

How do we respond to that? One way is to preserve and study the original texts, as is done with Shakespeare and Chaucer. Both the Buddhist and the Twelve Step literature have been preserved in this way. When I talk about the Steps, it's with this kind of respect. When I read the Steps in a meeting, I don't change the words "God" or "Him." These were the words written by the founders, and for me, they need to be honored.

Another response—not an alternative but an additional one—is to recast the language. In Buddhist history this has been done in commentaries. Each generation has its own voice that expresses its understanding of the teachings. With the Twelve Step tradition, likewise, there has been a great deal of such commentary, as our culture and language change and we need new interpretations of the original texts.

In one workshop, a student said, "I feel like I have to constantly be translating what I hear in meetings to fit with my Buddhist understanding." Rather than seeing this as a frustrating task, I recommended that she see this as a natural part of the process of finding her own spiritual path. You begin by doing a painstaking word-for-word translation. Then, once you've gotten comfortable, it's like learning a foreign language where the translation happens naturally without any thought. You just hear what others are saying and take it in with your own understanding. You know what the real meaning is.

Finding our own language for the Steps is a useful exercise as long as we don't forget the original intent. We have to be careful that we are only translating, not rewriting the meaning to let ourselves off the hook of doing the difficult work of transformation.

BALANCING FAITH AND WISDOM

In Step Two I explore the importance of faith in spiritual practice. Step Three is where we express that faith in our surrender to a Higher Power.

However, we need to take care with our faith, not allowing it to override our own common sense and wisdom.

One of the Middle Way teachings of the Buddha points to the need for balance between faith and wisdom, between openheartedness and discrimination. If we are to develop our spiritual life, we need to have both of these. We need to be able to access the soft, accepting, loving, and compassionate place in ourselves we call "the heart." Here we discover the sense of connection with others and with the universe; we learn to live with uncertainty; to trust in our intuition; to take risks based on this intuition. We need to be able to "turn our will and our lives over to the care of God" and venture deeper into the spiritual life, even though we don't know where it will lead or if it even makes sense. This is the power of faith.

We also need to question our assumptions; to look at many sides of questions; to study the texts of our faith and analyze them. To compare our experiences with the teachings; to contemplate and parse the meanings of myth, dreams, and visions. This is the power of wisdom.

When either one of these qualities dominates, we risk derailing our work. With too much faith, we no longer question anything. We take everything at face value so that the nuances of ancient poetic and mythic teaching are taken literally and lead us to rigid, irrational, and destructive beliefs. This is the faith of the absolutist, the fundamentalist, the fanatic. It is this kind of faith that leads people into cults in which they give up, voluntarily, their innate ability to question and come to their own understanding, and where one idea or teacher is accepted as perfect and unquestionable.

With too much wisdom, the hindrance of doubt comes to dominate the mind. There is an unwillingness to accept anything that is not before your eyes or that can't be "proved" through science or logic. You toss out your ability to understand things through subjective experience. The academic mantra becomes, "What are your sources?" This particular attitude is very common in our contemporary, Western, materialist culture. It has the effect of narrowing possibility to that which has already been known or understood. There is no room for imagination or discovery.

T OO   MUCH   WISDOM

One day I was working in my office when I got a call.

"Hi, my name is Lee, and James gave me your number. He said you might be able to help me."

I knew right away this was probably an addict or alcoholic, because those are the people James usually refers to me. I was right. Lee was a middle-aged, middle-class cocaine addict—although he didn't use that term. He claimed that he got high only occasionally, but the tone of his voice, and the very fact he was calling a stranger for help, suggested otherwise. Just as a person who gets pulled over by a cop for drunk driving always claims to have had just one or two beers, people who are considering getting sober are never addicts or alcoholics. This to me is like a homeless person saying they think it might be a good idea to consider a career change. As the fog lifts in sobriety, it's common for people to remember the truth very differently from the way they presented it at first.

It turned out that Lee had tried NA, Narcotics Anonymous, and hadn't felt comfortable. "It was a bunch of bikers and the pierced and tattooed set."

"Well, have you tried any other Twelve Step programs?" I asked.

"They're all holy rollers," he said. "It's 'God this, God that.' I can't take that nonsense."

Lee was a software architect with a Ph.D. in electrical engineering. He had a very logical and scientific mind. But he'd gotten into the habit of

76

overworking and bingeing. After putting in a couple ninety-hour weeks meeting a release deadline, it seemed two or three days of nonstop cocaine use was a great way to "unwind." Unfortunately, as he got up toward fifty, his body couldn't handle the abuse, and he was afraid his fiancée would find out and leave him.

"Well, what about the First Step?" I asked. "Do you believe that you're powerless over cocaine?"

"Sure. I mean, I might not use that word, 'powerless,' but yeah, I see how once I start there's no turning back. It's not the powerlessness thing that's bothers me, it's the God crap."

Aha. "So you're not comfortable with the concept of a Higher Power?"

"Look, I've been a scientist all my life. I work on facts, not flimsy fantasies. Science can look almost to the edge of the universe or down to a minute subatomic particle. You know what they've found?"

"Well, a lot of things, I guess."

"Yeah, but they didn't find God. You know why? 'Cuz he's not out there."

"I agree."

"What do you mean you agree? I thought you were into all these Steps."

"Sure, but I don't think God's out at the edge of the universe. God's inside. And everywhere else."

"See, that's just the kind of thinking I can't abide. If I have to believe that to get sober, then forget it. I'll manage on my own."

"Nobody's saying you have to believe anything in particular to get sober. The Steps are suggestions based on other people's experience. The main idea about God that I think's important is, 'I'm not Him.'"

"Well, that's not a problem." He sounded more subdued now. "If there's a God, it's definitely not me."

I encouraged Lee to hang out at some meetings and take what was useful from what he heard and ignore the rest. I could see that his belief system wasn't going to allow for the possibility of a Higher Power right now, but I didn't want him to give up on sobriety because of that.

Frankly, there are all kinds of reasons *not* to believe in God, scientific and otherwise. Certainly trying to prove to a skeptic the existence of God is fruitless. I take the idea of God as more of a practical one. It helps me. "Believing" in God allows me to see that I'm not in control of the world; that there is a value in committing wholeheartedly to a spiritual and moral path; that it's possible to have a sense of safety in an inherently unstable world. So, I *practice* this Step for myself, not for God, not for a religion, not even because I think there is a God. None of that matters; what matters is that I need the Higher Power idea to stay sober and to be free from self-centered suffering.

In Buddhism, the Hindrance of Skeptical Doubt is considered to be the most dangerous. Doubt has the ability to completely derail our spiritual work. If we lose faith, we might give up.

Doubt typically appears in three different ways: doubt of the teachings; doubt of the teacher; doubt of self. Lee's doubt was of the teachings, of Step Three and a Higher Power. With this kind of resistance, you cannot learn or progress on the path. The antidote to any of these forms of doubt is, firstly, practice. Try it out for yourself; don't take anyone's word for it. In Twelve Step programs we say, "Act as if," which means dropping our doubt just long enough to see if there's any value in what people, and the Steps, are suggesting. We can do this with Buddhism as well. One teacher uses "pretend meditation" when teaching children. He tells them, "Close your eyes, sit still, and pretend you are meditating." What's the difference between this and "real" meditation? Nothing that I can see. For the doubter, it's helpful to study the teachings from a variety of sources so that a clear understanding is established; we don't have to swallow it all whole. We can take what we need and leave the rest.

Trying different teachers can be very helpful too, as we all respond to different personalities. When we doubt ourselves, we might ask, "Am I truly different from these other people who are meditating? Am I really inherently flawed?" Check with other students and teachers to see if they've ever felt this way. A little reality check helps—usually others won't see us as uniquely unable to meditate.

TOO MUCH FAITH

My own tendency may be more toward too much faith than too much doubt. In Step One I mention the New Age guru I traveled with after the three-month meditation course I attended in 1981. Still several years away from sobriety, I'd been disappointed that a three-month retreat hadn't gotten me "enlightened." I thought that all my problems should have been solved, and when they weren't I kept looking around for another solution.

JUNE 1982

I'm sitting on a stool behind the counter at the Red Wing bookstore in Cambridge, reading the Hindu epic *Ramayana*, when I hear some giggling coming from the other side of the store. I look up to see a man in blue jeans and a blue oxford button-down looking at me.

"So *you* were the one pulling me," he says, coming up to the counter.

"What?" I put my book down.

"I was doing my laundry up the street and I felt a pull from this store."

This kind of New Age talk seems normal to me after getting into meditation, working in a health food store in California for a year, and now working in a spiritual bookstore.

"Do you want to get enlightened?" he asks.

I play along. "Yeah," I say.

"I can get you there in six months."

That grabs me.

His name is Ananda, which means "bliss" in Sanskrit, and he does seem inordinately happy. It turns out that he doesn't live anywhere—he isn't homeless in the typical sense, but he lives a wanderer's life for vague reasons that have to do with "energy."

I invite him back to my house and he begins to teach me his odd collection of Hindu, Christian, Jewish, and New Age practices. His main lesson is "living on faith."

Over the course of a few weeks I see a lot of him. He's traveling with a young blonde woman who has a car. They leave town for a while, then he shows up again. The two of them even come to my gig with an oldies band in a suburban bar.

He considers Buddhism to be archaic. He says it's lost its "juice," that what he is doing is drawing on fresh energy. He tells me that there is an old Buddhist guy blocking my spiritual progress.

To explain this, one day he shows me an image that he says depicts how we really look in our spiritual body; it shows a woman with a long tubelike light coming out of the top of her head and going into the sky. "See that tube? There's some old monk inside yours blocking the way. Your spirit has to escape out here to become enlightened. Have any idea who the monk is?" I tell him I don't.

Soon Ananda tells me that he's leaving Boston and heading out West. He doesn't know when or if he'll be back through. If I want to continue to study with him, I have to make a decision.

The whole thing is strange and disturbing to me. I don't want to believe Ananda, but I am afraid not to.

Since I started meditating four years ago, I've always wanted to find a real teacher, someone who would guide me. On the retreats I attend, the teachers are quite impersonal, and in between retreats there is no one. I want someone who can help me personally. Ananda is offering that. But at what price?

I'm afraid, but feel I should go with him, that I might be passing up the most important opportunity of my life. Ananda leaves it up to me, but I can't decide. We walk down to the strip of grass bordering the Charles River and sit down.

"Here," he says, and he hands me a piece of paper and a pen. "Tear the paper in two."

I do as he says.

"Now write 'go' on one piece and 'stay' on the other and fold them up."

I put the paper on my knee and write.

"Now mix them up and see which one feels lighter."

"What do you mean, lighter?" I ask.

"Close your eyes and hold them in front of you."

I take one piece of paper, close my eyes, and let my hand drift up in front of my face; then I take the other piece and do the same. While holding the second piece it seems that my arm floats up higher without any assistance from me.

I open my eyes. "I guess this one is lighter," I say.

"Open it," he says.

I unfold the paper: "go" it reads. And so I do. This is my first act of faith—or foolishness. I give up everything—my apartment, my job, my band, my friends, even my Buddhist beliefs—to go with Ananda, to wander with him, to achieve enlightenment. We drive cross-country, then he sends me back, telling me to hitchhike from Santa Fe back to Boston with no money. We travel to Hawaii, Boulder, Berkeley. We pick up others, often in bookstores like the one where he found me; and some people drop out along the way. We live in motel rooms paid for by people in his thrall; we eat fast food, chant Hebrew incantations, practice Yogic breath of fire, spread "light and energy" throughout shopping malls, perform "polarity balancing" in New Age bookstores. We make sure to walk always on his right side because the right side transmits and your left side receives. (Transmits what? I didn't ask.) Although I've been a vegetarian for five years, he insists I need to eat meat, so I do. He believes that, although I've worn glasses since I was twelve, I can regain perfect vision; one night while I'm behind the wheel he tells me to take off my glasses and I drive down the freeway outside Denver with the sight of splattered lights spread across the road in front of me. He rarely lets me meditate, because I'm "attached" to meditation.

By August I start to lose the energy and faith to continue. I'm done. When he sends me off on another hitchhiking-on-faith trip, I miss my connection. I wander around California for a few more weeks, finally drifting back to Venice Beach where I used to live with a band.

One day I find myself lying on the sand, homeless, jobless, and penniless. I also don't have a swimsuit, so I am fully clothed. A dry Santa Ana wind has brought smog and heat to the usually clear and mild coastline. I am lying on the sand because I don't have anywhere else to go.

I've lost not only my life in Cambridge and my tenuous grasp on security, but my faith in Ananda, too. The longing for enlightenment seems like a hollow, foolish dream; all I long for now is a hamburger, a beer, and a joint.

What Ananda demanded was absolute faith. His eclectic practices all came down to this: trust him.

This kind of unearned faith is dangerous. There was no room for argument with Ananda. Things were as he said they were, and that was it. Completely surrendering to him *was* his teaching.

It's easy to write Ananda off now as some wacky, New Age charlatan. Maybe he was. But if you read about saints and spiritual masters throughout the ages, many of them could be characterized the same way. In the end, it's not important who or what Ananda was. What's important for my story is who *I* was.

When I met Ananda I was advanced in my meditation practice but stunted in my emotional growth. I wanted to let go of self before I really *had* a self. The irony of spiritual practice is that before you can really let go of ego, you need to have a healthy ego.

Ananda didn't exactly run a cult. He wasn't accumulating money or power. But in some ways that's what the experience was like. What draws you to a cult is the feeling that you are going to be fulfilled, completed, by joining. When you join a cult it's because you sense something lacking in yourself and you want someone else to fix it. There's a weakness of personality that is drawn to the strength of the cult leader. And it's all done in the guise of spiritual growth—"love, devotion, and surrender."

What complicates the issue is that this kind of surrender *can* be an authentic and powerful spiritual path for someone who has the maturity to surrender out of true devotion and renunciation rather than out of personal frailty.

So, we have to be careful that when we "turn our will and our life over to the care of God" or a teacher, or Buddha, dharma, sangha, or a teaching, that we aren't doing it out of a need to be fixed, that we do it out of a sincere and healthy opening of the heart; a sense of connection that enriches our life and doesn't deplete it. The headlong dive into a relationship with a teacher or group is another particularly "alcoholic" behavior. Giving away all your possessions, cutting off relations with friends and family, quitting work, and giving up your home is extreme behavior, and extreme behavior is what addictive people do—not just alcoholics and addicts, but people afflicted by the scars and traumas of a painful childhood or abusive relationships.

Even now, when I'm having a bad day and I'm tired of my life—of living with my wife and daughter, of going to work, of being responsible—I'll get the idea that maybe I should "escape" to a monastery, just get away from it all. But then I remember what I've learned about the monastic life, the 227 precepts, the daily work, 4 A.M. chanting, the hierarchy and responsibilities, but most of all the continual inner scrutiny. I realize that there is no spiritual escape.

As we seek balance in our meditation practice as well as in our lives in recovery, one of the things we have to look out for is this tendency toward extremes. This doesn't mean that we might not have a calling for the monastic life, or for a very intense spiritual practice, but it does mean that we should move into these decisions very carefully, consulting with those around us—with friends, therapists, teachers, family. We should take our time. Ananda wanted me to decide *now*. Real-life decisions take time, and when people are pressuring us to make up our minds, there's often some agenda behind that.

In fact, many of our decisions in regard to our spiritual life don't even have to be decisions. If we practice sincerely, things will unfold naturally.

The invitation from my meditation teacher in Berkeley to facilitate a Kalyana Mitta group is an example of this. Here I was, after my retreat with Ruth Denison, feeling inspired and trusting in the dharma more than ever in my life, and my teacher saw that and gently guided me into the next step. Nothing radical or extreme, just a small step forward in practice. This turned out to be the beginning of my journey as a teacher, but it would be another four or five years before the next stage, so it takes time. With time comes confidence, wisdom, and appreciation.

Balancing Wisdom and Faith means keeping an open heart *and* an open mind. Not closing ourselves off from the unknown, from possibilities yet unexplored; and not seeking quick fixes or supernatural solutions to our problems. Life is a mystery; the mind an enigma; the possibilities for spiritual growth endless, if only we are willing to explore. As human beings we have amazing abilities to think, to feel, and to experience wonder. Step Three sets us firmly on the path of freedom, connecting us to the great mysteries of life and the heart. Our job is to keep opening to the mystery, with joy, gratitude, and bright attention.

Part Two

INVESTIGATION AND RESPONSIBILITY

In the Big Book, the first paragraph of chapter 5, "How It Works," includes the word honest three times. Clearly this pivotal chapter, read at many Twelve Step meetings, makes the quest for truth its central theme. Insight meditation is a quest for truth too—the truth of now.

Steps Four through Nine are where this quest becomes most challenging. By the time we get through them, there are few illusions left for us. We have bared our souls to ourselves and to each other; we have acknowledged in several different ways our failings; we have tried to let go; and we have sought to bring closure to the past so that it won't continue to haunt us.

These Steps are linked to the meditative processes of examining the mind, of letting go of the blocks to clarity, and of healing ourselves and others. As we investigate and take responsibility for our past actions and our continuing habits of mind, the light of truth shines on the shadowed recesses of our lives, and a new freedom imbues us with confidence and joy, as shame is banished and we are no longer dogged by secrets and guilt.

STEP FOUR

"Made a searching and fearless moral inventory of ourselves."

None of the Twelve Steps is easy. But certainly, Step Four would top many people's list as the most difficult (along with Step Nine, making amends). Taking a moral inventory can be wrenching, awkward, agonizing. Delving into the past—the sordid past—and exploring all the ways that we have caused others and ourselves pain is devastating to the ego. Most of us find it possible to do this Step only with the help of a sponsor or other spiritual advisor and only after firmly committing ourselves to our spiritual growth (Step Three). Once we know in our hearts unquestionably what our path is, we may look around to see what needs to be done next. It turns out to be cleaning house.

Typically Step Four is written down. Twelve Step literature suggests a specific format, and usually a sponsor will guide you through the process. There are many different approaches, but they all require rigorous honesty.

For the meditator, too, honesty underpins all the work. This isn't as obvious in meditation; it's implied, but if you don't want to hear it, you won't. (At least I didn't.) The tool of mindfulness could be called existential honesty—that is, honesty about what is happening in this moment of our existence, an unadulterated looking, not adding anything, not taking anything away. Just seeing what is.

For the addict/alcoholic, there is no substitute for the moral inventory; you can't meditate your way around it. I found that out. But, once you've worked Step Four on your disease, you can also use the tools of inventory for further spiritual development.

WHY INVENTORY?

When I admitted, at one year of sobriety, that I was using women addictively, I began moving toward an inventory. That led directly to my finding a sponsor, which brought me to the formal inventory process.

I'd finally gotten off the road, leaving the Hollywood Argyles and taking a room in a friend's apartment in West L.A., getting a job driving for a messenger service. At the same time, I began thinking about starting my own band. Driving all day through the business districts of L.A., from Westwood to Century City, from the Wilshire district to downtown, I pounded my poor little Subaru station wagon into the ground. Between deliveries I'd make phone calls to musicians and begin to set up auditions. In the evening I'd go to Twelve Step gatherings. Before bed I'd get out a notebook and write inventory, going back through my life and trying to recall all the people I'd hurt and looking at the patterns of my behavior.

I told the story chronologically because that's how I could remember it. Starting with early-teen romantic betrayals, struggles with my parents, and the messiness of my relationships with my brothers, my past exposed itself in a new way. I'd always looked at these events from the standpoint of the wronged party or the blameless innocent, and now I had to really examine what *I* had done, how *I* had hurt them, how *I* was responsible. It was totally unnatural, going against every self-preserving instinct I had. As I thought of the pain my parents had felt when I dropped out of high school, I wanted to say, "Yeah, but . . ." But I couldn't. Sure there were reasons, sure I was confused, in pain, frustrated, but that didn't mean my parents hadn't suffered because of my decision. I thought of the night in Portland, Maine, when, drunk and raging, I'd slammed the door on my girlfriend's hand. I wanted to say it was her fault, but it wasn't true. I committed the violence. It didn't matter what she had done. I was responsible for my actions.

Each of these memories was like a slap in the face, an awakening to another view of the world. This was, slowly, painfully, the beginning of compassion developing in me. Looking at my own behavior from the standpoint of how it affected others instead of how it affected me meant putting myself in their place and trying to understand their suffering. The fact that this suffering was caused by me made it more difficult to acknowledge, but once I did, something broke open.

In this new view, I saw not only the suffering that I caused in others, but the suffering in me that triggered my behavior. When the Buddha says we should "understand" the First Noble Truth, this is what he means: opening to our own pain and that of others. Some years later, soon after the Rodney King beating, I heard Thich Nhat Hanh, the widely respected Vietnamese Zen master, speak. He said that when he saw the video on television, he naturally felt great compassion for King, but he also felt compassion for the police who were wielding their nightsticks. He said he understood that they, too, were suffering, that the rage they carried inside that set off this behavior was painful, and that in order to fully comprehend these events and respond to them with real skill, we had to see this, we had to know the suffering of both victim and perpetrator. This is what opened up for me as I wrote these pages of inventory, August turning to September, the late summer heat sweltering in Los Angeles; I saw that this inventory, all of it—my pain and the pain of those I had hurt—was equally deserving of my compassion.

For weeks this went on. I committed to writing at least one page per night. Rarely did I exceed my quota. Recoiling from the memories, I had to drag the words out to paper.

What's odd about the inventory is that, for me, it was an admission that I had power in the world, power to hurt others, which I'd never acknowledged. Besides denying my responsibility, I'd also often denied that my words or actions could have any effect on anyone. So, even though what was revealed was painful and destructive, just admitting that I had hurt others was empowering. In fact, inventory is a review of past karma. To pretend that our existence doesn't affect others is to deny karma, to deny that every action has a reaction, to pretend that cause and effect aren't constantly in play. This careful parsing of our past forces us to become more cognizant of karma. When we see how our actions hurt others—and ourselves—we become more careful about what we are doing in the present. When we see our destructive patterns of thought, speech, and behavior, we begin to change, to unravel these habits, to act in ways that won't require more inventory writing.

At meetings I began to open up about the process and the feelings I was having. Stephen had asked me to commit to going to five meetings a week, and now I started to get comfortable with being part of things and with exposing myself to people. The initial, wrenching admission of my alcoholism was giving way to an acceptance of my failures. This immersion in inventory and meetings put me right in the middle of the program. No longer hanging out in the back of the rooms, I began to make friends, to connect with others, to feel part of a supportive community.

So, there was an odd sense of grace when, in October of 1986, my father called to tell me he was dying. I felt great sorrow, and yet I was grateful that at this moment in my life, perhaps for the first time, I was ready to say goodbye to him. For years he'd fought cancer with long, miserable chemotherapy treatments. When I went to visit him after his first round of treatments nine years before, I met a man who had gone from vigorous to old almost overnight. It was shocking to see him stooped, hair falling out, skin hanging flaccid from his body. He'd gone into remission from the cancer after the treatment, but he'd never be comfortable again, the ongoing therapies leaving him drained and miserable, like a constant case of the flu. During those years it seemed that he'd largely given up on life, withdrawing into depression and isolation. Now he was eighty-one years old and the cancers had returned with a vengeance. He told me he had only a few weeks to live.

As I continued my inventory, which was full of the conflicts I'd had with my father throughout my life, I felt an urgency now to come to completion. I needed to finish my inventory so that I could move through the rest of the Steps before visiting him.

WHY'S IT SO HARD?

When I look back at the inventory experience I wonder why I had such a difficult time reaching the point of being willing to admit my failings. From this side—from the side of sobriety and having worked the Steps— it doesn't seem like such a problem. But before I had the breakthrough of getting sober, then finding a sponsor, things looked very different.

JANUARY 1985, VENICE BEACH

I'm standing behind the dining room table, and Margaret is standing in the door of the kitchen of the little bungalow we've been sharing for six months.

"Would you just talk to me?" asks Margaret.

"What about?" I ask with false innocence.

"Something's going on with you. I want to know what."

"Nothing's going on," I lie. "Just leave me alone." I walk toward the living room and Margaret follows.

"I can't . . . this isn't working," says Margaret. "I need someone who isn't afraid of intimacy—"

"What the hell does that mean?!" I wheel on her. "I don't know what the hell you're talking about. God!"

"Kevin, I'm not attacking you," says Margaret. "But can't you see how you're acting? You come in at 3 A.M. after your gigs, then you sleep all morning. We barely talk. I just want a partner who will communicate with me."

"Fine!" I shout. "Get one!" I grab Margaret's red rocking chair and toss it across the room. I hear it crack as it hits the floor.

Margaret jumps away, and I look at her for a moment gripped with the urge to hit her; then I bolt out the door. I stomp through the verdant courtyard and push through the gate, moving quickly down the sidewalk toward the beach.

What's going on here?

I'm in the grip of the final stages of denial. Living with Margaret, a college professor whose insight into my dysfunction is sharp and penetrating, is pushing me into a corner. She loves me—and she wants me to look at myself in ways I've always avoided. I've made the concession of starting individual therapy, but she wants more. Soon she'll come home with the twenty questions used for determining if you're an alcoholic, and in six months I'll be sober. But right now I don't want to hear what she thinks about me or look at my "issues." I just want to be left alone.

When I met Margaret a year before, I had just joined a new band, playing New Wave music and dressing like a trendy English musician. The band had contacts for one gig: the Sheraton Hotel lounge in Anchorage, Alaska. After a couple months rehearsal, we flew north. This was typical of my relationships up to then: once I got seriously involved, I'd always manage to find a road gig and get out of town. Somehow this seemed like the best of both worlds. I had the security of a girlfriend at home without the actual commitment.

The other musicians in the band were ten to fifteen years younger than I, and so, it turned out, was most of the audience in Anchorage. Now in my mid-thirties, I was living the same way I had ten years before. Some things had changed, but there was a thick wall standing between me and emotional or spiritual maturity.

After the bar closed on the first night in town, the manager took some of us to a boarded-up cabin in an alley behind the hotel. He knocked and, just like in the movies, a little window opened. We were admitted to what turned out to be an after-hours drinking and gambling club. Illegal, of course, but one of many in the frontier-town atmosphere of Anchorage. A block over from the respectable Sheraton, prostitutes stood openly on the sidewalk in front of a strip club. This began four months of bingeing and chasing women as, once again, I struggled with my addictive cravings while trying to cling to some sense of my spiritual path.

That I could live this way, unfaithful to my partner, bingeing on drugs and alcohol, denying responsibility for my actions, was partly a result of my time with Ananda. His teaching was that I was already enlightened, and that any action could be performed from an enlightened viewpoint. I took this idea and distorted it to justify anything and everything I did. Stoned and half-drunk, I would convince myself that I was mindfully walking through the bar. Flirting with women, I would tell myself that it was all a game, that I wasn't creating any negative karma because my intention was pure. Which was, in fact, pure bullshit. My intention was to get laid. The true higher teachings assume that the student has gone through rigorous moral training and is certainly following the fundamental precepts of non-harming. To pretend that you are enlightened and that you can do no harm when you are in fact still driven by greed, hatred, and especially delusion, is a dangerous perversion of the teachings. It's this kind of thinking that supports cult leaders, adulterous gurus, drunken Zen masters, and child-abusing priests. It is, at root, a deeply cynical behavior. Only the cynicism itself is hidden as well, along with the true motivation for the destructive actions.

When I finally got back to L.A., Margaret had found us the little cottage in Venice where we would live together. Already, in less than a year, I'd hurt her badly—of course she knew I wasn't faithful to her in Alaska. When she tried to point out ways that I was cruel to her or irresponsible, this rage came over me.

The fear of facing my own failures with Margaret was the same fear I faced when approaching the Fourth Step: the fear of ego destruction. Any admission of weakness or flaws can trigger this fear. I felt that Margaret was threatening who I was, my very existence, and that if she were right it would invalidate me as a person. I thought that if I let in her ideas about me, I would be admitting to being a failure as a person, to being irrevocably damaged, to being small and cruel and stupid. So I fought— we fought. I blocked her attempts to talk with me, to explore our relationship and my part in its problems.

When I did get sober the following summer, my ego was finally able to take at least the First Step toward deflation. Another year later, as I began Step Four, I was ready for more.

Once there, at Step Four, I began to see how liberating these deflations were. Once I realized how admitting I was wrong about something could free me from so much pain, confusion, fear, and stress, I broke through. This is surely one of the stages of spiritual awakening that Step Twelve promises. In Buddhist terms, it's seeing the transparency of ego, realizing that actions don't define us; that thoughts are empty; that there's nothing to hold on to—nothing worth fighting over.

BUDDHIST INVENTORY

Inventory doesn't just happen in Step Four; it permeates the Steps. It also permeates the Buddhist path. In Buddhist meditation we take different kinds of inventory: we might do an inventory in relation to the Precepts, the Hindrances, the Eightfold Path, or any of a number of other formats.

This inventory can be quite personal, as when we look at how we harm others through actions or speech; or it can be impersonal, as when we see how thoughts of desire and aversion appear in the mind unbidden. Here we see how much of our mental activity is generic, human output—nothing unique to us, just patterns of neural impulse. In fact, the Buddha says that even those who are fully enlightened "in virtue, concentration, and wisdom" still do unskillful things, still make mistakes, and that they must be honest about this. The Theravada tradition includes a fortnightly "confession" in which the monks describe for their preceptor any rules they have broken that month.

The Buddha says that recognizing our mistakes and admitting them is how we develop our spiritual life. Ajahn Amaro, the Buddhist monk who taught me about the Refuges, paraphrases the *suttas* (Pali for sutra; Pali was the language the Buddha spoke) this way: "When someone blows it, getting lost or sidetracked, they'll go to the Buddha and say, 'Forgive me venerable sir because I was confused and deranged at the time.' And the Buddha says, 'It's good that you acknowledge this because to acknowledge our transgressions and to make the effort to do better in the future, this is called Furtherance in the Dhamma.'" So the Buddha teaches that recognizing our transgressions as such and setting the intention to do better in the future is the way to deepen our spiritual life.

The spirit of Buddhist inventory goes beyond any lists or set of rules to the core idea that in our hearts we know what is harmful. We could call Buddhism "a natural religion"; it allows us to discover for ourselves our innate moral nature. Harming others is painful; stealing leaves us fearful and ashamed; lying causes guilt and discomfort. Ultimately, we don't need Precepts or Commandments to know these things.

I've been confused by certain Buddhist teachings that suggest there is no actual right or wrong. When the Heart Sutra, the classic Zen text, declares, "Form is emptiness, and emptiness is form," I wondered if that meant nothing was real, nothing mattered. When I was walking around smashed saying, "I'm just a drunken Buddha," it came out of this confusion. You could also say, "Form is form, and emptiness is emptiness," meaning that everything has its reality, however transitory. Form must be respected. Traditionally, in the Mahayana Buddhist tradition, you make the vow to save all beings—the Bodhisattva Vow. In some cases, this commitment might cause you to break a precept. This would be done out of a selfless desire to serve, not out of a personal preference. One Zen teacher explains it this way: "Zen teaches that any form of duality is ultimately false. But, if you are acting out of 'I,' out of a self-centered motivation and desire, then you are already in duality, so you can't make the claim that you are striving to save all beings. You are only striving to bring yourself pleasure, or freedom from pain." He goes on to say that being clear about our motivation, exploring our conscious and unconscious intention, is much of what meditation practice is about. As this exploration deepens, we can see more clearly whether we are driven by the mind of greed, hatred, and delusion, or by our concern for all beings, our Bodhisattva mind.

I want to look at how we can use the Hindrances and the Precepts for inventory, and also how we might approach a "positive inventory."

HINDRANCE INVENTORY

One of the most powerful forms of meditative inventory is that of the Hindrances: Desire, Aversion, Sloth and Torpor, Restlessness and Worry, and Skeptical Doubt. These five qualities, unless clearly seen, block the development of calm and insight, carrying you away from the focus of your meditation into realms of disturbing thoughts, painful emotions, and physical discomfort. Working with them requires first clearly seeing and feeling their presence and accepting them as natural parts of our meditation—in fact, of our mind and body.

One way of using them to do inventory is at the end of each meditation session, to review what hindrances were present. Then you can consider, "How did I work with that hindrance?" and also, "What happened to the hindrance as I paid attention to it?"

We can also apply mindfulness, as the hindrances arise in the mind and body, noting the presence of "desire," "sleepiness," "doubt," and so on. We can begin to see the actual process by which the hindrances, and other experiences, come and go in meditation, and what their effects are.

The Hindrances appear in our lives all the time, not just when we're meditating. Learning to work with them in our daily lives, as well as our meditation, is critical to sobriety and happiness.

Desire. The Buddha said that desire is the cause of suffering. Addicts and alcoholics are experts on desire. We've seen it rule our lives. We've seen it ruin our lives. Addiction is desire run rampant. When we get sober, we finally start to stem the tide of desire, to refuse its seductive power. Seeing our powerlessness and then turning our lives over to a Higher Power are ways of dealing with desire. Much of the practice of meditation is directed toward letting go of desire.

Jody, a Twelve Step meditator, told me about her first experience of doing the Buddhist meditation practice of noting where she started to pay attention to the specific quality of each thought. "It shocked me to see how much of my thinking was oriented toward wanting something—clothes, vacations, relationships; my mind seemed to be constantly in the state of reaching for something, something *else*, something other than what was here, now." As she worked with this practice, she saw how painful this reaching was, how there was a quality of dissatisfaction to a greater or lesser degree in so many moments.

As she got more skilled in her practice, Jody began to have more balance. "I learned to first allow desire to be there—not create more tension by judging it or struggling to make it go away." In fact, just by being mindful of desire, something shifted for her. "It seemed like the attention itself would stop the desire. It was strange—here was this feeling that seemed so powerful, but then as soon as I shined a light on it, it scurried like a cockroach when you turn on the kitchen light." Once she saw that she didn't have to fear desire, she began to examine more closely how it felt, the visceral and energetic qualities of each moment of desire. As she felt the tension in her body from craving, she found that she would quite naturally relax. "Just like when you realize you've been clenching your teeth, you just let go."

When we see how desire is created out of focusing on the things we crave, we learn about restraint. As an alcoholic and addict, I knew how every day that I drank or took drugs reinforced that habit. If I went a week without smoking pot, then got high one night, the next day I'd crave it again. Through meditation I began to see how this principle worked on more subtle levels. Anything I indulged in, be it sugar, TV, or sex, I tended to crave more of.

Learning to live with desire may be the single most important act for an alcoholic. Our relationship to pleasure and self-gratification was distorted, and until it becomes relatively balanced, we will suffer, just as the Buddha said. As human beings, desire will always be there; the point isn't that we must achieve the fully enlightened state of desirelessness (although that's a skillful goal). Rather, we must learn to allow desire to come without acting on every impulse. It will go if we let it.

Aversion. The other side of desire is aversion, or Not-Wanting. While desire has the quality of reaching out, grasping at something, aversion has the quality of pushing away or resisting. The Big Book famously says that "resentment is the 'number one' offender . . . from it stem all forms of spiritual disease." Resentment is a form of aversion—we instinctively try to push away what we don't like. An inventory typically focuses on these resentments. As we deepen our meditation practice, we become more sensitive to how aversion or resentment appears. We can feel the physical qualities that rise up when thoughts of anger, fear, and judgment come into the mind. When we direct our attention this way we come to understand the Buddha's well-known description of how anger works: he said it is as though you were to pick up a burning coal to throw at your enemy. The person who is most certainly hurt by the anger is you; your enemy may or may not feel the sting. So, if our commitment to ourselves is to try to bring happiness and peace into our lives, picking up burning coals is probably not on the agenda. Ideally we won't pick them up, but if we do, we'll drop them before we throw them. In any case, mindfulness means seeing—*feeling*—the suffering, the pain that our anger causes ourselves, and finding ways to let it go.

One practice for letting go of anger is called "replacing with the opposite." This means trying to replace hate with love in our minds. This practice appears in Twelve Step programs when it's suggested that we should pray for those we resent. In Buddhism, we can use the lovingkindness practice in this way, sending loving thoughts to all beings, including those we resent or fear.

Alcoholism and addiction are diseases of self-hatred. Pouring lethal amounts of booze into our bodies, and smoking, snorting, popping, and shooting drugs of all sorts are ultimately acts of violence to ourselves. To stay sober and find happiness in our lives, we must come to understand the demons that drove us to this behavior. Meditation lets us see negative thoughts and destructive impulses at the moment they appear in the mind. With this clear seeing we can step in to stop the actions that often follow them. The Twelve Steps are sometimes called "a program of action," but in this way they are perhaps more importantly *a program of inaction*.

Sloth and torpor. Alcoholics and addicts know all about sloth and torpor. How many days have we written off to hangovers or crashing from drugs? Our bodies and minds were perennially drained by our substance abuse, and for many of us laziness became part of our lifestyle.

One old friend who still drinks heavily in his fifties simply takes Mondays off. He's arranged his life so that his boss accepts his four-day week, and, after every hard-drinking weekend, he simply lies on the couch reading all day Monday. Of course, many alcoholics are just the opposite, driving themselves intensely in their work and play lives. Still, these hyperactive achievers may experience crashing when they withdraw or break down. (Even in sobriety, these cycles of overactivity and collapse can continue.)

The mental side of this hindrance, torpor, is a dull, unmotivated mind. There's little awareness or effort. Unchecked, the combination of physical and mental dullness can lead to depression, which is why one of the antidotes to depression is activity and exercise.

With meditation we seek a balance of energy.

However, many times, when people first start to get relaxed in meditation, they find themselves falling asleep. This can be quite frustrating when you've set aside time specifically for practice. Our hectic lives may not allow for much rest, and so when we finally do get relaxed, the body just automatically shuts down. How to apply mindfulness to this?

It's quite tricky to be aware as you nod off, but it can be done. More important, though, is not to succumb to the sleepiness by lying down and giving up meditation. Very often during a period of meditation, sleepiness will come, and if you keep sitting, trying to maintain your posture and attention, it will pass. Perhaps the body just needs to fade out for a little while. Seeing how tiredness can pass is quite inspiring. It helps you to see that the experience of being tired doesn't necessarily mean that you have to catch up on your sleep. Energy is quite dynamic and changeable. On meditation retreats this becomes even more obvious, as the sustained attention throughout the day reveals a continual fluctuation of energy. Coming to equanimity around this energy, just being present without overreacting, helps us to develop a more consistent meditation practice that isn't diverted by the waves of sleepiness and restlessness that come and go. In our daily lives, handling energy fluctuations mindfully can help bring harmony as well.

Gabe, a sober parent of twin kindergarteners, told me about how his background in retreat practice helps him handle a hectic family life. "It used to be that when I got tired is when I acted out. A lot of my drinking happened when I was stressed or 'relaxing' after overworking. Even after I got sober, I found that being tired often set off my irritability. After a couple retreats where I tried to work with mindfulness steadily over long days of meditation, I started to see how I could relate to tiredness differently. I found I could kind of 'shift gears,' just feeling the tiredness and not fighting it, and not letting that physical feeling bleed over into my emotions." Applying mindfulness allowed Gabe to experience the tiredness without aversion, without reactivity. "When my wife and I had twins, I was amazed how at the end of the day, with all its struggles, I could maintain an evenness by opening to the feelings in my body and not telling myself a story about 'poor me, I'm so tired.' Those retreats gave me a whole different perspective on working with different levels of energy."

Sometimes our minds get cloudy because we are avoiding some thought or feeling which we don't want to deal with. When we repress disturbing thoughts, sometimes the mind becomes sluggish, trying to drain us of the ability to look clearly at what's happening because it's painful. Keeping the attention on the sluggishness may allow the difficult thought to come through and be processed. In taking time to meditate we create a space in our lives where such wounds can safely appear and get examined without trauma.

Classically, there are a few ways to fight sloth and torpor: strengthen the posture by sitting up straighter; take some deep breaths; open the eyes to let in light, which is stimulating; and, finally, if none of this works, do your meditation standing up. Standing meditation is much like walking meditation. You can follow the breath or move the attention throughout the body, examining all the sensations. Or, you can simply place your attention on the bottom of your feet, feeling the contact with the floor. A few minutes of this will often energize you enough to sit back down and be alert.

It's helpful to look at the ways we use energy in our lives. Do we stay up late watching TV? Do we eat too much of the wrong foods? Do we exercise enough? Too much? Do we indulge in sleep as an escape? Do we overwork? These and other questions can help us to find the places in our lives where we let our energy get out of balance. When sloth and torpor take over, our sobriety can be threatened, because exhaustion is a trigger for many addict/alcoholics and others. It can also threaten our emotional sobriety, triggering all kinds of negative mind states: anger, irritability, anxiety, depression. So, while the hindrance of sloth and torpor may seem trivial at first glance, when we are mindful of its effect on our lives, we see how it can be the source of real trouble. By learning to work with it, we can achieve a new level of physical and emotional balance in our lives.

Restlessness and worry. This hindrance is the flipside of sloth and torpor. Physically, restlessness is the feeling in the body that we can't sit still. Usually we don't even notice this feeling because we react to it so fast. Before we know it we've got the remote control in our hand, or we're driving down the street, or we're standing in front of the open refrigerator door. The mental side of this hindrance, worry, churns the same thought over and over in our head with no resolution. Closely related to fear, which is an aspect of aversion, worry often has a hidden cause.

Restlessness and worry drive alcoholics and addicts to drink and use. They can be terribly uncomfortable, growing into anxiety and even panic. Bringing mindfulness to them is critical to recovery and sobriety. Learning to be present with these feelings in a nonreactive way allows us to ride out those storms of craving that can lead back to drugs and alcohol.

In meditation, restlessness can be subtle: a little itch here that we scratch, a little tingle there making us move slightly. Or it can be gross, causing us to get up and stop meditating. Whatever the form restlessness takes, we can work with it only if we recognize its presence. That's why resolving to sit still is helpful in meditation. If we have this resolution, when the subtle or intense desire to move appears, we'll recognize it since it's pushing against our resolution. In that moment we have the chance to work with restlessness.

When that craving to move appears, we take our attention to the center of the sensation, feeling clearly the itch or tingle or anxiety, opening fully to the experience of restlessness. How does this feel? Where is it appearing in the body? Can I sit though it? What will happen? Asking these questions helps us focus clearly. Often there is an emotional energy behind the physical energy. You don't have to understand the emotions or figure out where they came from, simply feel them in the body. It can seem as though you're going to be hurdled off your cushion or chair, the energy is so intense. Or, it can be so subtle that you don't even realize that your forefinger is scratching your thigh very lightly. Keeping your attention on the sensation, you watch how it changes. You watch what it's telling you and what happens when you don't react. Restlessness can actually transmute into a form of alertness or even euphoria, it is so packed with energy. However, before that happens, it can seem unmanageable.

The antidote to this mad energy is concentration, which of course sounds kind of silly: if I could concentrate, I wouldn't be restless. But the idea is to do a concentration technique, counting breaths, repeating a mantra, something very simple and methodical that continually brings you back to a single meditation object. Eventually calming happens. Despite the fact that the energy may still seem strong and the thoughts may still be tumbling, with time, a quality of stillness will appear. Once we've experienced this, restlessness loses it ability to intimidate. It becomes manageable.

Doubt. When I first learned about the Hindrances, doubt seemed like the easy one. Desire—*whew!*—how could I ever get over that? On retreat I'd experience desire, aversion, sleepiness, and restlessness *all in the same sitting period*—the so-called multiple-hindrance attack. But doubt seemed less threatening. That's why I couldn't at first understand why my teachers said that ultimately it was the most dangerous hindrance.

In fact, for an alcoholic or addict, denial is a form of doubt. Many people never get sober because they aren't willing to accept the possibility that they have a real problem for which there is a solution. And many others, perhaps most tragically, lose their sobriety when their doubt becomes so strong that they decide to drink or use again. "I don't know if I'm really an alcoholic" is often the prelude to drinking. As one friend in recovery pointed out, "Why is it that the first thing people do when they decide they aren't alcoholics is go out and drink?" Hmmm . . .

Some aspects of our culture support doubt. As I talked about in Step Three, when we identify completely with the scientific materialism of contemporary society, we can become closed to anything new at all. The over-reliance on "objective" reasoning discounts subjective experience. Roger, who came to a weekly group I was leading, would often take the discussion off on intellectual and philosophical tangents. His skepticism made it difficult for him to accept certain Buddhist tenets. While I engaged him on some of these points, I also encouraged him to sit more, to simply have the direct experience of what the Buddha was talking about. He took my advice and went on retreat, as well as continuing a regular daily practice. He's still very engaged intellectually in the dharma, but two things have changed: he understands that his intellect cannot always grasp Truth, that if he remains open to possibilities outside his own immediate understanding that he develops a deeper and broader view; and he approaches discussions more gently, as he's become more aware of the effect of his words and attitude on others. This points up how practice shapes us. Through deepening meditation we gain wisdom and pliability and our behavior modulates toward kindness and compassion.

Bill Wilson, the co-founder of Alcoholics Anonymous, talks about "contempt prior to investigation" as the great danger in spiritual growth. Another problem is "contempt after limited investigation." Particularly because the initial stages of meditation are so difficult, some people give up before they experience the benefits. The Dalai Lama famously suggests that we shouldn't try to measure our growth over short periods, but rather judge our meditation practice by how much it's changed in five or ten years. This is a strategy for overcoming doubt. The longer view almost certainly will show significant change. Of course, it could also be a trick to get people to practice, since you'd have to be at it for at least five years before you'd question the value.

As we become more comfortable with doubt, it can turn into what's called, in the Zen tradition, Great Doubt. This is the doubt of the Don't Know mind I discussed in Step Three. Great Doubt, rather than being a rational dismissal of possibilities, is a radical opening to possibilities. In this way, instead of looking for answers to our difficult philosophical questions, we try to take a broader view, that many answers are possible; that the answers may change from day to day or moment to moment; and that, by continually questioning, our understanding has the potential to continually grow. For as soon as we settle for one answer, as soon as we think we've got something figured out, that's when we stop learning. Instead we see each answer as provisional, based on the information we have right now and our own ability to see clearly; as we get more information and penetrating wisdom deepens, our answers may change.

One of the things that makes the Hindrances a helpful model in taking inventory, both in meditation and in daily life, is their impersonal quality. Everyone's got them. They are part of the human condition. When we see them as natural forms of energy—"Oh, desire arising," or, "Well, here's restlessness again"—we don't tend to beat ourselves up so much about them. It becomes easier to be with them because there isn't the added emotional power of negative judgment along with the difficulty of the Hindrances themselves. This perspective takes us a long way toward a fruitful meditation practice. The more we defuse the power of the Hindrances, the more we are able to be with just what *is*. This has a healing effect on our whole life.

Precept inventory

The classic Buddhist inventory uses the training precepts. These are the fundamental moral principles that the Buddha recommended to avoid creating negative karma. They are taught as tools for spiritual growth. There is no implication that you are "bad" if you break them, rather that, as with all actions, you will bear the consequences. In the Buddhist tradition, rather than rigidly following a set of rules (which inevitably we will try to find ways to break), we are encouraged to investigate the meaning and effects of these precepts. In this way, because we aren't under a threat of retribution, there is much more likelihood that we will *expand* the meaning of the precepts, rather than, as often happens with rules, trying to *shrink* the meaning in some legalistic way. The idea is that we see the broader meaning of the precepts and find how applying them in imaginative ways improves our lives.

I struggle with the idea of rules. On the one hand I have this little Catholic boy in me who wants to do everything right and get patted on the head; on the other hand, there's a rebellious teenager who just wants to give you the finger. I went from being an altar boy in fifth grade to an atheist dropout in tenth grade. It seems to me that both of those guys continue to live in me, even today; my so-called inner adult mediates between the two. One of the ways I awaken my inner adult is through meditation. I need calm and focus to look at my failings. If I'm agitated; if the critical, perfectionist part of me is holding sway; if the rebellious, irresponsible part of me is strong; if my mind is out of balance in any way, I can't do a skillful inventory. Once I am calm and focused through meditation, I can turn my mind to the ways I can practice the precepts more skillfully.

In Buddhism the following Precepts are taught as "trainings," not Commandments. There's the understanding that we won't do them perfectly ("we are not saints"), but that we can strive to develop them ("progress not perfection"). In the Theravada tradition, they are repeated at a fortnightly ceremony. The idea is to keep them alive in your life.

I undertake the training Precept to refrain from killing living beings. In Buddhism, because we see how our human life is interwoven with all life, we commit not just to refrain from killing people but all beings. Realistically, this can't be done—when we boil water we kill microscopic beings. But the intention is to bring awareness and kindness into our relations with everyone and everything around us. Although we may not have literally killed any people in our lives, are there ways in which we stifle children's minds? Deny others their feelings? Ignore the suffering—or even the existence—of some people? In this way are we "killing" them: taking away their dignity, their freedom, their self-respect? In the same way that we try to escape our own lives through drugs and alcohol, we try to avoid contact with and awareness of others in our lives. By accepting this precept, we try to open ourselves to the whole range of life more fully, being aware of suffering and joy; letting others in; treating all beings with care and respect.

I undertake the training Precept to refrain from stealing and taking that which is not mine. Many of us had to deal with this Precept when we got sober. Through the years of self-centered drinking and using, it wasn't important who owned something if we wanted or needed it. An acquaintance once stashed a pound of pot in the basement of the band house I was living in. Over the course of several months, we nipped a little here, a little there. When he came back for his pot, a half-pound was gone. Oops! For many people, this precept is an encouragement not to overconsume. The Buddhist Peace Fellowship, an organization that promotes socially-engaged Buddhism, suggests we consider how the ways we accumulate and use the world's resources affect not just ourselves but those in other countries. When we waste oil, for instance, we are taking something from the planet and all its inhabitants. Contemplating our relationship to material things is a critical part of this precept.

Andrew, a high-strung sales manager for a software company, quit cocaine and started practicing meditation as part of the Twelve Step program he was attending. "When my meditation teacher started talking about the precept of not stealing, at first I felt good—I'd never ripped anybody off. I pay my bills on time, and I have good credit. But after a while, I started to notice that I was taking something else from people: time." Andrew realized that his tendency to be late for every appointment, whether social or professional, was robbing people of a precious commodity. "As I started paying more attention, I saw that I also stole people's attention." Every conversation he was in had to center around him—his accomplishments, his problems, his feelings. Gradually, through a conscious process, he learned to be more respectful of other's time and attention. "Now I always leave a cushion in my schedule so I won't be late. And I've learned to ask, 'How are you?' and really be interested in their answer." Andrew was surprised to find that through learning to listen mindfully, people were actually more interested in what he had to say, too.

Andrew's willingness to explore the precepts in this way meant bringing more integrity into his life. Now the people around him trust him more because of the way he treats them.

I undertake the training precept to refrain from causing harm through

sexual misconduct. Many of us acted sexually irresponsible before we got sober. Many of us continued to do so afterward. Sex is such a powerful energy—talk about craving!—and it runs so deep in our psyche. Obviously, we first need to try not to harm ourselves or others with our sexual activity. This really means not sleeping with people we don't have a commitment to. Otherwise, suffering is almost inevitable. I know people who say they can have sex casually and no one gets hurt. We each have to investigate our own hearts and our own actions.

Of course, for monastics, this precept means practicing celibacy, which is a time-honored form of renunciation in many religions. Celibacy can be very freeing, letting you use your energy and attention for other things. But even this practice can have its risks. One evening after a visiting monk spoke at a nearby monastery, I told him about my work with Buddhism and Twelve Step programs.

"I think I could use a Twelve Step program myself," he said as he gathered the notes he'd used for his talk that night. I looked at him with more than a little surprise.

"Really?" I was standing at the foot of the altar looking up at him.

"Celibacy can give you a lot of energy," he said. "I've become something of a workaholic." He put his bag over his shoulder and stepped off the dais.

It turned out that he spent a great deal of time working on his monastery's website and doing translations of his Thai master's dharma talks.

What an odd image this was for me: the overworked monk. One thinks of the monastic life as simple, serene. One sutta says we should be "unburdened with duties," and yet no robe, no vow, no practice protects us from our humanness. Whether a monk or a layperson, we all live in bodies, we all have minds and hearts that hunger for contact, for purpose, for meaning. If we take away one thing, another craving arises in its place. Our practice is to keep seeking after balance, extending and challenging ourselves but without overreaching and creating a backlash that could throw us into even more destructive acts.

I undertake the training precept to refrain from false speech, harmful speech, gossip, and slander. In Step Five I'll explore this precept much more. For now I'll say that on an ongoing, daily basis, it's the hardest precept to keep. Bringing awareness to how we speak is the best way to bring harmony into our lives. It's difficult, though, because our speech is habitual, so closely tied to our thoughts, which most of the time are what we use to identify our "selves." The way we create ourselves in the world, the way we let people know who we are, is through speech. Once we see how empty the concept of self is, however, the whole notion of asserting our identity in this way comes into question. Who do I think I am? Who am I creating with my words? Can I let go of that idea and, instead of expressing "me," try to express compassion, wisdom, and love? When I come from this place, the world appreciates "me" a lot more.

I undertake the training Precept to refrain from the misuse of intoxicants or substances such as alcohol or drugs that cause carelessness or loss of awareness. Hey, I found one I can do! I've already talked about how I thought my teachers under-emphasized this precept. Of course, had they emphasized it more, I wouldn't have listened to them anyway. There was a time when no Precept was going to keep me from drinking and using. Now I appreciate the power that comes through clarity of mind and body. I also see how keeping just one Precept can have an amazingly transforming effect on life.

Look at the ways we try to escape, using television, the Internet, the telephone, food, travel, exercise—and on and on. Letting go of the gross intoxicants is one step. Practicing moderation in these other forms of escape is another. It's helpful to notice when you are using something to numb yourself from life. This, in fact, takes us back to the First Precept, of not killing. When we numb ourselves we are cutting ourselves off from life itself, a not-so-subtle form of killing ourselves.

POSITIVE INVENTORY

Thich Nhat Hanh encourages us to look closely at suffering, to see the pain in our own lives and the pain of others. He also says that "suffering is not enough." We can't spend our lives focused solely on the First Noble Truth of suffering because we will lapse into despair. Instead, he says, we must find joy in our lives here and now. In this spirit, I find it helpful to make an inventory of my own positive qualities and actions as well as the negative ones.

The self-hatred that results in alcoholism can also make inventory a difficult process. There have been times when I've found my inventory to arouse *more* self-hatred, rather than defusing it. So be careful. It doesn't help to use self-examination as another way to criticize yourself.

Positive inventory, too, can be difficult. Ajahn Thanasanti, a Theravadan nun, tells about one of her students who was taking care of the monks and nuns on the Rains Retreat at her monastery. "I asked her to do some planting on the grounds, and she was delighted to have that job. Before she started, though, I told her, 'Every time you plant a tree, think of one of your virtues.' The look of anguish on her face was as if I'd asked her to clean the outhouses with her bare hands." Though an inventory of our failings may be difficult, an inventory of our virtues may be impossible.

This may be a cultural quality of Westerners. Asian teachers are generally dumbfounded by the concept of low self-esteem. Many cultures find self-appreciation to be quite natural and normal. Some years ago I played in a band with a brilliant Nigerian musician, Lofty Amao. When he introduced one of his songs he would often say, "Here's a beautiful song I wrote." The rest of us in the band would cringe. How can he be so conceited? Then, after meeting some of Lofty's West African friends, we began to see that they all talked like this. It was an accepted practice in their culture.

In fact, the Buddha instructed his monks to take pleasure in their skillful actions, to enjoy knowing that what they were doing would bear the fruits of good karma. I try to practice this in simple ways. When I give my spare change to a homeless person, I smile and engage him or her, allowing this tiny act of generosity to bring us both pleasure. There's the pleasure of giving and the pleasure of knowing that the giving is a good thing to do. When I taught meditation at a local rehab for homeless addicts, I would always come out feeling buoyant just from the pleasure of sharing the dharma. In those moments, as I walked back to work, I would try to appreciate my own kindness in giving my time and energy in this way. Even to say this now seems risky, as though people will think I'm prideful. But, that's not at all the point.

As a musician, people have often told me they enjoyed my playing. I used to be very uncomfortable at this, feeling almost as if I needed to apologize for my musicianship. After some time, I finally learned to say thank you. Now, I not only say thank you, but I often go on to say how much I enjoyed playing, and that it seemed the crowd was having fun, and wasn't that great? I can feel good about helping people to feel happy, and I appreciate that I can be part of something without being the whole thing. Now I emphasize the interactive aspect of performing. "I felt good; I felt I was playing well; and it seemed like people were enjoying it." Sweet.

Often people think of their meditation practice as two-dimensional: mindfulness and concentration. If these two aren't strong, they feel that their practice is weak. However, there are many qualities that the Buddhist path encourages us to develop. In one meditation group, one of the members, a single mother, talked about how bad she felt that she wasn't able to go on any retreats because she was in nursing school, and between that and caring for her son she couldn't get away. She felt that she wasn't progressing spiritually. I pointed out that Right Livelihood is a significant part of the Path, and that her schooling would enable that. Her care for her son was an expression of great love—another vital part of a spiritual path.

I take great pleasure in attending major league baseball games. When I enter the park, see the diamond in front of me, the fans filling the seats, and the players tossing the ball around the outfield, I feel great joy and rapture, and these very qualities are found in the Buddha's list of the Factors of Enlightenment. Now, I realize that there are higher forms of joy than baseball, but the awareness of the pleasure creates a deeper pleasure, an appreciation for the moment, for the experience itself. And this is healing.

Positive inventory can happen just in the moment: "Ah, generosity," or, "That was skillfully spoken"—or we can make a more formal inventory by taking one or more of these lists and writing about the ways we have expressed these qualities. It's amazing how a small moment of kindness can reverberate. When my father died, our family received a note from an old friend I hadn't seen in years. She told how she had never forgotten my father's kindness on the night her husband died. She felt and appreciated his goodness thirty-five years later. I wonder if he knew how his caring had so touched another human being. I hope so.

MORE REVEALED

Clearly there are many helpful tools for inventory to be found in Buddhist meditation. At some point, however, we may find that all of these lists and exercises become busymaking, turning meditation into just another attempt to fix ourselves. At that point it's best to stop and go back to basics, just being present with what is.

In the Big Book it says that "more will be revealed" as we stay sober and continue to work the Steps. The same is true of meditation. In some sense, we don't have to do anything, just sit. Recently I read an article

(continued on page 118)

MEDITATION EXERCISE: NOTING THE HINDRANCES

This is a guided meditation on seeing clearly into the habits of mind. Take great care when doing this practice that another layer of negativity doesn't appear; when we begin to see clearly how the mind behaves, it can be disturbing. Realize that the negative habits of mind are common to most people, and that they've been built up over a lifetime. Gradually we can chip away at them, but we can't expect them to disappear overnight.

As we work with the hindrances, we first try to recognize what is in the mind, noting its quality. Then we open the heart, not reacting to what we see, just allowing it to be present. As we open, we investigate the hindrance to see its nature as impermanent and (often) painful. Finally we see that the hindrances don't belong to us; they are human qualities shared by all people. In this way, we learn not to identify with these qualities as they appear in the mind. When we cease to identify, it's easier to let go.

Begin by relaxing with the breath, settling into the body. With each breath, make a soft mental note of "in-breath, out-breath," just following along as you breathe, feeling the sensations of breath and noting the action of breathing. The words in the mind are very soft, just helping to steer the attention to the actual experience of the breath. Feel the sensations of breath either at the nostrils, where the air passes in and out of the body, or at the belly as it rises and falls with each breath. Don't try to control the breath or do anything special with the breath. Just breathe, and know you are breathing.

When the mind wanders, make a mental note of "thinking, thinking," and return to the breath. You are acknowledging clearly that the mind has moved from the breath into thought. Each time you note a thought, let go and come back to the sensations of breath.

At whatever point you catch the thought, whether just as it arises or after you've been thinking for some time, just note it.

After a few minutes, try to refine your attention so that when you note a thought, you can determine whether it's a thought of wanting or not-wanting. Note "wanting, wanting," or "aversion, aversion." You can use other words if you prefer, but simply be aware whether the thought has either of these qualities. And then return to the breath.

When you notice thoughts, see if there's also a physical sensation associated with the thought. As you let go of the thought and return to the breath, open to and allow the sensations into your consciousness, relaxing around them. As you breathe, soften the belly; relax the shoulders; breathe into the tension and let go.

It may not always be immediately clear what kind of thought you are having. That's okay; just note "thinking, thinking" or choose "wanting" or "aversion," whichever draws you. In fact, many thoughts could be characterized as both: Am I "wanting" to be on vacation or having "aversion" to work? This isn't a test, just an exercise to refine awareness.

When you notice yourself thinking, see if a judgment arises. "I shouldn't be having all these thoughts." This is just more thinking, more "aversion." Or you might think, "I wish I could stop thinking." This is just desire. It's natural for the mind to wander. Note this and return to the breath. The moment of noticing a thought is actually a moment to enjoy—"Aah, waking up!" Enjoy the relief of coming back to wakefulness.

Notice the other hindrances in the same way: sleepiness, restlessness, doubt. If they appear, try to experience them with mindfulness, note them, then let go.

Notice moods. Are you sad, angry, bored, anxious? Happy, loving, calm, excited? Note these feelings as well. If you don't notice moods, they can lurk in the back of the mind and control the tone of thoughts.

You may notice that certain thoughts seem to have more authority than others; they may seem more "true" and deserving of exploration. Remember, a thought is a thought. Just let go.

Continue to note thoughts and return to the breath.

critical of meditation in which the author claimed that studies show that one gains the same benefit from sitting still for an hour as from an hour of meditation. When I tell this story to experienced meditators, they laugh, because they understand that, in some sense, all we are doing in meditation is sitting anyway. By taking this physical posture and staying still, free from distractions, we are opening ourselves to what is. When we sit with our minds, stuff comes up; you don't have to do anything, it comes unbidden. Once you've set your intention to grow on the spiritual path, you have no choice but to deal with the things that come up in this process. In this way, meditation is a gateway to the inventory process. Although meditation is only included formally in Step Eleven, I use it to facilitate all the other Steps.

STEP FIVE

"Admitted to God, to ourselves, and to another human being
the exact nature of our wrongs."

Step Five appears to stand in stark contrast to the Buddhist path of meditation. Typically Step Five involves reading our Fourth Step inventory to a trusted person, usually a sponsor. While meditation is silent, Step Five is spoken; while meditation is solitary, Step Five is interpersonal; while meditation involves looking at our own minds, Step Five exposes our destructive thoughts and actions to another. The spirit of this Step may be what, for me, really separates Buddhism from the Recovery movement. It was when I began to reveal myself, both through formal inventory and through informal group sharing, that the healing began for me. Even today, when I am agitated, angry, sad, anxious, or experiencing any difficult emotion, sharing at a group level is one of the most important ways I can return to balance. In these states, oftentimes meditation cannot penetrate. It's only when I speak, and am heard by understanding and sympathetic ears, that relief begins.

This Step, while formally being about the inventory process, really supports the entire group process, which is so important to Twelve Step programs. In Buddhist terms, it most generally relates to Right Speech, which I also will explore in this Step.

BREAKING THE SILENCE

I read my Fourth Step inventory to my sponsor on a sunny fall day in Southern California. After the regular Sunday morning Twelve Step meeting we both attended, we went for breakfast at an outdoor café, then over to his cottage on a quiet residential street.

I carried my notebook up the flagstone path, past a cactus garden. Nervously, I entered his house for the first time and sat on a couch.

I began to read, telling the story of my drinking, but also the history of pain in my life, the ways I had hurt people and been hurt. The girlfriend I had hit, the conflicts with my brothers, the battles with my parents, the bouts with depression, and more. Every sordid detail—or every one I could remember—from a life of drugs and alcohol, from years of frustration and failed ambition. I would stop to explain what I'd written, then continue on. Stephen nodded and even laughed—laughed!—at these tragedies. He also told me that it was all familiar to him, that he'd done many similar things, and that the rest he'd heard from many others in meetings and inventories. I was not unique.

Teri, another recovering addict, tells about her Fifth Step: "I started reading and my sponsor kind of checked off each thing: 'I did that; I did that; oh, I did that *worse*,' until, after a while, all my embarrassment just evaporated. Here I thought I had this wild story that she wasn't going to believe, and instead I wound up feeling like the whole thing was run of the mill."

This is the first revelation of Step Five: When you expose your hidden secrets and shame to your sponsor, you learn that you aren't alone. Your failings are common. Your shame, unnecessary. When I walked out of Stephen's house into the warm Southern California sunshine, I felt a huge weight had lifted, the weight of self-hatred, the fear of discovery, the fear of admitting my imperfections. The weeks of inventory writing had been so difficult. I felt like I was pushing against something heavy, barely movable. But, after reading all this to Stephen, the huge burden of fear rolled away. I drove home and collapsed on my bed.

Gail, a preschool teacher, talks about how the Step worked for her: "I used to mull over and over until I felt overwhelmed by my problems. I'd try to figure things out but instead would wind up getting nuts. When I started to do inventory, I saw that just speaking about my demons changed everything. Things became so much more clear when I wrote about them and told somebody, or if I shared in a meeting. Before I got clean I was always afraid to have people know my secrets. Now I see that when I hide what's happening, that's the real danger."

Before I did this Step, I, too, had the sense that my whole life would unravel if I pulled that little string of honesty. What is this fear? Why do we struggle so hard to avoid showing others our failings?

I don't know if I can really answer those questions—and I don't know if I have to. All I know is that I felt great fear and resistance to exposing myself—to myself and to others—but once I did there was great relief. For both Buddhism and the Twelve Steps, this is enough to know, because these two traditions encourage us to *act*, not to figure everything out. They encourage us to change our lives through behavior, and that's what this Step did for me.

When Stephen had agreed to sponsor me a couple of months earlier, one of the conditions was that I must share at meetings regularly. I'd cringed at this, but agreed. In my first year of sobriety I'd rarely raised my hand. Once I'd taken this Step, my involvement in meetings became much easier. With nothing to hide, I could share without trepidation. Having seen the benefit, even pleasure, of letting go in this way, I *wanted* to share. And with the sharing came more connection, as people came to know me better. And this acceptance from others grew into self-acceptance.

It was as though my recovery had been supercharged. I began to feel tremendous energy and a new openness. I started to look at my personal history in new ways. With a more honest view of my past, it became easier to assess where I was in my life and what I might need to do to improve things. In Buddhist terms, I didn't feel so attached to my identity— in this case, my negative view of myself. And with this easing of attachment, new possibilities began to arise. If I wasn't limited to who and what I had been in the past, I could become anybody, couldn't I?

For my own Twelve Step work, this new self-acceptance would prepare me for the difficult Steps to come.

RIGOROUS HONESTY

When I was young I thought of myself as incredibly honest because upon meeting someone I would launch into horror stories about myself and my family. I'd brag that I'd started in therapy at fourteen; that my depression had driven my parents to put me in a private mental hospital at eighteen; that my mother'd had a nervous breakdown; that my brothers had dropped out of the best colleges; that the whole family drank to excess; and that I'd been arrested for drug possession. But all this wasn't honesty, just bravado. I knew nothing about true honesty, about exposing myself on an intimate, emotional level, and, more important, about investigating and coming to understand myself, my motivations, and my destructive impulses. The first time I went to a Twelve Step meeting, before I actually got sober, I got a glimpse of what honesty meant.

OCTOBER 1983, WEST HOLLYWOOD

I climb the broad linoleum steps at the back of a church off Fairfax Boulevard with my friend Cat. I'm here to support her as she tries to deal with her cocaine addiction. A short, pretty blonde with a quick wit, penetrating intelligence, and complicated psychology, Cat has been working as a stripper at a club near LAX where her worst habits are encouraged and her real talents have been hidden.

I am still two years away from sobriety, still clinging to an image of myself as some kind of spiritual warrior. My connection with Cat came through a mutual friend I met on my first meditation retreat who also works at the strip club. This Buddhist/stripper connection is perfect for me right now: I've deluded myself into thinking that my spiritual development can include a Bacchanalian element, that "living on the edge," sexually and with drugs and alcohol, is some kind of exercise in nonattachment. And I've also convinced myself that I'm with Cat because she needs my help. I take cocaine with her so that I'll be on her level and she'll be able to receive my spiritual message. The layers of self-deception are manifold.

As we come up the steps, it sounds like we're entering a huge cocktail party. We turn right into a big meeting room with two hundred folding chairs set up facing a stage. In my first exposure to a Twelve Step meeting, I think, "These people aren't very spiritual. They're so noisy." Among my delusions is that being quiet is spiritual. (An odd delusion for a rock guitarist.)

Things quiet down when the meeting begins, although people are continuously getting up and going to the back of the room for coffee, shifting in their chairs, whispering to each other, and generally keeping the noise level of the room at a dull hum. I sit in my chair, upright, silent, still, and I continue to judge these addicts. Of course, I'm not here for myself—I'm not a cocaine addict (which is true, but an incomplete appraisal of myself).

When the main speaker begins to tell his story, I find myself laughing along. The outrageous behavior and confused thinking he describes from his years of using is familiar to me—very familiar. I smile and nod knowingly. Somehow the fact that I'm relating so closely to the story of a coke addict gets past me; I don't realize that the reason this all sounds so familiar is that *I am an alcoholic and addict myself.*

But I am impressed. Impressed with the incredible honesty and lack of pretense of someone who can get up in front of a couple hundred people and expose himself in this way. I can't imagine doing that.

Looking back, I see how in meditation it was possible to deceive myself. In silence, in my own mind, what appeared and disappeared was not seen or heard by anyone else. I got no feedback, and besides that, I didn't recognize the "nature of my wrongs," the destructive and dysfunctional quality of my thinking—not to mention my behavior. This is where the Twelve Steps have something to offer to Buddhism.

In Asia, the monastery is the center of social life for many people. The monks are teachers for the lay people, even confidants. They offer guidance on matters large and small. Buddhism acts as a social and spiritual support system. However, for lay Buddhists in the West, we've largely lost this element. Our prime focus has been on the practices and philosophical teachings of Buddhism, not in creating community. It may also be that Buddhists in the West, being a self-selecting bunch, tend toward introversion—after all, who wants to sit around silently all day but an introvert? In any case, in the typical Western meditation setting, be it a retreat or sitting group, there's little chance for interaction. Usually there is a teacher sitting in front who instructs with the students facing him or her in a typical hierarchical setting.

Many teachers have in the last decade or so tried to alter this dynamic, using interactive exercises, which pair up students with each other, helping to develop Kalyana Mitta groups, support groups of lay practitioners, and encouraging sangha activities like potlucks and group hikes. Spirit Rock Meditation Center in Marin County, California, has a family program and even began a monthly singles night. These are all positive and helpful attempts to bring the community of lay Buddhists together.

What's difficult to achieve is the kind of support that those in Twelve Step groups give each other. This may be because of a central difference in orientation between Twelve Step groups and Buddhist groups. In the Twelve Step groups, what brings people together is a common affliction, be it alcoholism, drug addiction, codependence, overeating, or something else. The members of these groups share a struggle, and also the willingness to engage that struggle with tremendous honesty. The Twelve Step tradition emphasizes the need for support, for "carrying the message," for an ongoing fellowship as we deal with our failings. People in recovery also have the sense of having survived something together, and like any group of survivors, they share a bond forged in pain, struggle, and eventual redemption.

In contrast, a Buddhist group is filled with people who, in some sense, are striving for Buddhahood, for perfection. Everyone is trying to learn Right Speech, Right Effort, Right Concentration, and on and on. In that context, there isn't the same tendency to talk about one's failings. You're "supposed" to be meditating right and being a good little Buddhist. There's a striving for this ideal. And in that striving, there may even be a touch of competitiveness. So, although the Buddhist teachings emphasize compassion and interconnectedness, in many Buddhist communities we haven't found ways to bring the kind of immediate bonding that newcomers to the Twelve Steps can feel after their first meeting when they are surrounded by people offering their phone numbers and asking how they can help.

Twelve Step programs, by starting in this dark place, allow for an honesty—require it—and a connection which doesn't necessarily happen when you tiptoe into a meditation hall, slip onto a cushion, close your eyes and sit for forty-five minutes, listen to a talk, and quietly go home. Of course, this isn't the way Buddhism is supposed to function.

NOBLE FRIENDS
AND NOBLE CONVERSATION

Although I'd practiced a lot of meditation before I got sober, I didn't have a broad understanding of Buddhism. I thought of Buddhist practice as the heroic work of the individual—hidden away in a cave or monastery, practicing in silence and isolation. I was many years into sobriety before I began to learn about how connecting with others fit into the Buddhist path.

One night, my teacher was talking about a sutta where the Buddha's cousin and attendant, Ananda, comes to him and says, "Venerable sir, this is half the holy life, that is Noble Friends and Noble Conversation." When my teacher read this, I thought that the Buddha was going to correct him, saying that these things weren't that important. Instead, the Buddha responds, "Not so, Ananda! Noble Friends and Noble Conversation are the *whole* of the holy life."

I was shocked. I'd always considered meditation to be the whole of the holy life. How could friends and conversation be so important? As my teacher talked about this sutta, I looked around and realized I knew only three or four people in the group, a group I'd been attending for several years. I noticed around this time that my teacher began to use more interactive exercises and integrate questions and dialogue more in his teaching.

I'd always thought of my Twelve Step program as a little bit of a poor stepchild to the "real" spiritual work of Buddhist meditation. But I realized then that "Noble Friends and Noble Conversation" exactly describes Twelve Step programs. That's what they're all about. Of course, the benignly anarchic form of these programs means that many less-than-noble conversations and friends will appear, but it's nobility that is at the heart of recovery. Sharing and sponsors; inventory and newcomers; going for coffee with the group after a meeting. These are all examples of Noble Friends and Noble Conversation.

When we choose a sponsor, this is essentially what we're looking for: in Twelve Step parlance, "someone who's got what we want." When I got sober I made a whole new set of friends—sober people—people trying to improve their lives. I also stopped hanging out in bars and with other drug addicts. This is highly recommended. In Twelve Step groups, the people we got loaded with or who helped enable our behavior are called "lower companions." These are the opposite of noble people. (Of course, nobility is a reflection of actions, not a permanent state. People who get sober go through the transition from lower companions, for someone, at least, to noble people.) After meetings we would go out and talk about our lives, our struggles, our joys, our recovery: noble conversation.

Immediately upon connecting with these new friends, my life changed. I had a whole set of companions who would listen to me talk about my difficulties, give me helpful feedback, and support me in my growth. In meetings, which are another place of noble conversation, I would hear how people had dealt with problems I was beginning to face. I would hear inspiring stories of recovery and growth. People would return to school, or get married, or have kids, or find more satisfying careers, or regain their health, or rebuild family relationships, and on and on. All of this helped me to realize my own potential and begin to consider the possibilities I had. My limited self-image had never allowed for the idea that I could be anything but a musician. Now those ideas began to change.

While it's true that our Western sanghas don't usually offer the same support as a Twelve Step group, a Buddhist community can help a great deal in establishing a meditation practice and learning about Buddhist teachings. At a weekly sitting group, you get the silent support of other meditators (a remarkably powerful aid to meditation). If you have a teacher, you will hear the dharma from an experienced practitioner who can help guide your understanding and practice. And you'll also hear the questions and concerns of other meditators, helping you to see your experience as less personal but part of a common path with common difficulties.

On most retreats, the teachers, besides asking for silence, suggest no eye contact. But one teacher at least, Ajahn Amaro, says, "Go ahead and look at one another and smile." Instead of trying to hold on to some inner quietness, he's encouraging us to open our hearts. Certainly quietness and solitude are powerful tools for practice, but the heart work of connection is equally powerful and vital to our growth.

RIGHT SPEECH

The simplest definition of Buddhist Right Speech is to say only "what is true and useful." If it's true but will harm others, don't say it. And even when we think we are helping someone with a lie, we are creating unforeseen consequences. Silence is usually preferable to falsehood. Can you imagine how your conversation would change if you followed this precept?

David, a therapist who's been practicing Buddhist meditation for many years, decided to specifically focus on Right Speech in his daily life. "As soon as I began to look at Right Speech, I realized there were these two critical questions: What is true? And, How do I know if what I say will be useful? It became evident that I couldn't actually answer either of these questions. The best I could do was say, 'As far as my present understanding goes, I believe this to be true.' " Seeing that he couldn't be sure about truth before he spoke made him more humble about speech. "I became less ready to make definitive statements," he says. "I thought about how many times I'd discovered that something I thought or believed later turned out to be inaccurate." As far as the question of what is useful, he realized he'd have to be able to see into the future to know the answer to that.

What to do, then?

It seems to me that we must speak and we must act, so the best we can do is make informed decisions. How do we inform ourselves? In two ways: one is to be very aware of our inner life, to understand our motivations, and to be present with our experience in the clearest way possible; the other is to study the dharma so that we may make decisions based on the timeless wisdom of the Buddha rather than our own less-informed understanding. When we understand the Buddhist teachings, or any system of constructive morality, we can use it as a template for understanding what is useful. This combination of our own mindfulness, along with the wisdom that comes from the Buddha, makes for a solid basis for Right Speech.

I've learned about Right Speech by watching one of my teachers and seeing the care with which he chooses his words. He has shown me how each word has its power, and that meaning is carried in the energy of these words. One exercise he uses is to ask people to say a harsh word to themselves—*hate*—and feel it resonate in the mind and body, feel how your mind hardens and your body contracts. Then, say a kind word: *love*. Feel that, the softness and openness.

Of course, when we speak, if we're thinking something painful or negative, it's not so easy to turn from hate to love. But, using this awareness, we might say, "I don't care for" instead of "I hate." This might sound like simple etiquette. It is. It turns out that Miss Manners was quite skillful at Right Speech.

Contemporary communications trainers have come up with some helpful approaches to speech. One is "I-centered" speech, whereby we recognize that most of our thoughts are based on opinion, so we shouldn't state them as facts but rather as personal thoughts or feelings. Instead of saying "You made me angry," we might say, "What you said triggered something in me." One dharma teacher says that blaming others for our feelings is never an accurate portrayal of events. No one can make you feel anything—they don't have the power to get inside your mind and heart in that way. The cause of our feelings is never the trigger but rather our own response to that trigger. If we are careful and attentive as these feelings arise, we have the choice whether to respond or not.

So, the beginning of Right Speech is this careful attention to our inner life, watching the habitual reactions, then considering how we *want* to express ourselves.

Our energy tone is also critical to speech. This is the quality that can turn the word "Please," from a polite request into a stern demand: "*Please!*" Speech includes our voice and our body. Bringing awareness to these makes us more sensitive to the unspoken messages we are sending. If our voice and body aren't expressing the same thing as our words, we can create confusion in our listeners—what is he really saying? This problem usually comes out of our own confusion about our feelings—we are angry, but we don't want to hurt anyone, or we're sad but we don't want anyone to know. These mixed messages can be a clue to ourselves that we are missing something about our inner experience.

In some circles, Right Speech becomes misdefined as what one friend calls "talking nicey-nice." This is the pseudo-spiritual habit of always speaking softly and avoiding anything resembling confrontation. The result of nicey-nice speech is repression and ultimately dishonesty and hypocrisy. No one's that nice, and if they try to be they are paving over their emotional truth, creating a false veneer that will eventually cause them and others suffering. Remember, Right Speech includes saying what is true. Also, what is useful may not always feel good. If we aren't willing to speak honestly, to speak our joy *and* our sorrow, we stunt our emotional and spiritual lives and leave ourselves isolated in a cocoon of false niceness.

Some communications experts talk about the idea of "matching" energy, so that if someone is speaking gently to you, you try to respond in a similar, gentle manner. Their thinking is that if someone is shouting, if you try to maintain an even, gentle attitude, it may actually make the communication worse because the person will perceive you as being either false or self-righteous. So, Right Speech also involves Right Listening.

RIGHT LISTENING

Most of us actually do much more listening than speaking in life, so developing mindfulness in this realm is a great tool.

In meditation classes, we often explore mindful listening in a formal way. In one of the exercises we do, everyone in the group finds a partner. We then address a question of some kind, for instance: "What quality would I like to develop in myself, and how might I do that?" The listener is instructed to look at his or her partner without reacting to their words; not nodding, smiling, or acknowledging them in any way. As they listen, they are to keep some of their attention on the sensations in their body. With the rest of their attention, they listen. If they find themselves wandering off in thought, in judgment, or into their own story, or how they would like to respond, or what they like or don't like about the exercise—whatever it is, when they notice that they aren't paying attention to the speaker, they drop the thought and come back to listening and feeling the body. This is essentially the same as meditation, only we pay attention to our partner instead of our breath.

Pamela, a regular member of a sitting group, found this exercise challenging. "I saw right away how I try to please people by looking interested and agreeable—even if I *don't* agree with what they are saying." She struggled not to nod or smile. "By *not* reacting I got to see how when

I'm talking to someone, my focus isn't so much on understanding what they're saying, but on making them like me for liking them. What an insight!" When we go back to our regular interactions, we will of course return to the common polite behaviors of nodding and smiling as someone else speaks, but we can notice that we are doing it. We can also notice how much of the time we are deciding how we are going to respond to the speaker, rehearsing our answer, or critiquing their words. All of this is the mechanism of mind playing out, the same thing we see when we sit in silent meditation.

For members of Twelve Step meetings who sit around listening to each other all the time, this is a great tool.

MEETINGS ARE MEDITATION

A friend recently told me about her struggles listening to others in Twelve Step meetings. Her problems with food had motivated her to join a very strict group in a neighboring town. The women in the meetings were socially different from her, mostly wealthy, middle-aged matrons, while my friend has moderate means and lives with another woman. While she sat in the meetings she found herself judging the other members and growing resentful of them. She resisted the program they proposed because she was afraid of its rigor.

When she finished telling me about these difficulties, I suggested she take a meditative attitude at the meetings, just watching her own mind and body as she does when sitting silently.

It's not uncommon to see people listening at meetings with their eyes closed. Most of the time we aren't speaking during a meeting, since our own sharing will usually last only a few minutes. We are also sitting still most of the time. In this stillness and silence, we can establish mindfulness of mind and body. With eyes open or shut, we notice the passing show of feelings, sensations, thoughts, judgments, and on and on. Each time our mind wanders into fantasy, boredom, or criticism, we come back to our present experience, checking in with the breath, sensations, or emotions.

In meetings we also develop compassion and sympathetic joy. As we listen to the suffering of others, we can practice opening our hearts. We can also share in the joys and successes of our fellows, appreciating how their efforts have borne fruit.

The tool of mindfulness can transform our experience in meetings. When we start to see that our boredom or frustration with someone's sharing is just our own judging mind, we can begin to investigate our own aversion. What was said that triggered those thoughts and feelings? What in me was reacting to those words? Is it possible to let go of these judgments and just listen with an open mind and heart?

With this approach, our compassion grows for our fellow members, and our own serenity is enhanced as the meeting becomes a place for calm and insight to arise instead of boredom and resistance. Many Buddhist groups use some of the Twelve Step meeting guidelines to create a place where Buddhist meditators can support each other and practice Right Speech in a safe environment.

MAY 1993

Eight of us are meditating in a circle on the grass in Live Oak Park, a small patch of trees and lawn straddling a creek in North Berkeley. It's 10:30 A.M. on a Saturday morning. Some of us are in lawn chairs, others on zafus—firm, round meditation pillows—and one person is sitting on a rolled-up sleeping bag. A pair of mourning doves coo on a power line nearby; a three-year-old screeches as her father tosses a tennis ball for their golden retriever. The splashing creek, distant freeway, passing planes, and rustling trees create a background drone.

I ring a small bell after twenty minutes, and people slowly open their eyes and stretch their legs. We begin to check in.

"My sitting's been really agitated," says Nova, a social worker from Oakland. "I keep worrying about this one client, a street lady who seems like she's going under."

We listen without responding. This phase of the Kalyana Mitta group is for people to talk about what's pressing in their lives. When Nova finishes, Scott, a soon-to-be graduate of Berkeley in environmental design, goes next.

"I'm totally whacked around all the graduation stuff," he says. "I can't even sit still for five minutes. But I'm trying to be gentle with myself. And I'm going to lots of meetings." Scott, too, is a recovering alcoholic who got sober at seventeen.

Around the circle we go, each person talking briefly about their practice and their life, and how they are trying to live by their Buddhist principles. When we complete the circle, we move on to the topic for the day: compassion.

"I thought I'd start with a reading," says Sheridan, my co-facilitator. She reads a poem by Thich Nhat Hanh about a girl who is raped by pirates while trying to escape Vietnam and jumps overboard and drowns. The poem says we should feel compassion not only for the girl, but for the pirates whose hearts are filled with hatred and violence.

The poem is remarkable, and we all sit in silence for a few minutes when its done, absorbing the lesson.

"I just don't think I can be that perfect," says Julie, a new member of the group. "When I hear that, I think, 'I wish I could have a heart that open,' but I don't. I hate that pirate." There are nods around the circle.

"I don't think it's so much to be perfect," says Sheridan. "But maybe just to see where we're stuck. I mean, the poem is more of a vision for me, a possibility. And it shows me how compassion doesn't have to be limited—just something you feel for 'good' people."

The exploration continues. People move through the park, kids in strollers, people walking their dogs, joggers and Frisbee throwers, while we sit in our little circle trying to understand the teaching on compassion.

After our teacher, James, convinced us to begin a Kalyana Mitta group, Sheridan and I contacted the people on the list he gave us, as well as inviting a couple friends who were interested. We set up a simple format: sit for twenty minutes, have a check-in, then a topic of discussion. We followed ground rules that I learned at Twelve Step meetings: no crosstalk, so people won't be interrupted when speaking; no advice, so everyone won't be trying to solve one another's problems and tell them how to run their lives; and everyone speaks, so that no one is left out. It's been interesting to see how the discussions have gone. A respectfulness has pervaded the conversation. People aren't jumping in to make their points but rather listening attentively and considering what is said by others, then responding with care.

A sense of support and intimacy has developed. Most of us had never had a chance to talk about our meditation practice with others, and few had talked about how the dharma impacted our lives. Much of our focus has been on "daily mindfulness," trying to see how we can apply the mindfulness practices and the teachings of the Buddha to everyday life. This isn't about having deep meditation experiences on retreat, but rather about seeing what the meaning and value of our practice is beyond the meditation cushion.

We are practicing Right Speech. If politics are mentioned at all, it's in the context of how they impact our practice and our emotions. Trivialities and gossip are out of place. A sense of nobility of purpose pervades the meetings. Afterward, I feel calm, joyful, and inspired. Through this merging of the power of Twelve Step group discussion with the Buddhist teachings, a new model is arising. Here the two traditions merge, bringing the best qualities of both together. Here we have the honesty and openness of Twelve Step meetings with the mindfulness and calm of Buddhist meditation. This commitment to attention and calm listening brings a peacefulness and consistency to the gatherings that some Twelve Step meetings can lack. At the same time, the effort to dig below the surface of our feelings, to truly expose ourselves in the service of spiritual growth, allows a personal exploration that silent meditation can overlook.

STEP SIX

Step Six brings us to the central issue of sobriety and all spiritual growth: letting go. This is how the Buddha said we would find happiness; he talked about many kinds of attachment and the necessity of letting go of each of them: attachment to material things and sense pleasure; attachment to views and opinions; attachment to relationships; attachment to your body, your thoughts, your sense of identity. This is a huge undertaking, and in the Buddhist cosmology it takes many, many lifetimes of spiritual practice to achieve perfection: freedom from attachment. Still, we can make a great deal of progress in letting go just by being aware of what is causing us suffering in this moment. When we see this pain clearly, it's easier to let go—who would want to hang on to something that hurts? Well . . .

Ted, a recovering alcoholic, talks about his experience of Step Six: "At first I thought that being 'entirely ready' to let go was no big deal. But then, when it came down to it, I realized there were a lot of things I didn't want to have removed: my lust, my laziness, my anger. In fact, I actually wanted to hang on to most of my character defects." This seems to be a common addictive pattern. Letting go sounds nice in theory, but when faced with the reality, change isn't so easy. Ted goes on. "Finally my sponsor pointed out that the whole point of sobriety was letting go—that's what I did when I stopped drinking, and of course, that wound up being the start of a new life for me. He showed how the other Steps, too, were about letting go. In Step Three I learned to 'let go and let God,' and even Steps Four and Five were about letting go of secrets, of shame and dishonesty. So he convinced me that it would be worth it to go ahead with Steps Six and Seven, that letting go of my character defects was going to be another kind of relief, just like getting sober."

Step Six pushes us further in our trust and commitment to a process that sometimes doesn't have much appeal. We've looked at ourselves honestly in Steps Four and Five, but now we have to do something about what we've discovered. We have to be ready to change. What gives us the courage to take this Step is the sensitivity to our own pain, which develops as we work through the Steps. At each Step and each level of honesty we see and feel more—in our minds, in our hearts, in our emotions. As this ability to feel becomes more refined with the increasing clarity of sobriety, it becomes more painful (or we become more aware of the pain) to hold on to the self-destructive aspects of ourselves.

Caroline, a pastry chef who has been sober for almost twenty years, still works the Steps on a regular basis. She's inspired by Bill Wilson's words on Step Six in *Twelve Steps and Twelve Traditions*. "The key word he uses is 'repeatedly,'" she says. "I think this should be called the 'never-give-up Step.' It's not a once-and-done deal." She goes on to say that Steps Six and Seven are what you have to use when you've been "brought to your knees over other issues" besides your addiction. This is how they worked for me as well.

When I first did Step Six, I looked at what I was clinging to that was causing me suffering: the rock-star dream; the perfect-relationship fantasy; the hope for escape and satisfaction through drugs and alcohol; the hope for escape and satisfaction through enlightenment; the scorn I had for the forty-hour-a-week day job; all the quick fixes and shortcuts, the instant salvation and lottery redemption. All of this had to go. I began this gritty work, each day asking myself what I could accomplish today, not looking too far to the future, not setting unreasonable goals. Just taking it slowly, carefully, and patiently. This laid the foundation for radical changes in my life. This is the Twelve Step work of Step Six.

Step Six in the meditation process probes more beneath the surface. Becoming aware of subtle forms of clinging allows us to start to let go at a deeper level. I'll use this Step to examine our relationship with emotions and how they influence and color our relationship with the world.

ARE YOU READY?

Willingness comes before any growth: willingness to stop drinking and using; willingness to try a new way of living; willingness to commit ourselves to our spiritual growth; willingness to put that growth before our personal comfort. In short, the willingness to let go. Step Six requires willingness. After completing Step Five, the Big Book suggests we take some time to reflect on what we've learned in the inventory process, then see if we are ready to let go of the destructive qualities we've uncovered.

In Buddhist terms, willingness refers back to Right Intention. How committed are we to the process of recovery? When I first worked Step Six, my desperate desire to pull my life together gave me the willingness to let go of my habitual behaviors and reactions, and to completely reevaluate my life and my approach to living.

In meditation, we also have to find a motivation to let go. As we struggle with learning how to calm the mind and bring equanimity to our experience, we may have to ask ourselves: How committed am I to awakening?

On the three-month retreat, I learned about how difficult it was to let go, how becoming "entirely ready" wasn't as easy as it sounded.

Fall 1981, Barre, Massachusetts

I've been sitting for weeks, months, forever. I signed up for the three-month meditation retreat thinking I'd become enlightened. I've experienced everything but.

When I began the retreat, I had a week or two of hearing songs in my head over and over. This as a result of all the music I've played and listened to over the years. These gradually faded away. Then, when we started doing chanting every morning before breakfast, I started hearing the chants in my head as I was meditating. Eventually these subsided as well.

As the New England fall, with its spectacular colors and clean, brisk air, has turned into a gray, biting early winter, a new phenomenon has appeared: original songs. In the middle of a long period of meditation, a song lyric will appear in my mind. Having written more than a hundred songs in my life, I have the habit, when I get a song idea, of following it. This is what I've found myself doing. I don't want to give them up, even though the meditation is supposed to be about letting go and returning to the present moment.

One day I spend a whole period of walking meditation, forty-five minutes, making up verses to one of these songs. As I sing them in my head I want more and more to actually hear them. I can imagine the chord progressions, but I want to hear what they will sound like. The pull toward my guitar, tucked away in the back of the closet in my dorm room, gets stronger.

Every few days we meditators check in with one of the teachers for guidance in our meditation practice. Soon after the songwriting episode, I find myself in an interview with Joseph Goldstein, one of the founders of the center where I'm practicing and a leading Western Buddhist teacher.

"I've been writing songs," I confess to Joseph. "I've just had this incredible pull. They seem so vital right now."

A tall, bearded man in his mid-thirties, Joseph exudes a confidence and clarity that is both inspiring and intimidating to me. He leans back in his wooden rocking chair. "You have to decide why you are here," he says. "Did you come here to write songs or to practice meditation?"

I'm ashamed when he says this. I feel I'm a failure, that I don't measure up to his standards, the standards that I want so much to reach. I respect Joseph above all the teachers. I'd read his book, *The Experience of Insight*, before I began to practice, and he's a hero to me. Yet I always have the feeling that I can't meet his expectations. Of course, if I were to ask him, I'd probably discover that he doesn't have any expectations of me—the expectations are all mine.

Eventually I stop writing the songs, but through this process I see how hard it is to let go. Here I am, on a three-month meditation retreat, supposedly fully committed to my practice, and even after many weeks of meditation, I can't let go of the craving to write music. The willingness simply isn't there.

Of course, writing songs isn't exactly a character defect. My creative life is my passion, my bliss. There's nothing inherently wrong with thinking about music. It's just that when you are practicing meditation, you are trying to drop discursive thought and bring the mind into the present. When we try to do this, to empty the mind, the habitual thought patterns fight back. It's these patterns that create our sense of self, our ego, and when stillness begins to pervade the mind, this sense of self is threatened. I see now that music is one of the ways—one of the deepest, most habitual ways—that I create my sense of self. Because I love music so much, and because so much of my identity is wrapped up in it, that's what appears as the last barrier between me and emptiness. The mind that is free, that has let go, can be creative without that creativity taking over and becoming an obsession.

Feeling feelings

Before we can be ready to have our "defects of character" removed, we must know what they are. When I first did Step Six, I equated the defects with the inventory itself: everything I did was my defect of character. But recently, after writing another inventory, I realized I'd missed a part of the process. To see what needs to be removed, we need to examine the underlying patterns, the substrata of our emotional landscape. This is particularly true in meditation.

In daily practice it can be even tougher to let go of habitual thinking than it is on retreat. At times I sit down on my meditation cushion only to realize ten minutes later that I've essentially forgotten that I was planning to meditate. I never even started. I went through the physical motions of putting myself into the meditation posture but never engaged my mind in following the breath or paying attention to the activities of mind and body. There's a willingness to practice but no engagement. Why do I get so lost, and how can I find my way back? Oftentimes I discover that the reason I'm not able to get present in my meditation is that something else is going on in my psyche that I'm not acknowledging.

Recently a handsome young man with long blond hair tied back in a ponytail approached me after a meditation class I'd been teaching. Brad had been sober for three years and practicing meditation for nine months. I'd seen him several times and gotten the impression he was very committed to his practice.

"I do an hour of lovingkindness practice every morning," he told me. "And an hour of Vipassana in the evening."

I was impressed by his rigor. He told me that another teacher had recommended metta practice as a counter to what Brad called "the voices in my head." These voices told him he wasn't worthy, that he didn't deserve love. But when he tried this, instead of metta quelling the voices, they only got louder.

Using metta to counter negativity in the mind is a classical Buddhist teaching called "replacing with the opposite"; in this case, trying to arouse a feeling of love toward oneself to get rid of self-hatred. It's a tricky proposition. If there is enough mindfulness and concentration, it can work, so that the negativity subsides as the forces of kindness and compassion pervade the mind. However, if there isn't sufficient strength of mind—of mindfulness and concentration—this practice can backfire in the way Brad was describing: every time you try to bring in an element of metta, the fierce, destructive aspects of mind throw back more venom, and instead of reducing the strength of negative thoughts, you actually increase them as they feed off the weak efforts at positivity.

As I listened to Brad, I thought of the passage in Jack Kornfield's book *A Path with Heart* that talks about "insistent visitors"—strong thoughts that repeat over and over. Kornfield suggests making a Top Ten list of such thoughts as a way of beginning to come to grips with these demons. He goes on to say, "When any experience of body, heart, or mind keeps repeating in consciousness, it is a signal that this visitor is asking for a deeper and fuller attention." In this model, you take an approach very different from the "replacing with opposites." Instead, you engage more deeply with the experience.

I had to do this for myself recently when I was in Colorado teaching a workshop. I awoke early the day after the workshop feeling restless and uncomfortable. I'd noticed the day before that the altitude was making me feel a bit shaky, and now I felt anxious. I lay in bed thinking that if I got up to meditate I would just spend the whole time spinning anxious thoughts through my mind. I thought it would be more productive to go back to sleep and try to meditate later with a clearer head.

But my body wouldn't cooperate. I continued to lie awake for some time until I decided to engage the energy. First I asked myself why I was anxious: being away from home, work pressures, the altitude. After making a list of stressors, I recognized that my feelings were valid; they weren't neurotic, but based in some reality. I was able to accept and not judge myself for having these feelings—a critical first step in engaging with emotions. Then, as I lay in bed, I tried to feel the emotions behind these concerns, to feel the visceral quality of them in my body. It was apparent that these feelings were quite powerful, as I felt tingling down my arms and back, a swirl of energy in my solar plexus, and a general sense of pulsing throughout my body.

I got up and went to the little meditation room my friend had in the basement. Sitting on a cushion, I once again felt the emotions in my body. Now, though, I felt a sadness behind the anxiety. What was this?

I remembered the previous day's workshop. My coteacher and I had participated in one of the exercises I'd taught the group. I'd asked people to investigate what the craving was beneath their alcoholic/addictive craving. While I talked with my friend, I saw that what was beneath that craving for me was a deeper craving just to be loved, a kind of primal, infantile desire to be unconditionally accepted, cared for, and nurtured. As I sat in my friend's basement, I allowed myself to take in that feeling, a tenderness in my chest, in my heart. Quite spontaneously I began to do lovingkindness meditation for myself. I began to say to myself, "May I feel loved"—not "May I *be* loved," getting love from someone else, from the outside, but actually feeling love inside. This was an acknowledgment that, no matter how much others loved me, my feeling of being loved came from inside me. I imagined I was embracing myself, holding myself with care and gentleness.

This wasn't metta as a replacement for something, but as healing. Not some impersonal, generic phrases but a true engagement with the power of my own need for love and at the same time, my own ability to give and receive my own love. After saying these phrases for myself for a few minutes, I began to think of others and how they wanted to feel that they were loved. I felt I was tapping into that vulnerable place in my wife, my daughter, my brothers, and outward. After ten or fifteen minutes, I stopped the phrases and checked back in with my emotions. The anxiety had been quelled, and a deep calm pervaded me. I moved my attention to this calm and began to practice Vipassana.

Sometimes we think that meditation happens outside the context of our lives. But we are meditating with the same mind we take to work and the same mind with which we argue with our partners and cut people off on the freeway. We are meditating with the mind that reads the newspaper in the morning and ignores the person behind the counter of the café. Whatever is happening in our lives will reverberate when we sit down to practice. That's why when I give meditation instructions—and when I myself meditate—I suggest people check in with their emotional state when they begin. If something is going on emotionally, we need to acknowledge that and sometimes just be with that before we'll be able to engage with the breath. Often, just by feeling our feelings for a few minutes, the feelings are calmed and we are able to move into a traditional meditation process. Perhaps this is because the act of giving attention itself is an act of love. Many times all our feelings are asking for is love. Also, when we are feeling rather than thinking about or avoiding our feelings, then we aren't adding more thoughts and anxiety to our existing feelings. We are practicing bare attention, non-interfering awareness, and this in itself is meditation.

After Brad told me about his struggles with metta, I suggested he focus instead on the feelings behind the thoughts of unworthiness. I told him that before the thoughts could carry him away, he should see what he was feeling in his body, just be with the preverbal experience of self-hatred. Where did it appear? How did it change? Could he be present with that feeling without trying to change it or fix it?

In order to get ready to let go, as Step Six asks us to do, we must see clearly what is going on, what it is that we are going to let go *of*. Without this clarity, we can't move forward.

FEELING FEELINGS II

My own experience with learning how to feel began on the three-month retreat. Up to then I had worked with the formal practices my teachers had offered: following the breath; noting thought, sounds, and sensations; and watching my experience arise and pass away moment to moment. Now I would have to learn a whole new approach to meditation.

FALL 1981, BARRE, MASSACHUSETTS

It's about two weeks into the retreat when I approach Joseph Goldstein after the morning instruction period. After breakfast, he guides us in our practice, helping us to navigate through the complex terrain that continues to open up over the days and weeks of silent meditation.

I step up onto the dais where he is gathering his notes to leave the meditation hall.

"Joseph," I say, speaking softly so as not to disturb the other ninety or so meditators who are moving about, preparing for a period of walking meditation. He looks up. "I'm settling in okay, I mean, everything's going fine, but there's kind of a dullness."

He looks at me with his dark eyes seeming to penetrate my psyche. "Don't be afraid to feel," he says.

What? Afraid to feel?

This is the strangest thing I've ever heard from a meditation teacher. I've always prided myself in feeling tons of stuff—I'm a feeler above all.

I've made a career out of feeling depressed; the sensitive songs I've written show how much I feel. Feelings have always been my problem—feeling too much!

I walk away befuddled.

It's early October, Indian summer in New England. I get a light jacket and go outside to do walking meditation. In front of the retreat center, a large lawn stretches out, and I find a patch where no one else is walking and begin to move slowly across the grass, walking a dozen or so steps, turning around, and walking back. Again and again, for forty-five minutes, I pace along with the other students. My mind is supposed to be on my feet and the sensation of movement as I walk, but instead I'm mulling Joseph's comment.

Am I afraid to feel? How could he say that based on my one little question? Is that just some stock response, or am I that easy to see through? Okay, I think, if I'm afraid to feel, let's see if I can feel. I stop walking. The sun coming over the trees touches my neck. I feel that, and the cool breeze coming up from the woods across the road. But what am I feeling emotionally? I feel . . . uh . . . kind of, I don't know, maybe nervous? I've been mostly silent for two weeks—some teacher interviews and a few words in the kitchen—and speaking at all, as I have with Joseph, disturbs my tranquility. I feel agitated, confused. Yeah, that's how I feel.

Two weeks later I'm in an interview with Jack Kornfield, Joseph's teaching partner. We're in his room on the second floor of the center. It's in the front of the building, looking out over the lawn and woods. The leaves are turning brilliant colors in the autumn light. The room is spare, the hardwood floors of wide boards worn from age. We sit in chairs facing each other. Jack is a thin man, much smaller than Joseph, with dark, Levantine looks, and a moustache.

"When I do the noting, it just turns into more judging," I say. One of the practices they teach is called "noting," where you label each thought, sensation, experience that happens to you in a continual stream, like "In-breath, out-breath; thinking, thinking; in-breath, sensation, hearing, in-breath, out-breath," and on and on. "I can't seem to get it."

"Your practice is to feel," Jack says in his smooth, comforting voice.

What? Has he been talking to Joseph about me? I know he hasn't, because there are just too many students and the teachers don't necessarily see the same students. But he seems to be saying the same thing.

"How do I do that?" I ask.

"Okay," says Jack. "Close your eyes. Now, notice the sensations in the middle of your chest. Can you feel that?"

"I think so."

"Good. That's where many emotions appear. But they may show up other places. Just keep paying attention to where in your body you can feel your feelings."

"Okay." Now I think I'm getting the idea.

As the retreat goes on, I make this my central practice, sometimes taking deep breaths as I feel strong emotions in my chest, my arms, my stomach. The noting practice falls away, and I begin to enter a new phase of practice, where I'm not paying attention to breath or thoughts, just resting in an open awareness, which feels warm, protected, comfortable.

Feeling my feelings turns out to be an easier, more natural practice for me than noting thoughts or watching my breath. As the three-month course goes on, the sense of solidity, of being able to sit through storms and earthquakes of thoughts and feelings grows. By the end of the retreat I feel as if I can sit like a mountain through anything my mind presents.

Of course, I'm in a special environment where concentration and mindfulness are fostered and protected. Still almost four years short of getting sober, I have no idea of the upheavals that are coming in my life. But over the succeeding years I will come back to this practice over and over, and it will serve as the foundation for my deepening experience with meditation, as well as my work in therapy and the Twelve Steps.

We are not saints

When I talk with people who practice meditation—Brad is typical in this way—often they are struggling with a sense that they aren't doing it right or that they don't have the ability to practice in the way they think they should. When we hear the meditation instructions, they seem so simple and unambiguous: follow the breath; notice thoughts, sounds, emotions, and sensations; stay attentive moment to moment. But what happens? You spend the time planning this weekend's activities; you try to figure out why your legs hurt and how you could sit more comfortably; you can barely feel the breath, and when you can, it's only for fleeting moments. Where is the mindfulness? The calm? The equanimity that you've heard about?

Or, perhaps you've been on a retreat or had some powerful moments of peace or joy or lovingness in your meditation, but now all you are experiencing is restlessness or sleepiness or anger. What are you doing wrong?

On my second retreat, a weekend spent crowded into a monastery in the Wilshire District of Los Angeles, I was sitting with forty or so other students through a warm February afternoon. I seemed to be sitting in anticipation of something—of whatever I thought meditation was supposed to give me. And it wasn't happening. Although I'd done TM for two years, I was relatively new to Buddhism, having practiced for about five months. So far I'd spent most of my time struggling with my thoughts. In the midst of that silent hall, the teacher spoke: "It's the nature of the mind to wander," he said. That's all.

That was enough.

Something shifted in me at that moment. I went from thinking there was something wrong with me to seeing that my struggle was a natural one. That it wasn't about me, but about mind. I still couldn't calm my mind, but now at least I wasn't blaming myself. So, while being "entirely ready" is an ideal, it's not one worth berating ourselves over. "Why am I not ready? What's wrong with me?" If we are willing to try, willing to put ourselves in the position of having our "defects of character" removed, that may be enough—or it may be all we can do sometimes, so it has to be enough.

The essence of practice is being aware of what is happening right now. But how often do we compare what's happening to some past experience or some ideal of what we think should be happening or wish would happen? This judging is not only painful and unproductive, but is, in fact, another trick of the mind to keep us from being present with what is. To be present with what is, we need to be accepting of the truth of our experience, not fight with it. This doesn't preclude making an effort to deepen our practice. But there's a difference between, for instance, *seeing* that our concentration is weak, and *judging* ourselves for that weakness. We can use the tools of practice to deepen concentration without stirring up feelings of failure or frustration.

In the Big Book, right after the presentation of the Twelve Steps, it says, "No one among us has been able to maintain anything like perfect adherence to these principles. We are not saints. The point is that we are willing to grow along spiritual lines." Is anyone ever "entirely ready" to let go?

WHO YOU CALLIN' DEFECTIVE?

When Brad talked to me about the painfully self-destructive thoughts that blocked his ability to practice metta, he was expressing a sense that he was somehow, at his core, defective. This tendency to view ourselves as inherently flawed can make the phrase "defects of character" a difficult one. It suggests something personal, something which is mine. In

Buddhist thinking, however, the self is a construction, a collection of processes and experiences that have no center and are inherently empty of substance. Although we may have tendencies and habits of mind, we don't have a hard and fast character. Who we are is much more fluid than that, more dynamic. Beneath the hindrances, beneath the thoughts, feelings, and sensations, is pure awareness: Buddha Nature, Buddha Mind. If we are anything at all, we are this luminous presence. And this nature cannot be defective.

And yet . . . And yet we can't always see this luminous nature. Sometimes letting go seems impossible. Sometimes we are completely lost in our negative thoughts and feelings and can't see the way out. Sometimes we're just not ready to let go. What then?

During a period of depression some years ago, I called one of my teachers. As I described my feelings and my struggle with negative thoughts, he asked me if there was any time when I wasn't depressed. My answer was no. "I'm depressed," I said. End of story. But he encouraged me to notice if there were moments or times in the day where I wasn't feeling this way. And, of course, there were. He encouraged me to notice these moments instead of focusing exclusively on the painful ones. What he was showing me was that my self-image was of a person who was "always" depressed, but in fact this was not true.

How you think about yourself is important to how you feel about yourself. If you think, "I'm defective," it can create a negative self-image. Sure, you need to admit your failings, but you don't have to see yourself as a failure. Taking the less personal, Buddhist view of self, as the unfolding of a set of elements, can soothe the sting of this admission. I can begin to deconstruct the elements of this solid identity, at the same time, breaking apart the solid opinions I have about myself.

On the other hand, it's important to recognize and admit the ways in which we are living unskillfully and creating suffering for ourselves and others; otherwise we can delude ourselves. In Step Four I talked about how in the last days of my drinking I fell back on a corrupted version of the Mahayana Buddhist principle that everything I did was just an expression of my Buddha nature. Drinking a lot? "Drunk Buddha." Chasing women? "Lustful Buddha." Cheating on my girlfriend? "Lying Buddha." I imagined I was "playing the edge," transforming what appeared to be unskillful actions into enlightened activity through my spiritually advanced being.

At the Red Robin, where I had my last drink, either a customer or the bartender would buy me beers. The waitress, Diane, and I would go out to her blue Corvette for a joint. As the night progressed, someone might take me into the bathroom for a line of cocaine. I recall the experience of winding my way through the tables toward the stage under the influence of all these substances, feeling as if I were very mindful: "walking meditation." In fact, when you're that loaded, you have to be mindful not to run into something.

As I admitted in Step Four, this was a particularly powerful strain of denial, one that had its roots in my distorted take on Ananda's teachings as well as my limited understanding of Buddhism. It may be possible that someone has achieved a state from which all action is sacred. More often than not, though, such behavior is hard to justify. Debates continue to this day over the actions of certain gurus and teachers. However, for me, and probably most alcoholics and addicts, the idea that I could be enlightened and loaded at the same time is simply a seductive way to avoid responsibility.

From this viewpoint, I had no "defects of character" to let go of. Anything I did was perfect. How convenient. I drove home drunk, washed my face and hands to get Diane's perfume off me, stumbled upstairs, and fell in bed with my girlfriend and felt that I was fine, no problem. Waking in the morning with a crushing headache and suicidal thoughts, I passed into despair—another place from which responsibility or constructive action was impossible. For months I swung on this pendulum from drunken delusion to depressive self-hatred, never reaching a middle ground from which I might address the truth of what was happening: I was abusing drugs and alcohol and betraying my own values of honesty, clarity, and kindness. I was too drained by day to meditate, and too drunk at night. My spiritual life was a sham, a fiction.

I'm not the only person who's ever fallen into this trap. Buddhism and other Eastern philosophies have been used as a justification for all kinds of behavior over the years. Compassionate acceptance of who we are can easily tip into denial of responsibility for our self-centered behavior. There's nothing to be gained, certainly, by harshly judging ourselves for who we are; on the other hand, pretending that we are beyond good and evil, that the precepts are just expressions of "duality," is usually not helping us but pulling us further into delusion.

The first stage of the Buddhist Path is sila, the development of moral and psychological purity. The Buddha, again and again, tells his monks that following the Precepts is the foundation for their growth. This includes the Precept on not taking intoxicants. The idea that we can skip this fundamental step in spiritual development and move right into enlightenment is seductive and dangerous. It fits well with our "you can have it all—right now!" culture, but not with the reality of spiritual principles. It may be true that beneath the surface of our anxious and neurotic mind lies the perfection of Buddha Nature. And touching this place can be a profound experience, whether sober or not. But what makes this place accessible, stable, and meaningful is having a practice whose purity of intention and action supports it. Yes, our essence is pure, but if it is silted over with lust, rage, sorrow, or addiction, our claims to purity, and to acting from that place, become suspect. There are very few of us who can really say that Step Six doesn't apply to us, that there's nothing from our character that needs to be removed, that there's nothing we need to let go of.

Feeling feelings III

The practice of feeling feelings has many levels. Many years after the three-month course, I discovered how getting too wrapped up in the psychological examination of feelings can obscure other truths.

April 1996, Yucca Valley, California

I wake up at 4 A.M. on the third day of the retreat. I have the job of morning bell ringer, so I need to be up before everyone else, but I'm not due to begin ringing for an hour. That feeling is there. I've felt it before on retreats, and I don't like it.

Whenever I'm up at this hour on retreat, I think I should start meditating, but something's telling me to stay in bed. If I start practicing at 4 A.M., I'll be so hungry in a couple hours that I'll be miserable. Besides, I probably need more sleep. If I get up now I'll wind up dragging through the whole day. I roll over and decide to wait for the alarm.

On day four I wake up early again. Same feelings. Yuck. It occurs to me that I should examine this feeling, use the mindfulness technique. That's what I'm here on retreat for, after all. I move slowly, pulling my legs out from the covers and placing them on the cool floor. I try to keep my attention on the feeling I'm having as I begin to get dressed. The oddly shaped room—it's actually a sharply pointed triangle—is part of Frank Lloyd Wright's design for this center, a compound built by a California Christian sect that believes in the power of pyramids. Many of the buildings use the three-angled motif. The door to the bathroom is wedged into the corner.

As I stay with the thoughts and feelings, it hits me that what I'm feeling is fear. How obvious. I wonder how I could have missed this. Fear of hunger, fear of sleepiness. Okay, I got it.

I stay with the feeling as I shower and dress. Before long, it's dissipated and I've moved into a more comfortable place. The close attention was my Step Six: watching my experience with the willingness to have it removed.

The next morning, I again awake early. Again, the feeling of fear. I connect with the feeling. It's there in my solar plexus. As I pay closer attention, I see that there's a fluttering in my chest, as though a butterfly were trying to escape my heart. This fluttering seems to be the core of the fear. Again I shower and dress, and the fluttering fades. I stand in the middle of my little room and contemplate what I've just felt and done. A flutter. A mood. Emotions. Thoughts. Rolling over and going back to sleep. Did all of this arise simply from this flutter? Are my thoughts, emotions, and actions all triggered by a tiny sensation in my chest?

I've learned the habit of examining my emotions through the body. In this way I've been able to maintain my balance around fear, sadness, anger. But when I identify these emotions, I also make them real. A story gets built around them. I'm feeling this because . . . I need to do such and such about this feeling. There are times when this can be helpful, but other times when the examination of emotions can become another form of obsession, always keeping tabs on what I'm feeling, always having a problem that needs to be solved. My life becomes this emotional drama. Feeling the flutter in my chest opened me to another view: Sometimes a feeling is just a feeling. It doesn't really mean anything. If I can stop at the visceral level, without labeling or analyzing, the feeling can just be there. There's no need to do anything about it, to solve it or cure it. In Buddhism, this is the recognition of "not self." The feelings are not me. And they have no intrinsic meaning. They are simply feelings. It's only my thought processes and emotional states that create the idea that these feelings are who I am.

Step Six asks us to be ready to have our defects of character removed. The deeper our attention to ourselves, to the processes of mind and body, the clearer we become about these so-called "defects." This clarity itself is the foundation for letting go. It's in being willing to examine closely how our mind creates suffering and clings to the creation of ego that we prepare ourselves to let go in Step Seven.

STEP SEVEN

"Humbly asked Him to remove our shortcomings."

When I first worked Step Seven, it was as a part of the formal inventory work. After reading my inventory to my sponsor, I went home and read Steps Six and Seven in the Big Book as he'd told me to do. This part of the book tells us to review the earlier Steps to make sure we've built a strong foundation for our sobriety. Then it suggests asking God to take away our defects of character so that we can be more useful in the world and do "God's will." After this prayer, the book says, we've completed Step Seven.

Those kind of instant results are what I used to use drugs and alcohol to achieve. I had always hoped that meditation, through a sudden spasm of enlightenment, would bring me such a quick fix, too. If only it were that simple.

While it's valuable to make a formal ritual out of this Step, showing our commitment and intention to let go of our negative qualities, what Step Seven really requires is an ongoing process. Certainly we may have moments of great insight or giving up that can be transformative; some of the most inspiring enlightenment stories, both ancient and contemporary, involve just such moments. But, most of the time, the removal of our shortcomings, and any real letting go, happens over time, a gradual chipping away that finally reveals a purified heart.

It's a process

Caroline, the pastry chef, says that Step Seven is what she does when she experiences another kind of powerlessness: powerlessness over self. "When I see how the emotional patterns and behaviors keep coming around, I experience real humility. I can't wish my defects away." When her ninety-four-year-old mother, blind, almost deaf, and one-legged after having a gangrenous limb amputated, demanded to be moved from one nursing home to another, never satisfied with the care, Caroline struggled with her impatience. "I had to keep working Step Seven. Here's this poor old lady suffering, and all I can think about is getting out of her room and back home." So, Step Seven helps us to see our habitual reactions and try to let go, or at least, not indulge them. Bringing awareness to these behaviors is the first step in change.

I saw how this could work when I started to deal with my problems around establishing a long-term relationship.

Around two years sober, after another failed, short-term fling, I began to talk more with my sponsor about how I could get what I wanted from relationships: a happy, healthy, long-term monogamous commitment. He gave me a tape of a talk given at a Twelve Step convention by psychotherapist Terry Gorsky. It described a whole different way of approaching getting involved with someone.

My habit had been to find someone who turned me on, usually in a bar, try to get her to sleep with me, and have an intensely passionate affair over a few months. Then, one of two things would happen: one of us would suddenly get turned off and break up, or we'd move in together. I'd lived with three women, and with each I'd engaged in more or less continuous conflict, ranging from bickering, to shouting, to throwing things, to, in the worst case in my early twenties, violence. Clearly I didn't know how to make a relationship work, and Gorsky's tape suggested that the place to start building a good relationship was the beginning. Specifically, he suggested no sex for the initial stages.

For me, this was a radical, and not particularly welcome suggestion. My dependence on at least the possibility, if not the reality, of sexual relations, had driven my life. Indeed, after my sponsor got to know me, when I complained about never having been successful in my musical career, he told me, "That's because your career was women, not music."

Another suggestion Gorsky made was to avoid people who triggered intense sexual longing because such partners wound up setting off an addictive pattern of craving, bingeing, and eventual revulsion. Instead, he suggested that you date people who you liked to spend time with on a friendly basis—a revolutionary concept in my dating life. But my commitment to change was strong, and I set out to find someone I could try out these new ideas on.

Instead of me finding her, soon, she found me. Katie, a young florist from Dublin, was one of the group of sober people I was hanging out with. I enjoyed her company, and she really seemed to like me. We started dating, and before long I told her about my new resolution. She wasn't particularly pleased but agreed to go along with it. Over the following weeks I found myself growing increasingly close to Katie, and when we did start to be intimate, the feeling deepened. Not only that, but over the next two years, instead of becoming bored, I became more and more drawn to her. And we weren't in constant conflict or drama. This was all new, and a revelation.

What had happened was that I'd done Step Six, becoming willing to change, *and* Step Seven, taking the simple, humbling actions that allowed for that change.

The Buddha, when talking about how to reduce craving and suffering, said not to focus on those objects that stimulate sensual desire. Just by taking our attention away from the strong triggers, we avoid having destructive cravings develop. I had always focused on women who set off bells and whistles, and my addictive impulses. By getting involved with someone with whom I was compatible and comfortable first, I was able to grow in true intimacy, without so many painful struggles and conflicts.

The same simple approach helps our recovery from alcohol and drugs: avoiding places where we encounter them and people who use them. The craving is much less likely to arise if we don't see or hear about our drug of choice. This can mean letting go of friends and activities that had been central to our lives. But if we expect our shortcomings, particularly our addictions, to be removed, we have to be willing to make major changes.

In meditation, the process of letting go happens on a subtler level. Appealing thoughts appear, and if we are mindful and have a strong intention, we don't move toward or away from them; we just let them be. They play out their brief life and fade away. Simple. Except that the strength of the thoughts' appeal must always be met by an equally strong mindfulness, concentration, and intention. Otherwise, we're caught. A human shortcoming, one that we all share, is the habit of repetitive thinking. This is so deeply ingrained that it's difficult to arouse enough spiritual power to address it. However, with determination and patience, and by just sitting with our experience, this power will arise. This Higher Power—the energies of mindfulness, concentration, and intention—eventually grows to the point that it meets these habitual thoughts; it sees them, and in that seeing, they wilt.

Concentration, which might be the most difficult of these qualities to develop, is mainly dependent upon two things: time and quiet. If we spend enough time in a quiet place, sitting relatively still, it grows. If we don't, it won't. This is why meditation retreats are so valuable, devoted as they are to stillness and silence. To develop the powerful kind of concentration that can see each arising thought, takes at least a few days, maybe more. And, once it's disturbed, concentration fades fairly quickly at the end of a retreat. For most meditators who are committed to deepening their practice, regular retreats are considered essential. For those with very strong determination, long retreats, or a commitment to the monastic life, is the only way to satisfy the hunger for a life devoted to awareness. But even for people whose life is fully committed to their spiritual practice, there is a continuous process of letting go.

As we work Step Seven, we confront the need to let go on many levels in our lives. Letting go of destructive behaviors; letting go of negative thought patterns; letting go of ideas of who we are. At every stage of our practice—whether newly sober or old-timers, whether beginning meditators or long-term practitioners—we face challenges. It's only through opening with humility to our pain, and being willing to change, to let go, to find new ways of being, that we can continue to grow on the path of freedom.

WHO AM I?

One of the hardest things to let go of is our own self-image. Our ideas of who we are start to form in the earliest stages of our lives, and by the time we are adults, most of us have locked down strong beliefs about our likes and dislikes; our skills and weaknesses; our personality and character. Unfortunately, our lives are often circumscribed by these beliefs, limiting the possibility for change or growth. Recognizing our alcoholism or addiction can shatter our self-image and allow for radical change. Suddenly, everything about who we are is up for grabs. The old rules don't apply, and new possibilities appear, perhaps for the first time in years.

When I got sober I was still working full-time as a musician. I was growing tired, though, of the struggling musician's life. My chances of real success, I knew, were virtually over. I didn't have a clear original musical direction. I was mostly devoting my time to playing oldies, which meant I'd never make it beyond the clubs I'd been playing. The one band I'd been with that had a chance at success had broken up five years earlier. Still, it was hard for me to envision life if I weren't a musician.

When I dropped out of high school and set my supposed course to rock stardom, it was partly because I loved music and thought I had talent. It was also because I didn't think I could do anything else. I didn't have the greatest sense of my own competency in the world, and besides, at seventeen I pretty much hated anything I associated with the word *work*. Being a musician, in my mind, meant playing—playing music—not working. After all these years, this view of myself as only suited for and, indeed, only *able* to play music for a living, had ossified into an unshakeable and inarguable truth. Buddhism asks us to question these assumptions about who we are with the simple question: "Who am I?" Over the last few years I'd tried a couple times to loosen the grip of this concept, to move away from "being" a musician—of using that as my prime identifier. But each time I came back to it, mainly because it was what I knew and I couldn't figure out what else to do— or who else to be.

Now, in sobriety, I began to experiment with different ideas. I took a part-time internship with a record company, thinking I might capitalize on my musical experience and go behind the scenes. Over time, however, I found myself so turned off by the way the company treated their artists that I realized I'd be betraying my own values—in fact, my own "tribe"—to work for them. However, from that job I got a clue: they had asked me to do some typing, and I didn't know how to type.

After leaving that job, I enrolled in a typing class at a trade school in my neighborhood. Near the end of the course, the teacher told us that the local school district was hiring, and I went for an interview. They hired me to do data entry on a temporary basis, and before long I'd found a permanent position in the personnel department. For the first time in my life, I was working in an office. I still was running the band, trying to book gigs on my breaks and playing on the weekends. After a few months I got pretty good at my job and started to gain confidence in my abilities. I had learned to type well and was learning more and more about computers. Unlike musical gigs, where you never knew if the club owner would pay you at the end of the week, or maybe fire you before the week was out, here I got a check right on time and I was under no threat as long as I showed up each day and did my work.

Over my years of drinking and using and playing music for a living, I'd always thought that people who got up to go to work every morning were losers. I thought I was living a life of freedom, spontaneity, and creativity. But now I realized that I'd been living a life of incredible insecurity. The stress and anxiety of the musician's life had been miserable, and only now, working this generic, uncool office job, did I see how painful it had been. I felt a great sense of freedom and comfort in being an office worker.

I gave up the belief that I could only be happy as a musician; that I couldn't do anything else; that I was incompetent; that day jobs were for losers. I allowed my concept of who I was to fall away and instead faced the facts of my life. My musical career was winding down and I needed a new career. When I began the process of going back to school, first for typing, then later at college, I discovered that I had a wealth of talent beyond music. My limited concept of who I was had not allowed me to discover or use these talents, but now a whole world opened up for me. Again, none of this happened in a blinding moment of insight, but rather it unfolded one step at a time, one moment of willingness to another.

In Twelve Step programs they talk about "putting one foot in front of the other," and this is what I had been doing. This means not knowing anything more than where your next step will fall. Not designing some grand plan for transformation, not questioning the value of small steps, but being willing to do the humbling work: typing, data entry, nine-to-five.

Eddy, a junkie from Chicago, got clean in Los Angeles. For almost twenty years he'd hustled for odd jobs, painting, driving cab, washing dishes, occasionally ripping off friends and family, anything to support his habit. After his head started to clear he realized he wanted to help people. He went to school to become a psychotherapist, and Eddy now heads the psychiatric unit of a major hospital. "The street was my life," he says. "I had no clue there could be something else for me out there. But after a couple years off smack, that didn't make sense anymore—I didn't feel like the same person. I had to find a new identity. For a while I thought I knew who I was—Super Shrink—and I built my self-esteem around that. After a couple of professional setbacks, I fell into a depression. I even thought about getting loaded again. I started to see how getting stuck in any idea of who I was was a setup. Now I try not to worry about my identity and just do what seems like the right thing to do."

The Buddha explains that any concept of I, me, or mine is inaccurate. Any time we try to nail down who we are, we miss something. We are a process; we are possibilities; and we constantly change. Every view of who we are can turn into a trap: "I'm a musician"—this could mean being a creative artist, but it can also mean staying up late drinking, taking drugs, and chasing women. And who am I when I stop enjoying that life? "I'm a husband"—this can mean I'm a loving, supportive partner, or it might cause me to play out some role I learned from my father, trying to achieve some stereotypical maleness that doesn't fit me. And who am I if I get divorced or my wife dies? "I'm a Buddhist"—this could mean that I act loving, compassionate, and wise, or that I think that I have to live up to some image of purity that doesn't fit me.

Each of our identities will change, and when they do we are faced with the pain of losing what we thought was "I." Step Seven teaches us to hold on lightly, and to let go gracefully. As we watch our identity change over time, we start to take pleasure in discovering how different aspects of our personality and character appear and disappear. We become more comfortable with not having to answer the question: "Who am I?"

A DIRTY WORD

Committing to going slowly in the beginning of my relationship with Katie was a big letting go for me, a kind of mini-celibacy. Of course, monastics make much greater sacrifices, but even mini-renunciation can be quite powerful. However, even suggesting this kind of spiritual practice can trigger a negative response. The word *renunciation* conjures up images of hair shirts and emaciated yogis. Often when I address the topic in Buddhist meditation groups I'm met with a certain resistance. "Isn't that self-deprivation? Aren't we trying to recover our self-esteem? Isn't that just masochism?" Our culture confuses self-deprivation and letting go. On the one hand, as we strive for material comfort we may push away anything that would get in the way of that. At the same time, perhaps we sense something missing in our lives, so the idea that we should give something up to find what is missing is counterintuitive.

Many of us have the tendency to judge ourselves harshly or to think negatively about ourselves. Through some combination of upbringing and cultural/moral conditioning, we've gotten the idea that we are not worthy of love. Renunciation from this standpoint can become anorexic—intentional self-deprivation meant to punish ourselves for our innate unworthiness. Perversely, then, in a culture of excess and obesity we value the thin and sleek body. This kind of renunciation is a constant struggle, a battle of self-will against the forces of greed and desire. Most of us experience this when we try to diet or impose a new exercise plan. When we finally, almost inevitably, falter in these efforts, bingeing results—all that repression of desire explodes in obsessive craving. Clearly, this is not a helpful form of renunciation.

And yet, many of us—certainly recovering addicts and alcoholics—know how valuable it can be to let go. Sobriety itself is a form of renunciation. When we renounce our self-destructive habits and substances in the First Step, it's not a repression or a masochistic effort at self-improvement, it's a spiritual release. When our craving for booze or drugs or food is removed, it's not because we willed it or because we have a strong character. It's because we've hit bottom, seen the suffering our addiction caused, and couldn't bear to continue to destroy ourselves in that way. In a "moment of clarity," of seeing clearly, we let go. It might not be pretty, or graceful, or as simple as all that, but once we do finally let go, it happens in this way, as a spontaneous response, as if dropping a hot coal. It is this clear seeing that prompts us to let go. This is why the Twelve Steps emphasize honesty and self-examination at every stage, showing us how our unskillful behavior causes our suffering. And this is why Buddhism emphasizes mindfulness. We don't let go because there is some rule or commandment that says we must; we let go because we see how our clinging is causing us pain.

If any group knows about the power of renunciation, it is recovering addicts and alcoholics. Many of us imagined sobriety as a bleak, boring place where all the fun was sucked out of life and we would live in an eternal purgatory of partylessness. Instead, most of us find an entirely new life, one we couldn't have imagined. Sobriety isn't just a matter of removing drugs and alcohol from our lives. In fact, that's only a small part of it. Sobriety is finding a new way of living that involves engagement where there was withdrawal; generosity where there was self-centeredness; community where there was isolation; joy where there was bitterness; trust where there was cynicism.

For some people who first encounter Buddhism, monasticism might carry the same sense of bleakness that sobriety does for the alcoholic who is still drinking. The Theravada monastic tradition is quite strict. Besides giving up sex, monks and nuns refrain from eating after noon; from watching TV and films and listening to music; from handling money and driving a car. And there's more, much more—for monks, over two hundred rules. Essentially, your whole life is scripted. There's little of what we would call personal freedom. And yet, freedom is exactly what monastics experience. Ajahn Amaro, the English monk, explains it this way: "It's not like ordinary human life with some bits cut out. It endeavors to manifest in the physical realm our innate, divine, transcendent nature. That's why many people find monasticism both appealing and frightening." True sobriety is much the same: it's not ordinary life with the drugs and alcohol cut out. It's a new way of living, of relating to ourselves and to the world. It's not a different version of the life we are living; it's a completely new life, one that can't be imagined until you are there. And it is both appealing and frightening.

Ajahn Amaro talks about the different attitude toward renunciation in Asia. "The word for renunciation or celibacy in Asia is *Brahmacharya*. In English, the implication is that it's a state of lack. The implication of Brahmacharya is a state of fullness. If you're not a renunciate, then you're in a diminished state. But if you're a renunciate, spiritually you're a much more full and resplendent person. The implication is completely the other way around."

For me, just being in the presence of this Brahmacharya is proof enough of the value of renunciation. He radiates a joy and wisdom that is enthralling. His appreciation for the simplicity of monastic life is contagious.

When I sat a ten-day retreat with Ajahn Amaro, I knew we'd be following the monastic rule of not eating after noon. On the days leading up to the retreat, I fretted about this sacrifice. I worried about my blood sugar—sometimes when I'm hungry I get dizzy or cranky. I thought of other retreats where, even when I did have an evening meal, I found myself hungry late at night. The hunger would often turn into sadness, a feeling of loneliness or deprivation. In fact, feelings about food had haunted many hours of retreats over the years. And now I was going to be faced with fasting every day from noon until the following morning.

On the three-month course I took years before, little treats started showing up in the dining hall late at night. Trail mix with M&M's. Hershey's Kisses. I couldn't imagine where they came from. The strict vegetarian diet we were fed didn't include any such sweets, and these items didn't seem to come from the kitchen. It never occurred to me that people were walking a few miles down the road to the nearest town and buying snacks to share. All I knew was that these sweets cheered me in my late-night practice.

Now, many years later, I'd adopted the practice of bringing a box of crackers and/or cookies to retreats. In my early retreats I'd had a rigid, rule-following attitude. Now I thought, Why suffer? Too many times I'd gotten dizzy or just uncomfortably hungry in late morning or late at night, and I'd decided that a mindfully eaten Stoned Wheat Thin would probably not delay my enlightenment significantly. Preparing for Ajahn Amaro's retreat, I stuck some crackers in my bag, along with some throat lozenges, which were officially sanctioned afternoon comestibles. The esoteric rules of the monks allowed for a few exceptions, called allowables, to the strict fasting.

My intention was to try to follow the Eight Precept standard and not eat after noon. But I also was allowing for the possibility that the hunger would become too uncomfortable to meditate effectively. In that case, I'd eat a few crackers.

The day of the retreat came, and I began to practice. During the first lunch I ate a little more than I usually would. Typically on retreat I limit my food intake because I've found that a full belly leads to sleepiness in my meditation practice. Besides, I'm not burning off a lot of calories. The afternoon wore on with alternating periods of sitting and walking meditation. Tea time came, the usual time for evening meal, and I drank tea and went back to my room. I got out a lozenge and sucked on it, then returned to the meditation hall. Nothing. No hunger, no dizziness, no sadness. Just an even, steady energy. The evening continued, and I actually felt less hunger than I normally would on retreat.

After a few days, I dropped the lozenge and didn't miss it. What had happened? Why didn't I feel hungry, even from the first day?

Oddly enough, one of the classical commentaries says that the antidote to lust or strong craving is to eat less. I've puzzled over this suggestion, but this retreat gave me some insight into it. It's about habit, or the way actions tend to condition us. Our gut-level feeling when we have a desire for something is that when we get it, we'll be satisfied, and we won't want it anymore. While that makes logical sense, the Law of Karma—cause and effect—works differently in most cases. Instead of satisfaction, getting what we want conditions us to want more. The most obvious case of this is the addict or alcoholic. Does having a drink satisfy our craving? On the contrary, it excites our craving. That's the whole idea behind the phrase "One drink is too much, and a thousand isn't enough." The Buddha understood this. When Mara the Temptor told him he should turn a mountain into gold, he said, "And were that mountain all of yellow gold, twice that is not enough for one man's wants." Craving breeds craving. Giving in to craving breeds more craving. Eating breeds hunger. Eating more just breeds more hunger. Now, with food, there are limits to this—we can't entirely give up food the way we can booze. But what the monastic rules show us is that, in some circumstances at least, we don't need as much food as we think we do, and that if we cut back, we won't be starving at all, but rather feel more satisfied. The advantage of this rule for someone who is meditating a lot is that limiting food intake allows more energy and time for practice. As for how this affects lust, we find that desire itself has a generic quality; we are often just looking for an object on which to place our craving. If we excite more and more craving through overeating, then sexual craving may appear as well.

There's more that we learn by restraining our desires. We learn the truth of impermanence. Whenever you give something up—smoking, drinking, biting your nails—you see that the craving isn't constant. There are moments when it's strong and you have to stay committed, and then there are times when the craving just fades away and it's no problem. Seeing this is quite freeing. The sense of being imprisoned by a constant hunger passes. We see that we don't have to suffer through eternal emptiness. In fact, what happens is that, over time, the craving scales back until it's at least manageable, and often gone completely. Again, this shows how not feeding the craving reduces its power. The problem isn't the substance, but the desire for the substance, and as long as we aren't reinforcing the desire by acting on it, the desire has no energy, nothing to feed it, so it eventually shrivels up.

When people struggle with the idea of renunciation, I like to point out that meditation itself is renunciation. When we sit down, close our eyes, and focus the attention on the breath, we are renouncing the world for this short time. We are turning away from sensory input, from pleasure seeking, from distraction. No entertainment, no shopping, no eating, and most important, no mental excursions. So renunciation, or letting go, is at the heart of the meditative process. Through this process we practice letting go in little ways—by sitting still for a few minutes a day, to start—and gradually build our ability to let go. As we see the joy and freedom that comes from this release, we may become inspired to find more and more creative ways to drop burdensome attitudes, belongings, relationships, or situations. Constantly playing with the edges of what we can manage, we learn more about our own self-imposed limitations and the rewards that come from moving beyond them.

Finally, the Buddha encouraged us to live simply, not as penance or to accumulate good karma, but because he was teaching us to be free from props of any kind. Freedom, in the Buddhist sense, comes not by being allowed to do anything we want, but by being less and less dependent on outside supports—supports for the ego or supports for the body. We learn to stop looking outside ourselves for happiness, for affirmation, for comfort. As we reach out for these supports less, we begin to let go more.

Don't overdo it

While renunciation is a vital tool, there are risks involved. If undertaken without a foundation in real wisdom, it can become a dangerous exercise in delusion. Before I got sober, I floundered with this practice.

Fall 1982

I'm walking, stumbling actually, down California Avenue in Venice Beach. It's after midnight—who knows what time it is? Who cares? I'm drunk (of course) and stoned, although at this point the pot is pretty much drowned out by the booze. It's been just about two months since I left Ananda; I'm living on the street, crashing on couches or in a friend's VW bus. I'm with an old friend from my hometown in Pennsylvania who lives in California now.

I'm wearing an embroidered jean jacket, a gift from a friend in Vermont several years earlier. The embroidery shows the Sufi heart, a symbol of spiritual awakening. When I was given the jacket I hadn't yet embarked on my spiritual quest, and since I began meditating it's always represented a kind of talisman and precursor of the journey, as though the gift-giver had known my destiny, or even helped shape it.

"I love your jacket," says Amy.

I smile a crooked smile and start to slip it off. I had "learned" from Ananda to give things away when people expressed appreciation.

"Here," I say, holding out the beautifully embroidered jacket to Amy.

"No, Kevin," she says, holding up her hands. "You don't have to give it to me."

We're in front of her house, standing beneath a streetlight.

"If you love it, you should have it," I say, pushing it toward her.

She keeps resisting, but I'm drunk, and nobody's going to stop me from giving my jacket away. Finally she relents, taking the jacket and going into her house.

I wander down the street heading to wherever I'm sleeping that night. In the morning when I awake, a terrible headache crushing in, my mouth dry, my stomach sour, I look around. Where's my jacket? Then it hits me. Oh, shit!

It's true that renunciation is a powerful tool, but, as with all aspects of spiritual practice, we have to make sure we are working within our own abilities, not trying to achieve some idealized state or behavior that doesn't suit us. When I abandoned my life in Boston to travel with Ananda, I was overreaching. This kind of excess spiritual grasping can be almost as dangerous as excess indulgence. When I gave Amy my Sufi heart jacket I was acting out a spiritual behavior that wasn't based in true understanding. I wasn't letting go, I was just drunk and stupid and trying to act spiritual.

Renunciation isn't a panacea. The Buddha's own journey shows the limits of renunciation, how he realized that his austerities needed to be balanced with proper nourishment, clothing, medicine, and housing. Some of us can get caught up in this movement toward letting go and lose sight of our own needs. At one daylong retreat, a participant at the end of the day said he was going to start wearing some uncomfortable clothing as a way of reminding himself to be mindful. Every time he felt the discomfort he would remind himself to pay attention to what was happening in that moment. This is, in fact, the reason for such austerities as the medieval practice of wearing hair shirts. Unfortunately, these kinds of practices can get mixed up with a sense of penance, of having to pay recompense for some sin—original or otherwise—and, even if we don't subscribe to a religious tradition that emphasizes this viewpoint, we may find ourselves, when trying to practice austerities, developing a self-abnegating attitude. Ultimately, it is our mental state, not our physical one, which we are trying to purify through spiritual practice.

Physical renunciation is a challenge that can train and purify us in many important ways, but if the mind continues unchecked, all external efforts are fruitless. Kabir, a fifteenth-century Indian poet describes this dilemma:

> *Friend, please tell me what I can do about this world*
> *I hold to, and keep spinning out!*
>
> *I gave up sewn clothes, and wore a robe,*
> *but I noticed one day that the cloth was well woven.*
>
> *So I bought some burlap, but I still*
> *throw it elegantly over my left shoulder.*
>
> *I pulled back my sexual longings,*
> *and now I discover that I'm angry a lot.*
>
> *I gave up rage, and now I notice*
> *that I am greedy all day.*
>
> *I worked hard at dissolving the greed,*
> *and now I am proud of myself.*
>
> *When the mind wants to break its link with the world*
> *it still holds on to one thing.*
>
> *Kabir says: Listen my friend,*
> *there are very few that find the path!*

Kabir shows how different forms of letting go can metamorphose into other forms of clinging, how physical renunciation doesn't necessarily transform the mind and heart. With Buddhist meditation, we keep watching the mind, noticing what appears there as we work with letting go. Am I developing peace or becoming more agitated? Am I dropping desire or simply changing its forms? As my experience deepens, is my pride growing, too?

Spiritual practices are not spirituality; rituals and forms don't free the heart; ideals and models of perfection can't awaken us. As we adopt a form of practice, we must watch carefully that it's working the way we intended. When we get sober, renouncing our destructive substance use, we have to be careful that we don't replace that behavior with another one. Many sober people become overworkers, overeaters, overexercisers, or overmeditators. We have to be careful that one form of letting go—sobriety—doesn't trigger another form of addictive behavior as a replacement.

When I was about four years sober, a friend told me, "You have to be careful you don't replace your old ideas with older ideas." He was referring to the Twelve Step suggestion that we let go of our "old ideas," the ones that supported our alcoholism or addiction. The point is to find a new, healthier way of living. When he said "older ideas," I realized that I had a tendency to fall back on concepts from my rigid Catholic training. Sure, I'd stopped drinking and using and dropped the destructive and cynical thinking that went along with it, but had I now replaced those ideas with guilt and shame associated with my earlier religious experiences? Was I trying to be a "good boy," following rules in a strict, indiscriminate way, without acknowledging my own needs and proclivities? I saw how difficult it is to be spiritually honest, to really shed my conditioned thoughts and actions and make decisions from a place of true freedom.

Whether practicing renunciation or adopting spiritual practices from a Buddhist tradition, we need to maintain the balance between effort and acceptance, between perfection and forgiveness, between letting go and taking care of our needs. Once again, the Middle Way acts as our guide, gently moving us forward on our path.

THE THREE P'S

One of the extremes that alcoholics and addicts often act out is perfectionism. Oddly enough, many sloppy drunks discover in sobriety this quality in themselves. People who have lived risky, careless lives realize that many of their destructive and irresponsible actions were perverse expressions of their wish to get things right—exactly right.

When I went back to school in sobriety I got into this mode. For the first year or so I maintained a 4.0 grade average. When it was threatened in a statistics course, I nearly dropped the class. Before I did, I called my sponsor.

"Do you remember the Three P's?" he asked.

This was one of those typical Twelve Step aphorisms he'd told me about: Because of your Perfectionism, you keep putting off doing anything, which leads to Procrastination; after a while, you can't function: Paralysis. The Three P's.

"If you drop the class now," he said, "you lose twelve weeks of work. What do you want? Perfection, or to get through school? Remember Step Seven: 'Humbly asked.' I think you could use a little humility here."

My ego didn't like it. I didn't want to be humble. I wanted to be perfect. Or at least close to perfect.

Stephen was right, of course. Dropping a course that you were passing just to maintain a perfect grade point average made no sense. Here I was, working full-time during the day and taking night classes year round; I didn't have the luxury of taking classes over just to feed my ego. I had to let go of 4.0.

Letting go of perfection may be one of the most difficult forms of surrender. My tendency was always to quit if I couldn't do something just the way I wanted. In meditation, perfection is probably impossible. And yet, how many of us judge our practice against this standard? One friend who has been practicing for years told me that she stopped sitting on a daily basis because it was "pointless." Now she just practices on retreats—which she can afford to go on only once a year. So, because her meditation practice can't be perfect at home, she's quit. On retreat she can put all her energy into practice and get concentrated. But what's the use of this kind of practice? It's as though she's chopped the Eightfold Path down to a Onefold Path: concentration. Accepting our imperfection and continuing on is the practice.

HUMBLY HUMBLED

If there's one thing that will humble anyone, it's sitting down and trying to control the mind, trying to hold our attention to the breath or any other object. There are different responses people have to this experience. One friend signed up for a six-week introductory meditation class, went for two weeks and said, "I can't do it. My mind just won't stay still." As far as I know, she never tried meditation again. Other people dig in their heels, putting in long hours of practice, determined to take control. Ultimately, though, even the most determined practitioner will find that effort alone is not enough to still the mind.

The first time I experienced quiet in my mind, it seemed to come out of nowhere. I was on a three-week retreat in the spring of 1981, my third, and longest, retreat since I'd begun practicing the previous fall. Ten days into the retreat, I still hadn't had a real moment of peace. Each time I sat down on my zafu, I tried to establish mindfulness of my breath, and each time my mind would fly away, jangling over anxieties, plans, memories, anything but the present moment. Hour after hour I struggled, finding respite only in the periods of walking meditation and dharma talks. I felt as if there were some key action I needed to take, some essential shift of perspective that would open things up, but I couldn't find the way in.

We'd arrived late the first day of the retreat and wound up sitting in the front row, a hundred other meditators crowded in behind us in the hall. The dawn meditation began with a few peeps from the birds out-side. As we sat, the sound would grow as more and more birds awoke and searched for their morning meal. This chorus, like a rising torrent, swept over us as we sat in stillness. The afternoons would grow hot and lazy as the desert breeze stilled and the sun bore down. While the lack of concentration frustrated me, the atmosphere touched me deeply, and I continued on despite my disappointment.

One afternoon as my mind wandered through its stories and I kept trying to find my way back to my breath, a sudden stillness came over me, as though someone had just turned off the stereo in the middle of a song. Just in that moment, my whole experience changed. A sense of quiet joy, of warm appreciation, of openness and presence pervaded my mind. I knew that this was where I had been headed, but I didn't know how I'd gotten here. One moment my mind was all over the place, and the next it was clear and focused. How did that happen?

Meditation is a kind of prayer, a prayer to ourselves and a prayer to awareness: "Come, be present." The Higher Power of meditation is this awareness. When we practice meditation, we turn our "will and our lives" over to awareness, and eventually, with our persistence, awareness brings us this peace and presence. After some time we see that it's not just effort that's at work, there is something else, an aspect of mind or spirit which is beyond our control. Showing up for our meditation, whatever happens, is "Humbly asking" for this presence to appear. Another way to say this is that the development of awareness removes the shortcoming of the wandering mind, of the hindrances. Through our continuous humble meditation, awareness dissolves what covers it. What made it clear for me that I wasn't making this happen was the way this first moment of stillness appeared—not in a moment when I was making a strong effort to be mindful, but right in the middle of my agitation. This is the grace of meditation, the grace that develops through persistent effort. This is the paradox: Nothing happens if we don't work for it, and yet our work alone doesn't make it happen.

The reason for this paradox is that if we strive too hard for quiet or peace, the striving itself creates disruptive energy that blocks the arising of that quiet. Or, as the Third Zen Patriarch put it: "If you try to stop activity to achieve passivity, your very effort fills you with activity." However, if we do nothing, make no effort, how are we going to develop any of these qualities? The art of meditation is learning to make the fullest effort possible without straining or expecting any results. This balance between striving and letting go is the "vigilant surrender" that allows peace to appear.

STEP EIGHT

"Made a list of all persons we had harmed,
and became willing to make amends to them all."

When I first looked at Step Eight, I thought, "There's not much to this. Just make a list." I picked up the inventory from Step Four and began to write down the names of all the people I'd hurt. But as soon as I saw the names on paper, the Step looked a lot tougher. I was faced with all my destructive history. Who did I hurt? Why did I hurt them? In what ways did I hurt them?

With Step Eight, once again we are challenged to be willing, to see the strength of our Right Intention. This emphasis on willingness and intention in the Steps points to the stubborn, willful nature of typical addicts and alcoholics. Our self-centeredness and pride often make it difficult for us to see that our way isn't always the best way to approach life and its problems.

One friend tells me that a woman she sponsors refused to do Step Eight. "She says she isn't about to make amends to anyone so there's no point in doing it." My friend and I look at each other with the shared understanding of people who have been sober for years. What a miserable place to wind up, hanging between one Step and another. Obviously, this list is a preparation for making amends, but if that's the only way we view it, we miss out on the greater value of looking honestly at who we hurt. Worrying about the next Step isn't in the spirit of "one day at a time," nor the spirit of "one breath at a time." Even if we never make any of the amends, writing this list and looking at it with discerning eyes help us to understand ourselves and our lives. It can also be a gauge of our willingness, as over time we work our way down the list to people we might have thought we could never make amends to.

As we approach this difficult and intimidating process of making amends, it can help if we look again at why we are involved in this work. First: to get and stay sober. The experience of millions who have worked the Steps suggests that cleaning up our personal relationships can help us let go of many of the destructive emotions that feed our addictions. Further, once we see that cultivating a spiritual life is the real route to happiness, we understand that we'll need harmonious relationships if we are going to live a life of serenity and joy. If we are going to journey deeply into our inner world, which has its own perils, we'll want to have as few external obstructions as possible.

THE WHOLE PATTERN OF OUR LIVES

Step Eight takes us to another, deeper level of honesty to consider who we really hurt with our actions when we were drinking or using. At this point it can seem as though the Steps are just an exercise in self-flagellation. "First I admit I'm an alcoholic, then I have to write this awful inventory, then I have to *tell someone* everything, and now you want me to *what*? Go through the inventory and make a list of everybody I've hurt?" No wonder it says in the Big Book, right after the Steps are enumerated for the first time: "Many of us exclaimed, 'What an order. I can't go through with it.'"

And yet . . . what choice do we have? Having seen the truth of our mistakes in the earlier Steps, and having made a commitment to let go, it's clear that we must get straight with our past. Otherwise we can never be free of the burden of guilt and shame, not to mention the practical problems that come with devoting years of our lives to consuming drugs or alcohol. If we are practicing meditation and trying to deepen that part of our spiritual lives, all this past history will very often keep coming up until it gets resolved. Part of the process of cleaning up our act is this very work of unburdening ourselves. Otherwise, true peace is never really available. Instead of meditation uncovering deeper levels of truth, it winds up being an escape, a covering over, and a numbing of the truth. While we can never completely resolve our past—some degree of regret almost inevitably follows us as we age—the more that we can face our past karma, the less we are likely to be attacked by painful memories in meditation.

Bill Wilson says that looking deeply at the roots of conflict with others can open real insight into our own basic flaws, which may be "responsible for the whole pattern of our lives." So, the list in this Step is only a window on the destructive patterns we act out in our relationships.

THANKSGIVING WEEKEND, 1980

My first retreat. Five days of meditation in the high desert. The tiny meditation hall holds forty young people, sitting in rows literally knee-to-knee. The only convenient way to come in or out is in line. Otherwise, you have to step between people's ankles and thighs.

I struggle over these days, especially with the pain in my knees. I pile meditation cushions high trying to find a comfortable way to sit, some way that my knees won't begin to burn and make the second half of every meditation period a battle just to sit still. Mindfulness? What's that? All I'm aware of is frustration.

On Saturday night, after the last sitting, I step out into the starry night, walking carefully down the sandy track toward the bunkhouse. As I walk

I hear my footsteps, the *scritch, scritch* of rubber-soled shoes crunching sand underfoot. I'm listening to the sound, the rhythm blending with the sounds of the night, the soft breeze, a distant bird call; I stop. This is it. This is mindfulness. I'm present.

Four days of meditation and it seems as though I haven't felt a moment of this in the hall. Now, on my way to bed, the natural simplicity of walking, listening, being, all come together in this clarity, this immanence. Ahhhh . . .

The next afternoon the retreat nears its end, and the teacher begins a guided meditation on lovingkindness, metta. He begins by asking us to think about people we have harmed and asking their forgiveness. Before we can open ourselves to love, we must forgive, emptying ourselves of the long-held resentments and guilt from the past.

Thoughts of long-ago girlfriends, my parents, lost band members float through my mind. I breathe and feel the sorrow—why did I hurt you?

Now we're asked to think of people who have hurt us. I think back and *the same people come to mind.* What's going on here?

Six years later, as I write my first inventory, I see the same thing. The people I hurt are very often the same ones who hurt me. I don't see this as some kind of tit-for-tat, but just the fact that intimacy triggers these struggles for me. I'm seeing the "pattern of my life." The inextricability of love and fear, of intimacy and alienation. And the truth of this paradox continues to open.

In lovingkindness practice we look at three types of relationships: with people we love, with those we feel neutral toward, and with difficult people. As I recently contemplated these levels of metta, I realized that my wife fell into all three categories. I love her dearly as my life partner; sometimes I hardly notice her as we pass each other in the hallway; sometimes she's the focus of all my frustrations. How convenient, I thought. I don't have to figure out who to do metta for anymore: just use Rosemary as the focus of all three types.

The self-examination that starts with Step Four's inventory (and really with Step One) and progresses through seeing what our defects are in Step Six brings the pattern of our problems into focus in Step Eight. Seeing who is on this list—my parents, my brothers, my ex-girlfriends, my wife, my former musical partners—all the people who were most important in my life, all the people I've loved most—shows me that the work I need to do is right here in front of me. My spiritual growth isn't contingent upon some transcendent meditative experience, but rather my ability to recognize that the person I'm sitting across the breakfast table from is a precious gift in my life; she is my lover, my teacher, my friend. And yet, how many times do I come into conflict with her? Feeling threatened or fearful. Wanting her to behave differently, thinking she doesn't understand me, doesn't appreciate me. On and on. Here again, I'm confronted with the whole pattern of my life. The blaming and judging. The wish to control.

What Buddhism tells me about this is two things: These habits, these patterns, are the results of past actions—*karmic resultants*; and I can change these habits this very moment. I can look up from the newspaper and smile. I can start again, a fresh breath, a fresh kindness, in this moment. If there's something a long-term relationship requires, it's this ability to let go of the last battle and begin again with kindness. When teaching about forgiveness recently, I found myself saying, "I'm an expert on forgiveness: I'm married." This got a big laugh, but indeed, if you can't forgive, your marriage probably won't last very long, or at least it will be a painful one.

This quality of forgiving and beginning again is the same one we need in meditation. Each time we find that we have slipped from our awareness of the present moment into some memory or fantasy, some judgment or analysis, right then we need to forgive ourselves and start our practice right in that place. When we come out of the dream, that's when we have the opportunity to begin again fresh. Like marriage, our meditation practice is a long-term relationship. It has its ups and downs, its bliss and its misery; and like a relationship, it needs gentle nurturing and persistent effort.

THE END OF ISOLATION

I've talked about how meditators may be a self-selecting bunch of isolators. A practice that requires so little human interaction can be quite appealing for people who struggle with personal relations. The Buddha recommended solitude for meditation practice, and many people take that to mean that living alone and limiting human contact is the most spiritual behavior. This conveniently overlooks the fact that the Buddha set up his monastic communities to be completely dependent on their lay followers and as communal living settings. Since the monks weren't allowed to store, grow, or purchase food, they had to interact with other people every day or they would, quite literally, die. Theravada monks continue this tradition to the present day. This isn't to say that meditating in solitude isn't helpful. Of course it is, and that kind of quiet is especially conducive to the development of concentration and the deeper meditative experiences. However, these activities are not the whole of the holy life. These experiences only give us the basis for a holy life, the tools. We still need to use these tools—mindfulness, compassion, and wisdom—in our lives with others. While deeply developing our meditation practice is a rich and meaningful experience, perhaps the truest expression of Buddhist wisdom is found in our relationships, when we act for the benefit of others.

Several years ago, my girlfriend of the time picked me up at the airport when I returned from a retreat. After ten days of sitting, I felt calm and centered. We had plans to go to a party, and as we drove back to town, I started to tell her about the retreat. The more I talked, the less calm I became, getting caught up in the excitement of describing my experiences. She, not being a meditator, wasn't all that interested, although she listened politely. However, when she didn't respond with the kind of appreciation I wanted, I became frustrated.

I started talking about how I wanted to go on longer retreats, and she expressed concern about my being away for that long. As we approached the house of our friends who were giving the party, I blew up, telling her that she was trying to control me, that meditation was the most important thing in my life, and that if she wasn't going to support me, I would go anyway.

We never made it to the party. Of course my calm was shattered, and it took a day or so for us to smooth things out. This experience pointed up for me how meditation itself isn't a solution to the problems in any relationship. In fact, meditation can put stress on relationships by taking us away for periods of time, and also by allowing us to become absorbed in the pleasure of solitude, quiet, and peace.

When we make the transition out of the retreat environment, it can be quite challenging to begin relating to others again. If we are attached to the states we've achieved in meditation, we will often struggle when returning. Just as we must work hard to strengthen concentration and mindfulness on retreat, we also have to work at letting go gracefully, at moving back into relationships with openness. In this process, we have to be gentle with ourselves, remembering to have compassion for the vulnerable places we have touched, and to be sensitive to those around us and how they are feeling in reconnecting with us. A period of intensive retreat is one of extreme introspection; we have virtually no responsibility to others, and this can become a kind of narcissism, where we are so used to looking at our own thoughts and feelings moment to moment that we forget how to pay attention to the needs of others. Step Eight reminds us that our spiritual life isn't all internal or solitary, that we must be sensitive to others, to see how we might hurt them in subtle ways, and be ready to make amends.

It's interesting that the Buddha's instructions on mindfulness suggest being aware of body, feelings, and thoughts "internally and externally."

But we don't often hear what being mindful "externally" might mean. We are mostly taught to pay attention to *ourselves* when we meditate. Apparently, though, the Buddha wanted us to be mindful of others as well. To notice what someone else is feeling or thinking by watching or listening to them and to respond to that with mindfulness, is the essence of compassion and the foundation of interpersonal harmony.

As we make our amends list, opening deeply to the pain we've caused ourselves and others, the heart begins to soften. The willingness to face pain—internally and externally—awakens love and compassion. The deepest veins of emotion start to reveal themselves in our heart. A sense of great sorrow can come over us, seeing how we—all of us—hurt each other, and ourselves. We tap into the Buddha's First Noble Truth, the truth of life's pain, but we do it not from a place of fear or distaste, but from a place of caring and kindness. The great sorrow can open into a spacious love and acceptance. Tears may come as we open the heart chakra, that part of us, physical (in the center of the chest, beneath the sternum), emotional, and spiritual, from which love comes and goes. After my first retreat in the desert, this happened to me. I cried every day for a week. And the tears were cleansing, enriching, fulfilling. When we spend years drinking and using, holding in our feelings, covering over our feelings, wreaking havoc in the lives of everyone we know, running, always running, never coming home to our true self, we bury some essential part of ourselves; we bury it alive. When, through this process of opening, we touch again the truth of our heart's deepest craving for love, something bursts forth, and often it flows in a river of tears. What joy!

MAKING THE LIST

The day I did my Fifth Step with my sponsor, reading him my Fourth Step inventory, he told me to go home and read the part of the Big Book on Steps Six and Seven. I was sharing an apartment with some friends in West L.A., and I closed my bedroom door and stretched out on the red futon, which was my bed. I looked over the Steps and said the prayers, trying to go deeply into the sense of letting go, of allowing my "defects of character" to be removed. I felt myself in the stream, swimming, yes, but also being carried along by the current of this process. The Steps were working.

Of course, I knew what was coming next. You don't sit in meeting after meeting for a year hearing the Steps read without knowing that on the horizon, lurking out there like some fanged monster, is the amends. I don't know if I'd thought about what amends I needed to make. I don't think so. I didn't want to face the reality of Steps Eight and Nine until I absolutely had to. And now I had to.

Here was my inventory beside me on the bed, twenty-five pages or so in a notebook, scrawled pages of furious writing in my barely legible, left-handed script. It roughly followed the chronology of my life, starting with the first girlfriend I hurt. My sponsor told me to prioritize my amends and not to try to make an amends unless I was clear about what I was apologizing for. None of these vague, "I'm sorry I hurt you" things. I had to be specific: "I'm sorry for the time I threw the sandwich you bought me against the wall because it was on rye bread." (This actually happened when I was nineteen—and now that I mention it, I never did make amends. As they say, "More will be revealed.")

I knew who had to be first on my list.

When I was twenty-one I was living with my brother who had bought a house when my father retired. This was my next older brother. (I'm the youngest of five boys.) Although he drank heavily, he wasn't into drugs. But I was. We moved into the house in late winter, and by the following fall, my so-called best friend, Rick, a drug dealer, was using one of the attic bedrooms as his crash pad. My room was the constant site of drug use. I smoked pot every day, often upon awaking; I drank every night, sometimes mixing booze with barbiturates or psychedelics; I snorted cocaine when it was available. Here I watched my friends shoot heroin and nod out. Although I never used needles, I would scrape up their leavings and snort it. And, as a drug dealer's friend, I was more or less involved in ongoing drug sales.

I had a job at the time waiting tables at a local bar. And I was working with some musician friends putting together a band doing original music. We'd become frustrated with the local music scene in southeastern Pennsylvania, and had decided we'd move to State College soon.

After hours at the bar, the employees would do rounds of ouzo and Rolling Rock until we couldn't drink anymore. One of those drunken nights I stumbled the few blocks home with a wild idea. In the flush of drunkenness, I climbed the attic stairs and found Rick in bed with someone he'd met earlier that evening.

Paying no attention to the girl, I said, "Let's split now. I want to get out of here. Let's head up to State College."

In the blur of that alcoholic memory, everything is white: the sheets, the freshly painted walls, Rick's pale skin, the cocaine.

Rick, naked beneath the sheets, looked at me thoughtfully. In a fine rock 'n' roll tradition, he'd agreed to be the "manager" of our band, a role often assigned to drug dealers, who were usually the only people hanging around with bands who had any money.

"Now?" he asked.

"Yeah," I said. "Let's just do some lines and drive."

He considered this. "I don't really have enough coke," he said.

"I don't need much," I said.

He reached over to a small aluminum foil package beside the bed. Peeling back the foil, he examined the white powder.

"Okay," he said. "We can probably make it."

So, by deciding that we had enough cocaine to travel a couple hundred miles—an odd form of measurement if there ever was one—Rick agreed to go. Soon we were on the road, both of us buzzing on cocaine and alcohol, speeding through the pre-dawn fall chill.

We arrived early in the morning and went to a friend's place in State College. We fell asleep, only to be awakened a few hours later by a phone call. Hung over, my mouth dry, my head imploding, my body aching from sleeping on the floor, I tried to take in the news: my brother's house had been busted. Everyone was in jail.

Apparently, just a few hours after our impulsive departure, the police had burst into my brother's house, rounding up everyone: two of my brothers, their girlfriends, and several other people who were either living in or staying overnight in the rambling three-story house. One person who had dropped by to make a purchase ran down the street, only to be tackled by the police as he tried to escape with a pound of pot.

Over the next months, charges were dropped for most of the people, but my brother who owned the house was put through a grueling and stressful legal battle. Here was someone who didn't even smoke pot who was being accused of possessing all sorts of things, including traces of drugs found in the carpet in my room.

I stayed away from my hometown for a few months, and when I returned I didn't say much to my brother. Somehow we got back to being friends, and the past was, at least theoretically, forgotten. A year later I left my hometown for good, and although my brother and I remained cordial, the dark past that I'd caused always lurked in the shadows of our relationship. And now, having written my Fourth Step and looked at the people I'd hurt in my life, it was clear what call I had to make first.

STEP NINE

"Made direct amends to such people whenever possible,
except when to do so would injure them or others."

The dreaded Step Nine. What person, when working through the Steps, has not looked ahead and feared facing the amends process? Here culminates one of the central themes of the Steps: admitting our failings and beginning to take responsibility for them. As this process unfolds, beginning with Step One and deepening throughout the inventory, something happens to us, a gradual but radical shift from shame, guilt, and denial, to openness, acceptance, and honesty. Revealing ourselves to ourselves and others through the Steps frees us from having to protect or hide parts of ourselves from the world. Once we discover the lightness of opening in this way, we can become almost playful about our failings.

Paulette, a longtime meditator who recently got sober, told me about her process with Step Nine. "Years ago I had a roommate who was very good to me and my family. He was a gambler, and one day I did his laundry, and out of his pants' pockets came about three hundred dollars. It was early December, with the pressure of Christmas already on, and I kept it. Once he even asked if I'd seen it, and I said no. My son had a better Christmas, and no one ever wondered where I got the money. The first time I heard about making amends, I thought to myself, 'I'll never make that one.'"

But, in the process of getting sober, something changed for her. "By the time I had gone through the preceding Steps, I looked forward to making the amends. I got three hundred dollars out of savings, told him the story, and gave him the money. He really didn't want it. 'You need it more than I do,' he said. But I was insistent." By coming clean with her inventory and embracing the honesty of the Steps, as Paulette says, she went from "No, never!" to "Maybe someday" to "Yes, I have to" to "I can't wait to do this."

Paulette's story points to the way that the Steps transmute from a burden to a joy; from dreaded task to freeing leap; from drudgery to vital activity.

Cleaning up our lives in this way is critical to the Buddhist path. The first thing the Buddha taught people was generosity. But how are we going to be generous if our work and financial life are in disarray? And, in practical terms, how are we going to be able to go on retreat if we can't afford to take a little time off work? The Buddha said Noble Friends and Noble Conversation were the whole of the holy life. But how are we going to have successful relationships if our histories are scarred and unresolved? In these very real ways, our practice requires a clean slate. Even more, we discover when we sit down to meditate the need to be free of excessive guilt and worries.

THE FIVE-HUNDRED-POUND PHONE

I lay on my bed thinking. A completely unproductive exercise. I knew that what I needed to do was to act, not think. I'd written and shared my inventory; asked for the failings revealed therein to be removed; made a list of the people I'd harmed. Now, all I had to do was make amends. The thought made me nauseous. The reasons why this was a pointless Step spun around in my mind: I can't really make up for hurting people; I don't have enough money to pay anyone back; there's no point in dredging up the past; what's the use? I looked at the telephone on the floor beside the bed; my arms didn't feel strong enough to lift it.

I grew up the youngest of five boys. As the "baby" in the family, I was probably spoiled, or so everyone told me. But it never felt that way to me. I adored my brothers, and I also resented them for being bigger than me. I had particular resentments for my brother Michael, my closest in age, who, in the typical ways that brothers will do, beat me up and tormented me as a kid. Of course, he would always say that I was a brat and that I only provoked his behavior. I suppose such arguments have gone on through the ages. Still, here I was with this list, and who was at the top? Michael. He may have tied me up and sat on me when I was eight, but I had been directly responsible for his being arrested and eventually losing his house. So I dialed his number.

The conversation was relatively brief. I told him that I'd realized that in all these years I'd never really said I was sorry. Then he told me more about what had happened: the police station, the interminable court dates, his anger and frustration. He didn't pretend that there wasn't some residual anger fifteen years later, but he also wasn't holding on to bitterness toward me. He'd pretty much let it go. The bottom line was, "You screwed up, but we're still brothers." I felt an appreciation for him, for his friendship and love that I'd never felt before. In fact, seeing his ability to forgive showed me something about my spiritual arrogance: Buddhists weren't the only ones who could let go.

Michael had been my best friend growing up. He taught me to play the guitar when I was twelve, which set me on my life's creative journey. With his brilliant intellect he introduced me to critical thinking in high school. For many years, his opinions were my opinions. As a kid he was ravenous in his interests: chemistry, photography, astronomy, chess, and reading—lots of reading. His imagination was prolific. With his friends he had dozens of in-jokes filled with word play and clever observations of the world. When he came into his sexuality, he taught me to girl watch, and he and his friends developed a set of acronyms for obscene insults.

I was Michael's fan, his assistant, his student. I felt I was in the presence of brilliance and authority when I was with him. I trusted him more than I trusted myself—or my parents. And now I recognized how much I had damaged his life. Could telling him how sorry I was make up for that? Probably not. This might be the first lesson we learn about amends: you can't take it back, you can't fix what you broke. So, ultimately, the amends process isn't for the other, but for the self. Even if you pay back the money you owed, you don't totally repair the damage you've done to someone's life.

I then called my brother Pat, who had also been arrested that early morning so many years before. Pat, who hadn't had to go through the same difficult legal battles as Michael, took my amends more lightly, but still was appreciative.

After talking with my brothers, something else became clear to me. There was another, messier resentment I carried. I had idolized them, but they had not lived up to my ideals. Growing up I had thought that being a Griffin meant something special. My first two brothers, Dave and Jerry, were very successful coming out of college, and I was proud of that. But Michael and Pat had trouble in college and both became heavy drinkers. When Michael became a carpenter, I was disappointed in him. He'd been my hero and I wanted him to achieve something great—*by my standards*—in the world. These feelings complicated my relationship with him.

It's these kind of complications that make the amends process tricky, as I saw in my first experience of the lovingkindness meditation in the desert. Painful relationships and situations rarely go in just one direction. We hurt each other. Many times we have to make amends to people who have hurt us—maybe even more than we've hurt them. Being willing to stay on our own side of the street, to not get involved in what we think others might owe us, is a huge step toward clarity in our lives. What I was seeing about Michael was that I was angry with him for something that was none of my business. If he was happy as a carpenter, why should I care? The fact that it affected my self-image or family image, really was my problem, not his.

And, after all, who was I to judge? While Michael was dropping out of college, I was dropping out of high school; and while I thought he was drinking heavily, I was taking drugs *and* drinking every day.

Even as I struggled with all these complicated feelings about the amends, relief poured over me. Sure, I was learning about more and more messy layers of my psyche, but I was also cleaning things up. I felt a freshness, a new freedom and sense of lightness. Unburdened of guilt, relieved of shame, I felt the possibility of a new life ahead.

BILL

My brothers and I always called my father "Bill." For some reason my parents didn't teach us to call them Mommy and Daddy, and it was only when my older brothers started school and learned that the other kids called their mothers "Mom" that they stopped calling her "Margie." But "Bill" stuck. I was always proud of it with my friends, another mark of my family's specialness (ah, the things children attach to). He and I were, at least on the surface, very different. He was meticulous, risk-averse, mechanically oriented, and organized (this is my own version—my brothers might give you a different description). I, on the other hand, was impulsive, impatient, irresponsible, clumsy; I was also creative, openhearted, emotionally sensitive, playful, and empathic. When I became, at seventeen, so depressed and passive that I had to be hospitalized, he fretted himself into a heart condition. When I dropped out of school and became a musician, he was angry and frustrated. When I was arrested for drugs, he turned his back. When I caused my brothers' arrests, I turned *my* back for fear of seeing his wrath. All of this happened before I was twenty-two, but by the time I was in my mid-twenties, miraculously, our relationship began to change. As I started to make my way in the world, I began to see that his concerns about my career weren't unfounded. And, as he saw me actually making a living as a musician (however meager), he started to respect me. One day he took me aside and told me he was proud of what I'd done as a musician. He said that his life had been easy because he'd followed a well-worn track: college, law school, and a career as a patent attorney. He thought that what I'd done, setting out to be a musician with no training and finding my way, had taken great courage and determination. I was stunned. It was one of the most important moments of my life.

When I learned he was dying, it had spurred me to finish my inventory so I could make some kind of amends to him. He was home then, done with treatments, lying in his own bed. "I'm sorry," I told him, "for all the ways I was a pain in the ass. I'm sorry I caused you so much pain." This was my awkward effort. I'd only finished my Fourth Step a couple weeks before and I didn't really know what to say. I knew I'd been a nightmare teenager, but what could I do about that now?

"Don't," he said, waving his hand. "We were different, that's all. It took me a while to see that you were going to be okay."

"We learned how to respect each other, didn't we?" I said. "I'm really glad we could do that. I didn't appreciate you when I was growing up."

"It wasn't easy," he said. "But it worked out."

There was an understanding in those moments, an appreciation for each other that neither of us would have believed could happen. I felt incredibly lucky. My own sponsor's parents had died before he got sober; he'd never been able to make amends. I didn't know if my father thought that my newfound sobriety was just another of my wild-goose chases or if he knew that a real transformation had started, but at least when we were together that final time we could be honest. We didn't pretend that our relationship had been easy, but both of us were able to feel and express the love that was beneath all the struggles. This was a true gift of sobriety.

The Buddhist teachings emphasize the transience of all things—even of fathers. When Bill died, I felt a bittersweet sadness. This was an honest pain, not the neurotic, self-centered depression or anxiety I'd tormented myself with for years; this was a deeply human grief. There was no confusion in my mind about my father's death—I hope the same will be true when I come to die. His passing was the natural unfolding of the dharma—all things that come into existence must pass away. I didn't want to shove my feelings of sorrow away or bury them, but I knew that in my busy life it would be easy to forget, to abort this grieving process. So I bought a book by Stephen Levine, *Meetings at the Edge*, which was filled with conversations with dying and grieving people, exploring the meaning and power of death and dying. Each night before bed I pulled it out and read a story, letting the sadness, along with the tears, come up again and again. In this way I stayed open to the grieving process for many months. It was a powerful cleansing.

LIVING AMENDS

No one act can overturn all our past transgressions. Surely telling Michael how sorry I was didn't compensate for the awful problems I'd caused him. And when I set out to gradually pay my brother Jerry back

money I'd owed him from years before, the tiny weekly payments I sent
were insignificant. What mattered was the movement toward healing.
When they saw over the coming years that I had changed my way of
living, I think this meant more to them than the small acts of contrition
I'd performed.

Typical of what's called living amends in Twelve Step programs is
Doug, whose eighteen-year-old son died driving drunk before Doug got
sober. Now, whenever he sees a young newcomer at a meeting, he gives
them his number. "Sometimes they even call," he says. "I know Larry's
drinking was a direct result of my own alcoholism, and there's no way I
can get him back or make up for his loss. But reaching out to kids and
trying to help them avoid the same fate is the closest thing I can do to
making amends to him."

If a life is a story, then living amends moves the narrative toward
growth and healing and away from destruction and pain. Our past actions come to be seen as mistakes on the way to recovery. The initial
amends become the benchmark for future behavior. We see them as the
point that marks the turnaround in our lives. And from there we begin
to live in a way that not only doesn't harm people and create the need
for more amends but actually serves others. My brothers' appreciation
of how much I had changed became much stronger as I moved further
into sobriety and the radical changes happened: returning to school;
completing a Bachelor's and then a Master's degree; getting married;
having a child; getting a "real" job; and on and on. If all I had done was
told Michael I was sorry for having set off the chain of events that got
him arrested, it wouldn't have meant much, but when he saw over the
following years that I really *had* changed, he expressed a newfound respect for me. And when I recognized his pain and the love he showed in
his forgiveness of me, I began to see him as he is today, and not as the
image of the big brother who had dominated my childhood.

Of course, living amends means more than making your family proud.

It means bringing the lessons of our spiritual growth into the daily activities of our lives. The way we lived as alcoholics and addicts caused indiscriminate harm. There's no way to track down every person who might have stepped in our path and been hurt over those years. So, with living amends we try to somehow balance that harm with healing. Our meditation practice and the teachings on lovingkindness, compassion, and sympathetic joy can be the underpinning for these amends.

SEPTEMBER 2000, BERKELEY, CALIFORNIA

I pull one of the mismatched folding chairs into the circle of twenty-five men and women in the large hall of the Veterans building in Berkeley. An ancient curtain hangs in front of the stage, and voices echo from corners of the cavernous room as people come together for the Friday morning meditation group. I take a little silk bag out of my backpack and bring out a set of Tibetan cymbals. The two small chimes are attached with a strand of leather, like a shoelace. I hang the leather over my thigh, a chime falling on either side.

"My name's Kevin, and I'm an alcoholic and addict," I shout.

"Hi, Kevin," they shout back. They settle in and the room gets quieter.

"I'm here to share some meditation with you," I say. "Meditation is part of the Twelve Steps—Step Eleven—and I've found it to be very helpful in staying sober."

Most of the group is listening with interest. They are here, many of them, because they were arrested for drug possession and diverted to this program. "Options," it's called. Largely homeless, the population served by Options is pretty far "down the scale," as the Big Book says. With poor health, bad teeth, jobless, friendless, they really don't have much going for them.

"This kind of meditation has two main purposes: it helps you relax, let go of stress, which is really important when you're trying to get sober; and it can help you notice your negative thinking, so when you say to yourself, 'I need a drink' or a drug or whatever, you can notice that and not necessarily react to it. You can make a decision not to act on those thoughts."

Some nods, some grunts of appreciation. This is not the typical middle-class meditation crowd. Some slump in their chairs looking bored, while others have a hard time sitting still without fidgeting. I ask them to close their eyes, and I strike the chimes together. I take them through a simple relaxation exercise, scanning the body and softening any tension. Then I lead them in the breath meditation, and finally in noticing thoughts.

The majority of the group really try, sitting still and upright; while a few of the younger ones mumble and poke their neighbors, making fun of the exercise. After about fifteen minutes, I ring the bells again, and everyone begins to stir and open their eyes. I ask if there are any questions, but most of them are already up and heading for the door, the meditation being the last part of the morning program. A few people walk by and shake my hand, nodding a thanks.

One older black man walks up as I'm putting my bells away.

"Beautiful, man," he says, putting out his hand. "I needed that."

"Good," I say. "It really does help, doesn't it?"

"Yeah, I used to do some meditation a long time ago," he says. "It's good to get back to that." He smiles and walks off.

I step out of the musty hall into the sunlight of the courtyard garden and down the steps, smiling as people greet me and thank me, these downtrodden, hard-luck street people looking light and buoyant in the bright fall morning. I feel the same, turning the corner and heading back to my office. This morning I've given something back, made a small offering to people whose addiction took them even further down than mine took me. This is my living amends.

Forgiveness

Ultimately, Step Nine is about forgiveness. Forgiving others, being forgiven, and forgiving ourselves. For many people, this is one of the most difficult tasks in spiritual development.

Many people in Twelve Step programs have painful (to say the least) personal history with parents, siblings, and partners. Often our substance abuse was in part a reaction to our upbringing, and stories of childhood abuse are not uncommon in Twelve Step meetings. I was not the victim of abuse as a child, but on the other hand, my parents failed me in some pretty serious ways. As a teenager and beyond, I felt quite angry with them, probably for fairly typical things, which fall under the "You don't understand me" umbrella. Later, as I got into therapy, I began to understand more specifically their failures: their inability to show their love for me; their inability to show love to each other; their alcohol abuse; my mother's instability and my father's passivity. With these understandings, my teen anger turned into a deeper, self-righteous anger. Ironically, of course, this was when my own alcoholism and drug-addiction kept me out of the reach of my parents—and most everyone else.

When I did get sober, and particularly as I wrote my first inventory, my feelings began to change. I began to see my own part in the problems I had with my parents, to feel compassion for the difficulty they had raising me. Finally seeing and accepting my own failures helped me to accept my parents' failures. I realized that they too had had parents who were less than perfect, and that they had tried very hard to be good parents. Their emotional limitations weren't something they had chosen. In fact my mother had gone to therapy for years trying to overcome her anxieties and depression. No, my parents weren't demons, they were humans, with all the failings we have. And at the point I realized that, I largely forgave them.

In that process of passing from a state of holding on to certain beliefs about my parents and myself into seeing them on completely different terms, it became clear that the only thing that had changed was how I was thinking and feeling. In forgiving my parents I was freeing myself. Forgiveness is a mostly internal experience. At one daylong retreat I was teaching, people talked a lot about how they didn't want to let someone off the hook, absolve them of responsibility, by forgiving them. I think it's important to draw the distinction between forgiveness and absolution. Forgiveness is something we do in our own hearts to relieve ourselves of the pain of resentment. It's not saying that the person is off the hook for any harm they have caused. In fact, we aren't capable of letting someone off the hook—the Law of Karma is responsible for that. If we can be very clear about this distinction, it helps as we enter into the delicate work of forgiveness. We forgive others so that we can heal ourselves. For no other reason.

Right now, as you're reading, think of someone you resent or fear and haven't forgiven. It can be someone you know—a parent, sibling, ex-partner—or even someone you don't know, like a political figure or criminal. When you think of that person, what do you feel? Probably something uncomfortable—a physical tightness or queasiness, an emotional cloud. Who is suffering in this moment? The answer is obvious: the object of our resentment doesn't feel pain, *we* do. So, the irony of resentment, of the lack of forgiveness, is that, even as we are holding this thought and feeling, we are allowing this person to harm us *again*. This fundamental insight is the basis for forgiveness: I am the one who suffers for my lack of forgiveness, and I am the one who benefits from my forgiveness. The Buddhist teaching on equanimity says, "All beings are the owners of their karma. Their happiness and unhappiness depend on their actions, not on my wishes for them."

The other insight that makes forgiveness possible is the recognition of our own failings. Here, looking at our inventory can help. When I think of a murderer and wonder how he could have committed such an act, all

I have to do is think of my own experiences with anger. Have I ever said or thought, "I want to kill you!" Have I ever hit someone? Driven dangerously? Drunk myself into a blackout so I had no control over my actions? A great many of the people in prison committed their crimes while under the influence of drugs and alcohol. Imagine waking up in a prison cell and not knowing why you were there because you were in a blackout when you were arrested. For addicts and alcoholics, often the only thing that separates us from people who are in jail is luck—however short-lived.

Such contemplations can aid us in our forgiveness practice. Certainly once we've become parents it becomes much easier to understand the mistakes our own parents made. And even if we aren't parents, just seeing our own failings clearly and knowing how hard life can be may be enough of a revelation to open a door to forgiving them.

Finally, I ask myself, what am I getting by holding back forgiveness? Am I staking out some position of moral superiority? Does it allow me to excuse myself for my own destructive behavior? Am I afraid of shattering some long-held worldview? When I really look at the results of not forgiving, what I see is my own pain. The anger, resentment, pride, or fear I feel only hurts me. Maybe we need a new word for forgiveness so that we don't think that it means we're losing something or letting the object of our resentment off scot-free. Perhaps we should call it "for-taking" not "forgiving."

TOP OF THE LIST

After I'd begun to make my amends, I started to get the sense that my list was incomplete. Somehow, the damage I'd done in my life seemed more pervasive than the discrete incidents that I'd remembered. For several days I was dogged by a feeling of missing something. I pondered my list;

I pondered my life. Then it came to me: the person who had been hurt the most by my actions was me.

What does it mean to be willing to make amends to ourselves? Eva, a woman who came to one of my workshops, talked about this type of amends. "Most of my amends are amends to myself, and also living amends to my two daughters (now eighteen and twenty), which para-doxically are also amends to myself. Ultimately I found that all amends are amends to ourselves, since while hurting others we hurt ourselves in the process."

The entire path of sobriety can be seen as an amends to ourselves. When we stop using and drinking, that in itself is of great benefit to us. Each Step is an amends to ourselves, repairing our connection with the spiritual life, becoming honest with ourselves and others, making amends, and passing on the gift. For me, going back to school so many years after dropping out was a big amends to myself. So was delving back into my beloved meditation practice, and learning to be more com-passionate toward myself, more forgiving, each of these was a way to re-pair past damage. Making amends to ourselves means "following our bliss," pursuing our heart's true desire. This may touch our lives in many ways, through our spiritual work, through our livelihood, through our relationships, through service, fun, or art. There's no particular way we make amends to ourselves, rather it's a spirit we bring to our lives, the spirit of joy and engagement, of generosity and possibility, of openness and imagination. Isn't this why we got sober? To live?

The Buddha said we could search the whole world and not find a person more deserving of love than ourselves. Is it possible to see your-self in this way? As equally precious as anyone else on earth? Seeing our-selves as worthy of love can take some work.

Part Three

FULFILLMENT

The last three Steps are the culmination of the spiritual path. Here we try to thoroughly integrate the work we've done into our lives. We learn to maintain the honesty and responsibility we developed in the earlier Steps, to deepen our spiritual connection, and to serve others.

Buddhism teaches that the real value of the spiritual life isn't found in moments of great bliss but in the daily application of mindfulness and lovingkindness. Steps Ten, Eleven, and Twelve point to the same truth: It's our ongoing effort that is most important to our spiritual development. We can't rest on yesterday's calm and insight, we must renew our commitment and energy each day.

These Steps are the cornerstones of maintenance. They are also the bridge to a life that is "happy, joyous, and free." Our spiritual awakening brings liberation, as we enter a new life, one free from the encumbrances of addiction, and one guided by the principles of wisdom and compassion.

STEP TEN

"Continued to take personal inventory and when we were wrong promptly admitted it."

There are some formal ways to work this Step, such as writing a regular inventory or making a daily or weekly phone call to a sponsor. These are important maintenance tools. Some people stop and take the time during the day, whenever they feel the need to process some experience, and do a quick written inventory, followed by a prayer to have the defects removed and a moment of reflection or meditation.

The main point is to not let a new set of mistakes build up so that we find ourselves back where we started at Step Four, with a whole list of people we have harmed and actions we must correct. Or, worse, that we *don't* wind up back at Step Four, but instead back with a drink, a drug, or whatever destructive substance or activity got us here.

With Step Ten, I try to catch things as they come up, so that I'm just making amends for one thing at a time. Step Ten implies a moment-to-moment attention to our behavior, keeping the Precepts and watching the places our mind is taking us—and being careful that we aren't headed for trouble.

* * *

Admitting we're wrong

Before I got sober, the idea of admitting I was wrong was distasteful. As I talked about in Step Four, I went to great lengths not to admit my failings. But, once I'd experienced the relief that came with Steps Four and Five, my attitude practically reversed. Once I saw how admitting I'd made a mistake could free me from the burden of having to defend the indefensible, I started to willingly offer my apologies. One of the places this immediately helped was at work.

At three years sober, I got my very first office job. Up to then, most of my day jobs had been whatever fell into my lap: factories, retail, deliveries—the kinds of jobs you take when you don't really want a job, when you're just waiting to get back to being a musician. I'd learned to type and was working in the personnel office of the Santa Monica–Malibu Unified School District. I was helping people to get employment, learning about computers, and getting paid regularly—unlike many of my music gigs where I didn't seem to be helping anyone, I didn't learn much except the latest Top 40 song, and getting paid at the end of the week was often a difficult negotiation. Being a beginner at this kind of work, filing, writing letters, maintaining a database, and administering tests, I made a lot of mistakes. But I found that, having recently been through the inventory process, when I messed up, or when someone pointed out something I'd missed, it didn't disturb me in the least. It wasn't that I didn't care—of course I wanted to do a good job and not look like an idiot—but I didn't take it personally. Having heard so many stories of addicts and alcoholics in those three years, and having talked with my sponsor and many others, I realized now that mistakes were normal—not a sign of deficiency, but a sign of humanity. What a relief.

This sense of welcoming criticism—as the Buddha says, being "easy to admonish"—is so freeing. One doesn't tiptoe through life afraid to make a mistake. And this same ease can make our meditation practice more pleasant and productive as well. As Suzuki Roshi says, meditation can be called "one continuous mistake" or one mistake after another. We go off the breath, we come back, we go off, we come back. If every time our attention wanders we get angry with ourselves or think there's something wrong, we'll just be creating more suffering in our practice. When we can freely admit that we've lost it without letting that fact bother us, just seeing the wandering mind as a natural part of the meditative process, then we can begin to settle in. In our daily lives as well as our meditation practice, we try to cultivate the same attitude of watching the mistakes arise with acceptance and kindness.

At the school district personnel office I tried to apply Step Ten by letting people know right away when I'd made a mistake. This usually resulted in getting the situation straightened out quickly. Most of the time my supervisors appreciated my willingness to let them know what had happened. After all, if you don't admit a mistake, you can't correct it.

There have been many other times in my sobriety when I didn't react so fast—didn't "promptly admit" as the Step says—but this is my intention, at least. Often I learn during my meditation what I need to make amends for. When I sit down to practice, recent transgressions often pop up in my mind. The stillness and quiet seem to give space for these simmering problems to come back to consciousness. So, meditation is a great aid to Step Ten. When you discover yourself sitting with anger or fear, there's an immediate desire to get rid of it.

On occasion, I've tried to sit after having had a fight with my wife, and, right in the middle of the meditation, stopped, gotten up, and gone to her to apologize. Seeing the suffering I had caused, my part in it, and the suffering I was experiencing as a result, prompted me to abandon any attempt at sitting and go take care of that amends. Sometimes it's not possible to so quickly address the object of our amends, so we have to sit with the discomfort. This, too, is a powerful lesson. Staying present and engaging directly the feelings that appear as we realize how we have hurt someone acts as a strong motivator to make amends and to not repeat the behavior. This is one of the ways that the sensitivity developed in meditation practice serves to purify our thoughts and actions.

OVER AND OVER

Step Ten is what I try to do in meditation: be continuously aware of what is appearing in my mind and body, and promptly let go of the attachments and aversions that form around those experiences. In meditation I don't stick the label "wrong" on what appears, but rather put what I see in the context of *dukkha*: Is this going to cause me suffering? If so, then I might as well let go, if I can.

This comes to the heart of meditation, the repetitive nature of practice. If we are going to reap the benefits of meditation we need to be willing to repeat this process over and over. This requires a certain determination. It helps if we recognize how imperative it is that we continue to practice.

There have been times over the years when I've had a hard time keeping my practice up. At about two years, sober life was very exciting but not peaceful. I was leading a band and working two jobs. I had a new girlfriend and had just moved. When I sat down to practice, nothing much happened. I'd had many deep experiences of meditation before, but now they were all gone. It seemed pointless.

I talked to a teacher about this situation and he gave some simple instructions about trying to just follow my breath for the first few minutes of meditation until I got settled in. But that was the problem: I couldn't follow my breath. I couldn't keep my mind steady for three seconds. But more than that, I felt that what I was doing wasn't even meditation. How did I weather this difficult period? Essentially by doing what they say at the end of many Twelve Step meetings: "Keep coming back." Although the memories of pleasant meditative experiences were having the negative effect of making me feel my current practice was a waste of time, they also had the positive effect of giving me faith in meditation. I knew that if I stuck with it, eventually things would change. I also knew that if I gave up meditation, I would never get that peace of equanimity back.

At other times I've felt that I didn't need to meditate because my practice was so solid. After a long retreat it can seem as though everything is meditation, so there's no need to formally sit.

The Big Book addresses this issue when it says:

It is easy to let up on the spiritual program of action and rest on our laurels. We are headed for trouble if we do, for alcohol is a subtle foe. We are not cured of alcoholism. What we really have is a daily reprieve contingent on the maintenance of our spiritual condition.

In the late seventies, I lived with one of my brothers in Brooklyn for six months. He was interested in the human potential movement and had recently taken the EST training. With some of the same insights that come out of Buddhism, this movement helped many people have breakthroughs in seeing the illusion of self. When they did, the common description of the experience was to say that they "got it."

The trouble with "I got it," is that, like every other experience, it's impermanent. Many people have similar moments in meditation, therapy, sobriety, and other psycho/spiritual practices. If they fall under the illusion that what they got is good for all time, they are setting themselves up for disappointment at least, and possibly worse.

As Jack Kornfield points out in *After the Ecstasy, the Laundry* (which is essentially a Tenth Step book), even after his enlightenment, the

Buddha encountered Mara the Temptor, regularly. "There is no state of enlightened retirement," says Kornfield, "no experience of awakening that places us outside the truth of change."

He goes on to tell about a young man who experienced very high spiritual states practicing in India during the sixties. Returning to America, he was feted as a guru—at twenty-five! Soon, getting caught up in the glamour of spiritual celebrity, he lost his commitment to daily practice, fell away from the path, and wound up selling used cars in Santa Cruz. Only after twenty years did he eventually find his way back to his true path.

This reminds me of the many stories I've heard in Twelve Step meetings of people who got sober and thought they'd "got it." As the excitement of a restored life grew, their attendance at meetings dropped, as did their commitment to the spiritual life and principles. Soon follows a "slip," a return to drinking or drugging, and then, depending on the story, perhaps years of using before finding their way back to sobriety. Obviously, the ones who do get back are the lucky ones, because for an alcoholic the price of losing your spiritual lifeline is likely to be much more severe than just a job selling used cars—it's as likely to be prison, institutionalization, or death.

For a Buddhist practitioner, the need for maintenance is equally vital. While our meditation practice certainly grows over time, it seems that there is no point at which we can say we've "got it" and can now let the meditation take care of itself. The Twelve Step cliché is that while you are staying sober, your disease is in the next room doing push-ups, waiting for a chance to disrupt and take over your life; in Buddhist meditation we see that what's doing push-ups in the next room is the sense of self.

Robert, an environmental engineer with a Ph.D. from Berkeley, took his first meditation retreat at ten years sober. Afterward he told me that he thinks we're all addicted to "I." "What I kept seeing," he said, "is how the mind continually creates this identity. If I want to maintain my spiritual condition I have to let go of I, me, mine, moment-to-moment. It's like a constant Tenth Step. But when I do that, I feel this spaciousness, a feeling of pure awareness."

Indeed, the ego is a subtle foe, maybe even more subtle than alcohol or drugs, for it is out of this sense of self that suffering is created in all its forms. When we see how our own tendency toward creating identity is, in fact, that which causes us the most problems in our lives, a sense of urgency to practice can develop. This urgency, called *samvega*, mixes a certain disillusionment with worldly things with a growing faith in the efficacy of Buddhist practice. Our practice goes from an interesting sideline in our lives to center stage. Step Ten has this same quality, as it prods us to make "continuous" our self-examination, and "prompt" our corrections. This makes explicit the fact that the Steps are not meant to be worked once and then forgotten; instead, like mindfulness itself—and indeed, all spiritual qualities—the greatest value is in applying the Steps, and their principles, continuously.

For most of us, this development of our spiritual lives and letting go of ego is an ongoing process, one at which we fail as often as we succeed. Some very special people may come to a point when they are no longer creating ego, but they seem to be rare. For the rest of us, we need to remain vigilant—gently. There are a few qualities which will help you to maintain a long-term commitment to meditation and letting go.

First among these qualities is forgiveness—again. Just as we needed forgiveness in Steps Eight and Nine as we went through the amends process, to maintain our practice, we need ongoing forgiveness. The ups and downs of spiritual practice mean that sometimes I will feel that "I've got it." In fact, almost every time I go on an intensive meditation retreat, I come back with this feeling: my sittings are peaceful and clear; I'm able to be mindful and relaxed in my daily activities; my heart feels open and caring; all the qualities that I want to develop are strong. The first time this happened, after a three-week retreat in 1981, I thought I'd simply moved to a new plateau from which I would continue to rise. Gradually though, these qualities weakened, and eventually my sitting practice and daily experience stopped being so satisfying. I thought, "I've lost it."

I began to see that I couldn't sustain the depth of stillness, the strong mindfulness and concentration, outside of retreat. So, like any good addict, I decided I needed more retreats—my drug. I started to see practice as an attempt to connect the dots from one retreat to the next, so that the qualities I treasured—and which gave me pleasure—would never dip below a certain level. After a time this proved to be unsustainable, and eventually I gave up. I became somewhat cynical then about the whole enterprise, swinging from a greed for mindfulness and concentration to an aversion—a sense that trying to sustain a solid practice wasn't realistic.

Over time I came to see that a more helpful way to react to the loss of mindfulness and concentration was forgiveness: realizing these qualities were impermanent and that I had done my best to develop them. If they had weakened or passed away, I wasn't to blame; it was in the natural order of things. They would come back again when the conditions were right. If we are to practice meditation for the rest of our lives—as I intend to—we will need forgiveness because we will "fail" a lot.

I love baseball, and what impresses me most about professional baseball players is the way they handle failure. The very best, Hall of Fame–level batter fails two-thirds of the time. If each time he struck out or hit a weak grounder Barry Bonds allowed himself to fall into despair, he'd never get through a nine-inning game. He'd be curled up on the bench, saying, "I'm no good," and quit. The same is true of meditation. We have to recognize that the task we are attempting, to be awake and aware with love and compassion in each moment, is enormous. Just to have a few moments of mindfulness is more than many people have in an entire lifetime. To string together a whole series of these moments is remarkable.

APPRECIATION

Part of the practice of Step Ten is to recognize the opportunities for spiritual development that are in our lives right now—and acknowledging as well those qualities that aren't growing at this time.

Recently, a friend, Anne, who was a longtime meditator and new mother, came to me to talk about the frustration she felt with her meditation practice. She said that when she was able to find the time to meditate at all, she would either fall asleep or spend the whole time thinking, seemingly never remembering to follow her breath or be in the present. Did I have any suggestions for how to get her practice back?

We have to be realistic, I told her. Mindfulness and concentration are probably not going to be strong if we aren't getting enough rest and our practice time is sporadic. When that's the case, some teachers will suggest increasing the effort, bearing down with determination. That doesn't work for me—or at least it hasn't worked. My approach is to try to take another step back, to just let the thoughts, the sleepiness, the restlessness—whatever is going on—happen, not struggling or trying to perfect my meditation. Sometimes when I do that, I'll drop into a place of stillness; other times not. In any case, I'm not creating another layer of suffering as I battle with my own mind and body. This approach to practice can give us the needed relief or relaxation and rest that are the initial benefits of meditation.

That's what I told her about meditation. But then I told her that I thought there was something more important than worrying about her meditation practice. Instead of focusing solely on meditation, I think it's more helpful to look at the whole of the spiritual path. New parents typically are weak on concentration especially, as sleep-deprivation and the stresses of caring for an infant make stillness and calm rare. However, what new parents have in abundance is love—metta.

A few weeks after my daughter was born, my wife and I were invited to meet a Thai monk named Ajahn Jumnien. We gathered with a small group in a friend's living room. Ajahn Jumnien, a jolly, round figure whose English is limited to a few words—"Happy, happy," apparently being his favorite—sat in an easy chair in the corner while a translator sat at his feet. When Ajahn Jumnien saw that my wife was carrying a baby in a sling around her neck, he gestured for us to come forward.

Smiling and waving a kind of wand over us, he repeated "Happy, happy," then started to speak in Thai.

"He says, 'Metta is mother love,'" the translator told us, referring to the Buddhist word for lovingkindness. "He says, 'Without metta—mother love—the human race would not survive.'"

This simple insight struck me. Since our daughter had been born, I'd been feeling this love—I hadn't thought of it as metta or as mother love, but those were good words for it. It was a feeling beyond any love I'd ever felt—beyond what I felt for my wife or my own mother. It was a force of nature—of survival—as Ajahn Jumnien had pointed out. Even though I'd been practicing meditation for many years and had very rich experiences with the lovingkindess meditation, I'd never known anything like this feeling.

This is what I told Anne: the path is broad and involves many aspects. Sometimes we are focused on developing concentration or investigation or some other quality. New parents have to work hard at cultivating and maintaining a lot of spiritual qualities: patience, generosity, renunciation (as they give up so much of their freedom and time). But the gift that they receive is love, as well as what's called *mudita*, or appreciative joy. There's no work involved, no effort in developing metta and mudita for our children, they just blossom. Appreciating that this is happening for us can help us to be easier on ourselves when other aspects of our practice seem to be crumbling.

Sometimes we have to focus our attention on a career transition, Right

Livelihood; or perhaps we're trying to improve our communication skills, Right Speech; other times we are drawn to study of the dharma, trying to grow in Right View and Right Intention. Perhaps our faith is blossoming as we work with a teacher, or our understanding of suffering is deepening as we sit with a dying parent. There are many ways that we grow in the dharma, that our spiritual life ripens. We can use Step Ten as a reminder to pay attention to what is happening now in our practice.

Practice doesn't just mean the time we spend sitting on a cushion. Practice is life. Life is practice. Many times it's possible to see that there is already natural growth happening, we just have to appreciate it. Other times we'll see that some work needs to be done, that some struggle in our lives is pointing to a place that needs work. The investigation of our spiritual condition on a regular basis is our guide.

REALLY PROMPTLY

The recognition of our mistakes and failures often takes years. I drank and used from age sixteen to thirty-five before I realized it was a problem. I was in therapy for years before I came to some understanding of my relationships with my parents and brothers. When I wrote my first sober inventory I discovered things I had done twenty and thirty years before. Even as I've written this book, past events have come up that I've tried to make amends for.

If we don't have a process for dealing with our past, it can all pile up. It's tragic to see people as they approach death finally reconciling with their estranged children, or finally admitting that they have been living a lie. My own father waited until all of his sons were full grown to announce one night at dinner that he had never believed in the Catholic Church.

"Why did you send us all to a Catholic school then?" asked my brother

Michael in frustration. "Why did you make us all go to mass every week?"

"I was hoping you'd get something I didn't," said my father. How sad, to have to pretend to believe in something for all those years. And how sad that, after making this sacrifice, every one of his five sons ended up rejecting the Church.

The sooner we recognize and admit the truth, the less negative karma we build up. The longer we wait to correct our mistakes, the more we hurt ourselves and others. The repercussions of our actions continue outward until we correct them. And if we wait too long, it may be impossible to correct them. Meditation gives us a tool for recognizing the truth in the moment, making it possible to avoid a great deal of potential suffering.

When Step Ten says "promptly admitted," it refers specifically to ways we may have acted unskillfully toward others—or ourselves. Typically this means apologizing right away when we get angry or quickly admitting a mistake. There's another way to think of this promptness: the immediate recognition of a thought appearing in the mind—particularly an "I-creating" thought.

Recently I attended a retreat that began with five days of silent meditation, then moved into some interpersonal meditative work with Gregory Kramer, who teaches a practice called Insight Dialogue. The group on the retreat was composed of fellow teachers, and at the end of the five days of silence some of us were disappointed to learn that the interpersonal work would involve silence outside the meditation hall, although we'd be speaking with one another in the workshop setting. After dinner on the first day of the interpersonal work, I took a walk with one of the other participants to talk about the silence (yes, we were breaking the rules).

The setting for the retreat was central Massachusetts in early July. We walked down a tree-lined dirt road, a drizzling rain falling, mosquitoes searching for any exposed skin. Just as we started our walk, Greg, the teacher, came up behind us and asked if he could join us.

Embarrassed at being "caught" talking, my pulse jumped and I quickly started to speak, a defensive reaction. I told him why we were talking, that we felt that the group would prefer to have more time to talk outside the formal constraints of the workshop, since we were all friends and this was a rare time to be together and catch up. As I spoke, I tried to maintain the mindfulness that he had encouraged in the interpersonal workshop. After a long, wet, and buggy walk, Greg agreed to change the rules. He said he would ask the rest of the group what they thought before the evening session began.

As we came back to the meditation hall, Greg moved ahead of us. My friend and I gave each other a silent thumbs-up, feeling that we had gotten our way—and done a service for the group as well.

As the evening session began Greg explained what had happened in our conversation, telling the group of fifteen or so meditators that we had asked to alter the rule about silence and that he wanted to know how others felt.

The first person he addressed said that, no, she didn't want to stop being silent; she felt it was helping her do the exercises he had offered. I was surprised, but thought she would be the exception.

She wasn't.

As Greg went around the room, virtually every person said that they wanted to keep the silence. As it became clear that I had misjudged what people wanted, I felt the terrible embarrassment of public failure. In a matter of seconds, a wide range of emotions appeared in my mind: humiliation, sadness, self-judgment, anger. I saw that my normal reaction to these events and these feelings would be to envelop myself in depression, to start to tell a story to myself about what a jerk I was.

But I didn't do it.

Instead of following the well-traveled emotional road to depression, I let go. In that moment I looked ahead, knowing that it was typical for me to have resistance to workshops and exercises but that whenever I came out the other side I felt better. Having attended lots of retreats and workshops, I knew that I would look back and say, "Why did I get so uptight about this?" And I would see the experience as a great learning process. So, right in the moment where I would typically fall apart or withdraw, or get angry and depressed, I just let go of it all. It was like seeing my whole personality structure dissolve before my eyes. All the defenses and fears and self-judgments looked completely pointless, and I didn't let them catch me. I saw through the illusion of self. It's this kind of promptness that insight meditation allows.

Usually it's only in silent meditation that such insights are possible, but the purpose of the Insight Dialogue workshop was to bridge the gap between silent meditation and interpersonal relationships. Although I'd resisted some of the work that day, I'd tried to maintain the close meditative attention in my interactions with people.

Just a few minutes later, as we split up into smaller groups, I sat in front of the person who had spoken first about wanting to keep the silence, and she asked how I was. Clearly everyone in the group knew that I had been put on the spot, and that it had probably been really uncomfortable.

I smiled and said, "Great," and I meant it.

"Really?" she asked.

"Yeah, I'm fine," I said. I had a sense of spaciousness and lightness, just as I do when I'm deep in meditation.

Dukkha of maintenance

Every weekday morning when I was a boy, at exactly the same time, I would hear my father go into the bathroom and take a shower. This would be preceded by calisthenics, and followed by a soft-boiled egg, eaten standing up. He would arrive at work between 8:00 and 8:05 everyday, and get home at exactly 5:20, just as my mother poured her first martini. When he came in the house he would say, "I'm going to go change my socks," then disappear for about fifteen minutes. When he returned he'd have not only changed his socks, but his jacket, pants, and shirt. Yes, my father was a man of routines and schedules (and a quirky sense of humor). He had a great deal of discipline. And I hated it.

There was nothing less appealing to me as I grew up than the idea of doing the same thing at the same time every single day. I saw myself as creative and spontaneous, so when, at eighteen, a psychiatrist told me that I needed structure in my life, I flew into a rage. Structure! Who wants that crap! I'm an artist—I need to *breathe*!

In my twenties, I started to get up around noon every day (after playing a gig and being up till four A.M.), take a shower, eat breakfast, roll a joint, smoke it, then practice scales for an hour and work on my songwriting. I didn't realize that my so-called artist's life was falling into its own kind of pattern—of structure and discipline, the very things I'd rebelled against.

When I first learned meditation, it was easy for me to commit to practicing twice a day, twenty minutes at a time. As with many people, I'd inherited the qualities in my father that I'd hated in him as a child. And these qualities began to serve me—certainly better than they did when routine meant routinely getting stoned and drunk.

The Buddha identified different kinds of dukkha. One of them—the one that relates to Step Ten—is the Dukkha of Maintenance. This is the tedium that comes with daily life: having to wash ourselves, brush our teeth, eat, clean dishes, clean clothes, go to the bathroom, exercise, sleep. Over and over we repeat these activities, many of them daily, spending our lives performing repetitive duties that serve only to sustain our existence, seemingly adding little pleasure or meaning to life. Even on retreat, where our focus is on doing nothing but meditation, we find that these maintenance needs constantly intrude—we sit for an hour and we're thirsty or have to use the bathroom; we walk for an hour and our legs grow tired; hunger arises; sleepiness; we need to brush our teeth or wash. It can begin to seem that there's hardly any time for what we came for. (Friends who have taught meditation in prison say that something similar happens there; prisoners often say, "I'd like to start meditating every day, but I can't find the time." Huh?)

Just as we have to maintain our bodies in this disciplined and somewhat tedious way, so, as the Big Book points out, must we maintain our spiritual life. Daily meditation is a cornerstone of any Twelve Step program and any Buddhist practice. And, just like doing dishes or washing your clothes, it can come to seem like a tedious duty.

Although I fortunately inherited some of my father's discipline, it's still sometimes difficult to show up at my zafu every day, as it is for many people. However, if we can get ourselves to start doing it, after a while, if we are fortunate, our addictive nature will kick in and we'll *have* to meditate. I compare it to flossing. When I began flossing it was hard for me to force myself to do it, but after a while my mouth didn't feel right if I hadn't flossed that day. In the same way, after practicing meditation every day for some time, your mind won't feel right if you haven't sat.

MAINTAINING JOY

Recognizing the First Noble Truth of suffering isn't the end of the spiritual path. We need to move beyond that, to find joy in our lives and in our practice. Especially when we recognize how pervasive dukkha is in life—including the Dukkha of Maintenance—we are going to hunger for relief, for ways to inject lightness and pleasure into our lives. In fact, the

Buddha even includes joy as one of the Factors of Enlightenment—the qualities we need to develop to be free. So, sitting around being serious, meditating, and flossing all day isn't the whole spiritual path.

One of my teachers helped me to understand this when he came up against what he felt were the stifling aspects of Buddhism. He'd been studying with some pretty severe Asian monastics who emphasized the difficult aspects of practice and the necessity for continuous, heroic effort. After several years of this challenging work, he came to see that an important part of him was being left out—the playful, joyful, spontaneous part. Through these years he'd maintained a closet love of pro football—especially the San Francisco Forty-Niners. Finally, he couldn't restrain himself anymore, and he decided he was going to let people know that he loved football. More important, he was going to let himself enjoy it instead of feeling guilty about it. What he discovered was that the joy—the rapture!—of cheering on his team could be done with mindfulness and that these feelings were uplifting for him.

I find the same rapture in rock 'n' roll: dancing and playing madly, caught up in the release of the moment, of feeling life's intensity moving through my body and spirit. And, just as I need the discipline of formal spiritual practices, sometimes I also need the wild release of music or sports or sex or ice cream to remember the richness and beauty of life. Each of us needs to find a way to bliss, this path of rapture, if we are going to have balance in our lives.

This isn't to suggest that the monastic life of renunciation isn't equally—probably *more*—rich. My monastic teachers show me through their joyful countenance and serene presence that they have found the way to rapture *through* renunciation. In fact, meditation itself, when developed deeply, is probably the source of the greatest happiness and release.

Ajahn Amaro tells a story of a Hindu saint who found it hilarious that her followers thought her asceticism was a sacrifice.

A delegation of politicians and businessmen came to offer her *dana,* gifts of money, food, and other items. It was quite lavish. After all the offerings, she asked them why they were treating her like this.

"You are the epitome of the great renunciation," one of the men said. "You have given up everything."

She started giggling and they smiled. Her giggles turned into guffaws and finally convulsions of laughter. By then the businessmen were wondering if she'd lost her mind.

"Me, the renunciate?" she said. "It's you who have given up everything. Here you are businessmen, politicians. Your minds are completely taken up with money and power and position and family, so that you've given up all the spiritual riches imaginable. I should be bowing to you because you're the ones who have surrendered everything that's valuable."

We don't have to be afraid of joy. Like dukkha, it's a natural part of life. The Buddha's teaching is often put in negative terms—"letting go of suffering"—but doesn't this just mean finding happiness? Isn't that the whole point of letting go of suffering? There are many pleasures in life: the pleasure of food and friends; the pleasure of insight and concentration; the pleasure of nature and the senses. Learning to enjoy these pleasures without becoming attached—addicted—is what both Buddhism and the Twelve Steps allow.

STEP ELEVEN

"Sought through prayer and meditation to improve our
conscious contact with God *as we understood Him*, praying only for
knowledge of His will for us and the power to carry that out."

If it weren't for Step Eleven, this book wouldn't exist. I've told you that the first time I saw Step Eleven posted in the front of a meeting I was encouraged to believe that perhaps the Twelve Step program could work for me. I was hopeful because meditation was something I trusted, and seeing its importance affirmed from another source gave me more confidence in the Steps as well as in Buddhism.

Step Eleven leads us directly into the fullness of spiritual life; it shows a direct line between our spiritual practices and our connection with ultimate truth. Once we've weathered the storms of inventory and amends, this Step leads us to a safe harbor where we can begin to live the promises of peace and serenity. While Step Ten helps us maintain our sobriety through inventory, Step Eleven may be even more important in our spiritual maintenance.

* * *

THE SEEKER

I was sober for many years before it occurred to me in a conscious way that the word *sought* in this Step was the past tense of *seek*. Seeking was very familiar to me. I'd been seeking all my life. The seeker is an archetype that has great resonance for me—one who sets off on a journey of discovery, moving beyond the comfort of the familiar to find meaning and richness in something greater than common, everyday experience. From the time I discovered music, then started exploring different spiritual paths, and even as I drank and used drugs, a part of me was seeking freedom in the extraordinary.

Many addicts and alcoholics share this trait of seeking. Once we redirect our energy away from seeking oblivion and toward improving our lives, this quality can be put to good use. The thirst for (alcoholic) spirits can be turned toward reaching a higher spirit.

When we come to this Step and need to find a way to practice meditation, many people want to explore Buddhism. What's appealing about Buddhism is the fact that, as Reverend Heng Sure, a Buddhist monk, says, while most religions are orthodoxies—that is, they adhere to a system of ideas, of rules, of words—Buddhism is an orthopraxy: it adheres to a set of practices, through which you can come to your own understanding, not one imposed from the outside. Indeed, this practical aspect of Buddhism is one of its main corollaries to the Steps. Twelve Step programs don't care *how* you believe in a Higher Power or *what* you believe in; there's no requirement that you practice a certain form of meditation. The only requirement for membership is the "desire to stop" your destructive behavior. The Twelve Steps are interested in results, just as the Buddha was interested in enlightenment. He overturned much of the orthodoxy of his day, not out of rebelliousness but simply because he found it didn't work. The same is true of the Twelve Steps: Bill Wilson didn't put meditation and Higher Power and inventory and powerlessness in the Steps because he *thought* they would be good ideas, or even because he was particularly devoted to God or these other principles, but because he found that he and others could stay sober using these guidelines.

In the same way, as the Twelve Step literature says, meditation is an intensely practical tool. In the sixties, when I first heard about meditation and things like enlightenment and "cosmic consciousness," I imagined meditation as some otherworldly experience, something that would carry me up and away from my mundane existence. Now I see it, first and foremost, as a way to support and heal my mundane existence: a tool for developing calm, acceptance, self-inquiry, and examination. And while sometimes I have experiences of great joy and bliss in meditation, that is more of a sideshow. The real meat—or tofu, if you prefer—is the way that meditation helps me to connect with my own inner wisdom and thus engage more fully with my life.

CONTACT

SEPTEMBER 2002, GREEN GULCH FARM

I'm sitting in a small circle of meditators in a small building in a meadow away from the main complex of this Marin County Zen community. I'm one of the students on a "Zen and Recovery" daylong retreat, exploring what the Zen tradition can offer my understanding of Buddhism and the Steps. We're approaching the end of the day, and the teacher begins a discussion of Step Eleven.

People share about how meditation has affected their lives, how they've used the idea of "prayer" from a Buddhist perspective, and what "God's will" means to them. Having been practicing meditation all day, my mind is relatively quiet and open. I let the words of the Step flow through my mind, and as I do I'm struck by something. I open my eyes and raise my hand.

"For me, I think I can just say: 'Sought through prayer and meditation to improve my conscious contact.' That's enough. Once I'm making contact, I'm there—I'm in tune with God's will. Practicing meditation for me is trying to come into contact with what *is*."

This idea of conscious contact—which is really just another way of saying mindfulness—solves a lot of the Higher Power problem. Indeed, for Buddhists trying to reconcile their practice with the Steps, the immediacy of mindfulness, of contact, gives a nonverbal, direct experience of something greater than ourselves, something that doesn't have to be explained or defined—indeed, defies explanation or definition—and allows us to rest in our understanding, born of experience, of the mystery, power, and majesty of life and the manifest world.

There may be a tendency to overcomplicate the idea of a Higher Power. One woman came to me on the verge of tears at the end of one of my classes. She'd struggled with sobriety and especially with understanding a Higher Power for years, trying to come up with some intellectually satisfying understanding of God. But now, the simple idea of mindfulness as a Higher Power had transformed her ability to work the Steps and stay sober. All her resistance had melted away, and a strong feeling of safety, of being held, had arisen for her. We both felt a great humility and gratitude for her breakthrough.

It's important, in terms of the Buddhist understanding of ultimate truth, not to stop here, though. Mindfulness is usually applied to "objects," things like breath, sounds, thoughts, tastes, and so on. If we are seeking after ultimate truth, however, at some point we have to let go of the objects of mindfulness. At that point—and this is probably most possible when the mind is quite still, perhaps on retreat—we can turn our attention to the quality of awareness itself. This is a little like the fish trying to notice the water; a very careful attention is required, a subtle turning of the mind in on itself. Ajahn Amaro, in his remarkable book *Small Boat, Great Mountain*, which is devoted to an exploration of this kind of attention, says, "We simply withdraw our attention from the objects of the mind and incline the attention toward the deathless, the unborn. This is not a massive reconstruction program. It's not like we have to *do* a whole lot. It's very simple and natural. We relax and notice that which has been here all along, like noticing the space in a room." We might call this a shift from paying attention to *content*, to noticing *context*. Instead of "doing" meditation, we are simply "being" meditation— or more simply, just being.

We can see this process of experiencing contact as one of moving from the more obvious, external experiences of contact, to this increasingly subtle, ultimate, inner contact. We begin with what is readily apparent: the phenomenal world. As we become more experienced with working with mindfulness, and our concentration becomes stronger, the mind clearer, we pay attention to more and more subtle experiences, until finally we are just paying attention to the attention itself.

I describe this as a linear process, but of course it's not. My own experience is that there are times when my attention is quite sharp and subtle, and times when it's not. With practice, I've become more able to incline the mind toward the finer states, but I can't count on that happening every time I sit down to meditate.

THE LORD'S PRAYER

Many Twelve Step meetings close with the Lord's Prayer, a distinctly Christian and somewhat archaic voicing of human pleas to God. For people with a Christian orientation, it's quite natural and comforting to repeat these words in a group. For others, it's a disaster.

Recently a newcomer to the Twelve Steps called me and said that she couldn't stand going to meetings.

"What's the problem?" I asked.

"That damn prayer," she said. "I can't stand that patriarchal 'Our Father' crap."

"Aha," I said. "Are we having a little aversion?" I teased. Since she was a Buddhist meditator I knew she'd recognize the language I was using.

"It's not just that," she said. "I just can't personally relate. It doesn't make any sense to me."

I began to talk to her about my understanding of the Lord's Prayer. First I said that if we take an external, God-being out of the picture, who are we talking to? Well, strictly speaking, we're talking to ourselves. Then I said that everyone can interpret the prayer in his or her own way, but that I saw it, from a nontheistic perspective, as a setting of my own intention.

"Our Father who art in Heaven . . ."

For me this is addressing my highest self, the place in me that is wise, patient, peaceful, loving, and compassionate—Heaven. So, I'm beginning the prayer by calling on my best qualities.

"Hallowed be thy name . . ."

If I'm not praying to something outside myself, then I'm just showing appreciation for my higher self here, reminding myself what is important and what I value. There's a sense of humility being evoked here, too, which Bill Wilson says is "the foundation principle" of the Steps. I often rebel against this kind of praise of God, but, oddly enough, I've found very similar language in Buddhist chants: "Homage to Him, the Holy One, the Pure One, the Fully Enlightened One."

"Thy Kingdom come, thy will be done, on earth as it is in Heaven."

Here, as I say the prayer, I imagine my highest wisdom coming down into the nitty-gritty details of my life, down to earth, with the Kingdom of Heaven—that is, the place of purity and wisdom in me—becoming manifest through thought, word, and deed. "Thy will," refers to Right Intention, acting from the desire to be of service to all beings.

"Give us this day our daily bread . . ."

I understand this as an appreciation of interdependence, recognizing that the whole universe is supporting my existence: the atmosphere for air, the earth for food and water, and everything else that allows me to live in this moment. In that sense, it's a recognition of powerlessness; if not for the bounty of the universe, I wouldn't even be alive.

"Forgive us our trespasses as we forgive those who trespass against us . . ."

Obviously this echoes the Golden Rule, treating others as we would like to be treated. The recognition of our own imperfection is vital to accepting the imperfection of others, and for a meditator, the moment-to-moment forgiveness as we fall off the meditation object and into wandering thoughts is vital to settling in, to allowing the process to unfold naturally. If we are judging—not forgiving—ourselves each time we space out or forget to pay attention, we only create more suffering. So, we set our intention here to be kind and accepting of ourselves and our failures.

"Lead us not into temptation, but deliver us from evil."

For an addict or alcoholic, these words are important—and point to something real. In practical terms, we need to avoid situations and people that might trigger relapse; you don't hang out in bars if you don't have business there, and you don't drop by your drug dealer's house for a social call. In Buddhist terms, this is the aspect of Right Effort called prevention, where we try to keep negative thoughts or emotions from even appearing. The Buddha, knowing the tendencies of the mind to veer into desire and aversion, encouraged quite strong effort to counter these destructive habits. So, although I resist the Biblical language of "temptation" and "evil," the meaning beneath the words is relevant—if you can just let go of the judgment.

BUDDHIST PRAYER

If I want to fully work the Steps, I know I need to find a way to pray, and yet, at times, this has seemed difficult in the context of my Buddhist practice, just as it was for the woman who struggled with the Lord's Prayer. I've had to come to my own understanding, not just of the Lord's Prayer, but of prayer in general.

One way of understanding Buddhist prayer is as "setting our intention." This means making conscious and explicit our highest aspirations. A lot of times, as with the Serenity Prayer, I find this to be more like reminding myself of what is true—"Hey, there're some things I simply can't change, so I better get over it!" Prayer is meant to break through the mind's barriers of negativity and pain and open the heart. By using ritualized language, we remind ourselves that these are timeless truths, reliable words. Still, sometimes these traditional forms of prayer can be limiting.

In his book *Gratefulness, the Heart of Prayer*, Brother David Steindl-Rast says, "If what is called 'God' means in the language of experience the ultimate Source of Meaning, then those moments that quench the thirst of the heart are moments of prayer." He says that often when we are saying formalized prayers, our heart is not engaged, so they have no meaning for us.

When I was a boy and had confessed my boyish sins, the priest would typically give me a penance that involved a certain number of prayers: "Say six Hail Marys and three Our Fathers." Going back to a pew and kneeling down, I would repeat the words, keeping close count of my work. It's hard to imagine that counted prayers can engage the heart. In those circumstances, the meaning is being drained from the prayers.

Steindl-Rast talks about this when he says, "Suppose, for example, you are reciting Psalms. If all goes well, this may be a truly prayerful experience. But all doesn't always go well. While reciting Psalms, you might experience nothing but a struggle against distractions. Half an hour later you are watering your African violets. Now, suddenly the prayerfulness that never came during the prayers overwhelms you. You come alive from within. Which was the real prayer, the Psalms or the watering of your African violets?" He goes on to say that what allows this authentic prayer—the "watering your African violets" kind of prayer—is mindfulness. But more than that, he talks about "wholeheartedness" a turning over of this moment fully to the experience of prayer.

Prayer isn't just words, it's a state of mind, of sinking into the truth, into the meaning. To believe that just repeating some stock phrases will bring results is magical thinking.

Still, it doesn't seem like enough to say that prayer is just setting our intention or talking to ourselves, or even "quenching the thirst of the heart." People say that their prayers are "answered;" they claim to have had real-world results from prayer. Sometimes this happens because the prayer puts them into a place of acceptance and openness that is able to "hear" or experience the answer they needed. In other cases, perhaps the prayers are having real effects. We see studies that suggest the power of prayer. How might this work?

The Buddha said that the power of a highly concentrated mind was unknowable. He didn't explain what this meant, but this might be how prayer has real-life effects. The deep concentration practices described in the Buddhist literature are almost other-worldly; these same states are documented in the writings of Christian mystics such as St. Theresa of Avila. In these states, the mind becomes malleable, glowingly clear, and breaks loose from the ego-bounded mental states of daily life. As though traveling in celestial realms, one might see visions or have mystic experiences such as unlimited consciousness or the sense of being in vast space. These are altered states brought on not by drugs but by extended stillness, silence, and focus. They occur naturally (which is why they appear in all the mystic traditions). In these states we may be connecting with something greater than our limited mind/body, with what some call universal consciousness.

If what the Buddha says about the power of these concentration states, called *jhana*, is true, then a prayer sent out from there *could* have real-world effects. This would be a very powerful kind of prayer.

In the end, it's not so important whether prayer "works," whether it has real-world effects. If we are caught up in trying to change things—people or the material world—we are living in desire and aversion. Then, no matter what other effects our prayer is having, it's really not giving us its greatest benefit: the calm and insight that comes from aligning the heart with what is true.

After a recent workshop I got an e-mail from a participant named Doug who said that as he'd become more involved with Buddhist practice he didn't know who or what to pray to anymore. This is certainly one of the difficulties of Buddhists working with the Twelve Steps. In Step Two, I talked about the gradual dissolution for me of an external, solid Higher Power, a God-being. After this happened, I encountered the same problem as Doug, feeling adrift when trying to say prayers but still wanting some kind of focus for my praying. What I think now is that if a Higher Power is in fact the ultimate truth, then we cannot be separate from that, so there's nothing outside ourselves to pray to. You could say that prayer to an external Higher Power doesn't make sense. However, most of the time we aren't living in awareness of ultimate truth, and pretending to be there doesn't help. It's more helpful to recognize that, although we know there is an ultimate truth, at any given moment we might not be able to experience that—our minds are mostly caught up in duality, so it's more realistic to act from the place we really are than from some idealized perfection. Otherwise, all we have is this "knowledge" of ultimate truth, which is solely intellectual, and our hearts have no refuge. We can be left with a sort of existential loneliness.

The Buddha's always trying to pull us away from extremes of thinking, often giving answers that don't allow us to rest in any one way of seeing things. What this tells me is that it's okay, when the heart yearns for some outside support, to pray to "God." For me, God is not a being but more like praying to the universe or the dharma. At that moment I feel separate, so to express that with a dualistic prayer is appropriate—it's an expression of where I am at that moment. At those moments when I feel totally in tune with the universe, the heart open and flowing, there's no need to externalize God. My prayer is my being itself.

To me, my spiritual life is meant to be a support, not an intellectual exercise, so, "God as I understand him" can, and should, be whatever I need it to be at any given time. I don't have to answer to some logic or some rule-making body, just respond to what my heart is calling for in this moment.

METTA

If it's true that resentment "destroys more alcoholics than anything," as the Big Book says, then metta, or lovingkindness, may be the most important practice for addicts and alcoholics. Metta is a complex practice because even as we try to arouse this sublime emotion, we must face those aspects of ourselves that are less than sublime. Before we can even begin to practice lovingkindness, we typically work with forgiveness, as I described in Steps Eight and Nine. On the other hand, just in practicing mindfulness deeply, metta can spontaneously arise, without any formal practice.

On the three-month retreat I experienced this. One day the teachers posted a notice that Oxfam was asking people in developed countries to fast for a day in solidarity with those in the world who live in hunger. Having been practicing meditation continuously for many weeks, my heart was very open, and as I began to contemplate the suffering of hungry people all over the world, a wellspring of compassion burst forth. I did fast that day, then I went to my teacher and asked him if I could continue fasting because I felt so moved by my contemplation of the suffering of hunger. He told me that it wasn't such a good idea to combine fasting with intensive meditation practice at this stage. I was disappointed but realized that I could still continue my compassion and lovingkindness practice. What struck me most from that experience was seeing how open my heart was and that the slightest thought of suffering triggered this great feeling of caring for others.

Many people practice metta as their main practice, and entire metta retreats are taught in which people do this practice instead of following the breath or watching thoughts. I have never done one of these retreats, partly because I saw that no matter what kind of practice I did, metta would arise; I didn't have to cultivate it specially. For addicts and alcoholics, I think it's probably most important that we practice metta in our daily lives. Developing a loving and compassionate heart, learning to react with kindness rather than judgment or anger is critical both to our sobriety as well as to our serenity. My tendency to react negatively to others was brought home to me on an early retreat.

One afternoon I started to notice the sound of someone repeatedly swallowing in the meditation hall. The silence on a retreat is so deep that such a sound is quite audible in a room full of a hundred meditators. Hearing that sound was unpleasant, and I found it annoying. "Why don't they stop swallowing?" I thought. "What's wrong with them?" I tried to let go of my aversion to the sound, but I had difficulty not being judgmental.

The next day I was in a group interview with Jack Kornfield when someone brought up "the swallower." Everyone agreed that it was annoying and that the person should stop. Jack said, "You might try to practice compassion for this person. They probably don't want to be swallowing."

Of course they didn't want to be swallowing over and over! What had I been thinking? My own self-centeredness was driven home to me. The idea that I could consider the problem from someone else's point of view broke something open for me.

A few years later, I was working for a magazine distributor in Venice Beach, and we were talking about one of his other employees who spoke harshly and critically a great deal of the time. I was complaining to my boss about it when he said that whenever someone talked (or yelled) like that to him, he just remembered that the person was also talking like that to themselves, inside their head. Instead of being frustrated or angry with them, he felt compassion. When he said this to me, it struck me as a wonderful insight—of course we speak the way we think!

Making a habit of bringing lovingkindness and compassion to mind in daily life can shift our entire outlook. And this is a practice—a real practice. It requires first noticing when our thoughts are angry or judgmental toward someone (Right Mindfulness); then consciously shifting our focus to the other person and how we might view them and their behavior differently (Right Effort). When someone cuts us off on the freeway, we can consider that they might be rushing to the hospital to visit an injured relative; we can also consider that *whatever* is pushing them to behave like that is certainly painful—the stress and anxiety involved with driving dangerously is very unpleasant, and when we are in that place, we are usually completely unaware that it's happening and so are not able to change. We've all been there; can we feel compassion for someone stuck in that suffering?

One of the places it's most useful to practice metta is in Twelve Step meetings. Here we often find ourselves reacting to the sharing of others. Forgetting that they, like us, are there because they need support, we might find ourselves thinking, "I wish he'd stop talking about his stupid boss every week. Why doesn't he just quit the stupid job?" Or, "She slipped again?! Why doesn't she get it together?" Here we are in a support group trying to share our common difficulties, judging the others there, as though *they* had a problem but we didn't. So, in meetings, I find it helpful to use the mindfulness practice of noticing my thoughts; then, when negative judgments come up, practicing either formal metta, repeating phrases to myself, or simply taking a breath and feeling my Heart Center, that place in the middle of the chest just beneath the sternum, where the sense of lovingness focuses in the body. Softening my Heart Center, I drop down into a nonverbal state of acceptance and kindness, remembering, virtually on a cellular level, that we all suffer (the First Noble Truth), and that we all need love. When I do this practice, very quickly I feel like I'm part of the meeting again, participating in everyone's pain and joy in a supportive way.

Of course, it's one thing to be compassionate to strangers, and once we get in the habit, it's not that hard. But what about those we love? With them it's more difficult to disidentify with our feelings. And this points to one of the paradoxes of metta practice. Typically we think of love as a very personal, intimate expression of human emotion. But with metta practice, we move to a different level of love, to the impersonal, unconditional level, the level that's not responding to the other person or being but rather drawing from our own, inherent quality of heartfelt caring and openness. While our intimate relationships are typically reciprocal arrangements, in which we cosupport each other, with metta, there is no expectation of a return for what we give. In fact, with metta, we discover that the giving itself is the return, it is the reward.

As I mentioned in Step Eight, my feelings for my wife can range from love to boredom to frustration. While it's powerful to expand the heart to love all beings, directing it toward *one* being can be a challenge. Just as prayer helps me set my intention, metta practice does the same. It reminds me to bring this lovingkindness back into the practical realities of my life, back to the person upstairs drinking coffee in her bathrobe. If I can't love her, if I can't offer her my metta, then how authentic is the rest of my "unconditional love"?

Metta, lovingkindness, is a rich and layered practice. Exploring its boundaries—expanding the boundaries of our own self-imposed limitations—is an ongoing practice. I include metta in virtually every period of meditation I do. I practice metta for myself, for my family and friends, my teachers, politicians, the hungry, sick, and dying, for animals, bugs, fish, birds, for the earth itself, and for the entire universe. The universe is a great sponge of metta, absorbing all the love we can give and giving it right back to us.

WHOSE WILL?

When I hear someone—a politician or preacher or someone else—claim that they were told to do something by "God," I tend to be suspicious. Was it a voice in their head? Are they just schizophrenic? Or did God single them out specially to hear His message, and not the rest of us? Why would God do that? I think we have to be very careful how we go about determining what God's will is.

In Step Three I talked about having too much faith and my time with Ananda, the New Age guru whom I followed for a few months in 1982. Ananda taught various methods for inferring God's will in the moment, ways to "feel the energy," and, supposedly know what was the best next action. When I met him I was living in a spacious apartment in Cambridge, Massachusetts, working at a spiritual bookstore, and playing in an oldies band. Based on his suggestions on how to know God's will, I left all of that. At the end of my journey with him I was homeless, with no money, no job, and no prospects. My life was shattered; I entered a long period of homelessness and depression, only coming out the other side because of the help of friends and some basic survival instinct. Was it really *God's* will that I go through this?

The Big Book says that before we become adept at intuiting God's will we might get involved in "all sorts of absurd actions and ideas." This certainly was my experience. What went wrong?

With Ananda, all decisions were urgent. We had to know God's will *now*. There was no time to consider the implications of a decision, no time to consult family, friends, or even our own inner wisdom. Essentially, it was hold your finger up and see which way the wind blows—then follow the wind. This, to me, is magical thinking—the idea that some special power is singling you out for special treatment. Ananda's attitude, and indeed his teaching, was that we were a kind of chosen people, New Age underground warriors, traveling the land, spreading our special power to all the lower beings. And, since we were such special, higher beings who were already practically enlightened (and in his case, completely enlightened), everything we did was automatically good and right. In other words, it was a miniature version of most of the religious movements that have started on our planet.

I try not to make my decisions so quickly these days. In fact, when someone comes to me for advice or with concerns about some decision they have to make in their life, I ask, "When do you need to decide?" Usually it turns out that they don't have to decide right this minute. So, I counsel patience. It's hard, of course, living with uncertainty. Sometimes it can seem easier to make a decision *now*, just so you don't have to live with that discomfort. But what I often find is that I don't have all the information, and that if I wait, I'll be better informed. In fact, what often happens is that some circumstances arise that make the decision for me. Problem solved.

So, what do we know about "God's will"? Well, first of all, if it's already happened, whether we want to believe it's what God wanted or not, there's nothing we can do about it, so we need to accept it. Might as well call it God's will. If it's happening in this moment, it's real, so you can't deny it—that must be God's will, too. However, in this moment we can make changes to what is happening, so here we might use the Serenity Prayer to guide us to see what we can change and what we can't (assuming we *want* to change it). Finally, we come to the future. What should I do next? This is the tough question, where our decisions determine our future life to some degree. The Buddha has a very specific teaching on this question, called Clear Comprehension.

CLEAR COMPREHENSION

Clear Comprehension, in the general sense, is the aspect of mindfulness that looks at the broader context of our moment-to-moment situation. While Bare Attention might help us to be very attentive to walking, just feeling our feet and legs moving down the sidewalk, Clear Comprehension notices that we have come to an intersection and need to look both ways so we don't get run over. Specifically, Clear Comprehension has four components, and they are expressly designed to help us make decisions, to know what "God's will" is in any situation.

The four components of Clear Comprehension are:

Question my purpose. Why do I want (or not want) to do or say this? Is my intention to help others or to further my own self-centered wants? If I can see that, at least to some extent, my motives are good, I go on to the next question.

Question my means. Do I actually have the personal ability, as well any material things I might need, to accomplish what I'm thinking about? If my motives are positive and I see that I probably have what I need to get it done, then I can go to the next question.

Question my alignment with the teachings. Is what I want to do or say in accord with the Precepts, with lovingkindness and compassion? Will it lead to less suffering? If I've answered all these questions positively, then there's a good chance things will work out. I take the leap.

Question the results. After we've done or said something, we look back at how it worked out. What can we learn? If the results were good, it's helpful to see how we got there, so maybe we can do or say something like that again. If the results aren't so good, what went wrong? What part of the first three stages did we foul up on?

There are a couple things that are apparent about Clear Comprehension. First of all, it takes time to ask these four questions. In that time, hopefully, passions are cooled and rash acts and words are avoided. So, taking time, whether it's five seconds or five months—whatever's needed—really helps us to make skillful decisions.

Second, and even more important, is how carefully we must examine ourselves and the teachings before we can successfully follow these steps. Just the first question—what are my motives?—takes a great deal of contemplation. As we practice meditation for some time, we see more and more clearly the layers of deception, of self-justification, of craving upon craving, and finally come to know that virtually *all* motives are mixed. Perfect motivation or Right Intention is beyond the reach of most of us. Instead of expecting perfection, we try to achieve some reasonable level of Right Intention. If we didn't allow ourselves to act or speak until we'd achieved perfectly pure motivation, we would wind up passive and mute for the rest of our lives.

When I question my means, I'm really saying, "Am I ready to do (or say) this?" So often we get ahead of ourselves, wanting to be someone we aren't, wanting to skip the steps involved in achieving our goals. One night, after I gave a dharma talk to a large group, someone approached me and said, "I want to be a meditation teacher. What do I have to do?" I was taken aback. It was as though the person wanted to know what graduate studies program they could sign up for to get a certificate. The real answer might be, "If you want to be a meditation teacher, you already have the wrong motivation. A more skillful goal is to practice deeply to develop wisdom and compassion for all beings. If you are meant to teach, it will arise out of your own practice."

I am trying to learn to apply this teaching to my communication with my wife. When I ask myself, "Do I have the ability to say this to her kindly?" (usually something critical, of course), the answer is often no. When I decide *not* to speak, I usually get into much less trouble than when I decide *to* speak.

Working with the third question, my alignment with the teachings, is, first of all, a great motivator to study the teachings, because, after all, if I don't know what they are, how can I know if I'm in line with them?

The first set of teachings that we need to study are the Precepts, because breaking these is the most obvious way we cause ourselves and others pain. Fortunately, if we are in recovery, we already have the Fifth Precept down. This is no small accomplishment. As I talked about in Step Four, the thrust of the Precepts is non-harming: not to kill, which in Buddhism means not *any* beings, and also implies a gentleness toward others; not to steal or take what isn't offered to us, which can have broader implications socially, politically, and even with things like time—"Am I wasting someone else's time?"; not to harm others with our sexuality, being careful before we enter intimate relations, and even in the ways we flirt with others or display our bodies; not to lie or use harsh language, becoming more sensitive to the ways we talk about others, gossip, criticize, express anger; and not to use intoxicants—easy if you're sober—but beyond alcohol and drugs, being aware of the ways we use TV, music, sex, food, or any other diversion to stifle, numb, or alter our awareness and feelings.

When we consider the Precepts before acting or speaking, as part of

Clear Comprehension, we avoid making a lot of mistakes.

Other core Buddhist teachings guide us in decision making as well. Impermanence reminds us that things will change whether we do something or not; suffering reminds us that there is no perfect answer, all decisions will include some discomfort or unsatisfactoriness; Not-Self reminds us not to take things so personally, that much of what we think, say, or do is conditioned by forces out of our control; lovingkindness and compassion remind us to love ourselves and consider the needs of others no matter what we decide. These and many other teachings help guide us as we seek our Higher Power's will and try to live skillfully in the world.

DEPTH OF PRACTICE: RETREATS

I like to think of the development of my spiritual life as having two major aspects: depth and breadth. In Step Twelve I'll talk about breadth of practice as I address the idea of "practicing these principles in all our affairs." For Step Eleven, it may be helpful to talk about depth.

Depth of practice most commonly is developed on retreat. On retreat we take some time away from our common daily life and focus exclusively on our inner life and the development of special qualities. The qualities that typically head the list are mindfulness and concentration. But many other qualities grow on retreat as well: patience, lovingkindness, compassion, Right View, Right Effort, faith, wisdom, and more.

A typical Vipassana retreat is conducted in Noble Silence, which means that the students don't talk with one another but speak only during interviews with teachers and during question-and-answer sessions. (If there's an emergency, of course you can speak to staff members.) This silence has an amazing effect, helping to quiet the mind and turn our attention inward. I find that people who have never sat a retreat find the idea of silence to be one of the most intimidating when considering taking a retreat. I felt the same way before my first retreat, the one I told you about in Step Eight.

It was the fall of 1980 and I was taking my first weekly class in Vipassana meditation. When my teacher, Akasa, told me that he was going to hold a five-day retreat over the coming Thanksgiving weekend, my girlfriend, Jane, signed up and wanted me to come along. She had already taken several daylongs and one ten-day retreat the previous summer. I was intrigued and felt a strong desire to develop the qualities of calm and clarity I'd heard about from her and others who had taken retreats. But two things frightened me: my knees and silence.

Whenever I went to the class and meditated for forty-five minutes, I spent what seemed like ages—probably just fifteen or twenty minutes—struggling with the burning sensations in my knees. I was afraid that a retreat, which involved many such meditation periods each day, would be agonizing.

As for the silence, I just couldn't imagine not being able to talk to people. I suppose it was a fear of loneliness. Even now when people express concern over trying to be silent, I'm not sure what the fear is. But I had it. For days I vacillated. Jane and Akasa encouraged, cajoled, teased—and finally I agreed that I would go.

Ironically, I turned out to be right: many of the sittings were painful for me, plus I felt a profound loneliness in the silence. But even though these fears were realized, I left the retreat with a great sense of faith and commitment. Yes, it was difficult, but, more important, a vision of a new way of experiencing life had opened up for me. I saw more clearly than ever how bringing a mindful attention to each moment enriched and deepened my experience of life. This was precious, more important than the physical and emotional struggles involved. I felt on that retreat that, in some ways, I was experiencing life, real life, for the first time.

As you sit on retreat, mindfulness becomes more and more precise. You begin to notice the sensations of every movement; the subtle shifts of thought and mood; colors and sounds and tastes are all amplified and clarified. You sit and watch a bee dancing on a flower as though you were at the Russian Ballet; you savor the simple rice-and-veggie fare as though it were being served in a four-star restaurant; you listen to the birds at dawn as though you were attending the London Philharmonic.

With this mindfulness comes a powerful concentration. During particularly calm sittings, you may feel the sensations of the breath as though observing in slow motion with a laserlike awareness and mountainlike steadiness. The mind becomes so still that you are able to sense when you are just about to have a thought, noticing the vague stirrings that indicate thinking about to happen. And, in that moment, you can actually choose not to think.

This kind of depth of practice is probably only possible on retreat. Afterward, you might be able to preserve something of this depth for a few days or weeks, but eventually it fades. What we're left with, however, is not just fond memories. Retreats teach us profound life lessons which can carry into our daily lives in vital ways if we let them.

On retreat I see that my common, everyday vision of life is only one version of the way things are. I'm reminded that much of what I believe is just a mental construction. When I remind myself of that in daily life, I'm relieved of some of the burden of solving the "problems" of the world. I remember that there is a deeper way of seeing things.

Practicing on retreats, I see the cyclical flow of practice: one sitting I'm concentrated, the next restless; later I'm sleepy; and again, I wake up and feel sharp and clear. Retreats remind me that even under the best of conditions my practice isn't perfect. Retreats teach deep lessons about impermanence, suffering, and not-self that get under my skin, into my understanding of life and the world. These insights transform my daily experience in subtle and not-so-subtle ways.

In every spiritual tradition, withdrawal from the world—retreat—has an important place. Jesus went to the desert for forty days; the Buddha sat beneath the Bodhi Tree vowing to become enlightened; Native Americans go into the wilderness on vision quests. This time of inner solitude opens us to the deeper reality of our lives, of our minds, and of our bodies. Forsaking the distractions of daily life, facing squarely our demons, and finally touching the place of stillness and wisdom inside, we come to know life in a new way, in a way that inspires and invigorates. This gives us courage and faith. People enter retreat to seek guidance and find peace; to uncover personal and universal truths; to find the deepest love and the most profound wisdom; to find forgiveness and joy. Retreat, finally, acts as the foundation for all of our spiritual development.

I'm no theologian, and I don't mean this as a definitive interpretation of the Lord's prayer by any means. However, it's important to me to understand the prayer for myself. We can find the wisdom in these traditional prayers if we are ready to make them our own.

MEDITATION EXERCISE: CULTIVATING THE WHOLESOME: MUDITA AND KARUNA

Some forms of meditation are used for developing positive qualities in the mind. Here are two practices, one on appreciation, or *mudita,* and the other on compassion, or *karuna.*

Begin by focusing the attention on the Heart Center, the middle of the chest just beneath the sternum. Feel the breath moving there, rising and falling. Soften the heart; let yourself be open and receptive, letting down any defenses. Very slowly move through these phrases in your mind, contemplating their meaning and letting their meaning penetrate beyond the *idea* to the actual feeling itself.

"May I be appreciative and grateful."

"May I be aware of beauty and joy."

"May I be open to beauty and joy."

"May I respond to beauty and joy with appreciation and gratitude."

Think of those who are dear to you and offer them the same wishes. Say their names to yourself as you repeat the phrases, "May . . . be appreciative and grateful." Envision them experiencing mudita.

"May . . . be aware of beauty and joy."

"May . . . be open to beauty and joy."

"May . . . respond to beauty and joy with appreciation and gratitude."

After wishing those who are dear to you mudita, move out to people more neutral: neighbors, colleagues, people you see in your daily routine. Instead of using names, you can visualize them and say, "May you be aware of beauty and joy." You can see many faces as you repeat the phrases.

Finally, wish mudita for those who are difficult, people you resent or fear, or someone who has harmed you.

Then radiate mudita outward to all beings nearby, and gradually out to the whole planet, and finally the entire universe.

At the end, come back to an awareness of breath and the Heart Center again, returning to the reality of your own body and this present moment.

The Karuna practice has the same structure, only using different phrases. As with the Mudita practice, begin by setting the intention for the quality you want to develop: kindness. Then try to become aware of the pain the person is experiencing. Once you're aware, relax and allow yourself really to take it in. Finally, try to respond with love.

"May I be kind."

"May I be aware of my own suffering."

"May I be open to my own suffering."

"May I respond to my suffering with love and compassion."

"May I respond to my suffering with love and compassion."

Now that you've opened to your own suffering, turn your attention to others, starting with those who are closest to you.

"May I be kind to . . ."

"May I be aware of the suffering of . . ."

"May I be open to the suffering of . . ."

"May I respond to the suffering of . . . with love and compassion."

Spread compassion to those you love, to neutral people, and to those who are difficult (your enemies). Then radiate compassion outward to all beings nearby, and gradually out to the whole planet, and finally the entire universe.

At the end, come back to an awareness of breath and the Heart Center again, returning to the reality of your own body and this present moment.

STEP TWELVE

"Having had a spiritual awakening as the result of these Steps, we tried to carry this message to other alcoholics, and to practice these principles in all our affairs."

Step Twelve traditionally means service. It's this Step that encourages us to sponsor people, to greet newcomers, to take on a commitment at a meeting such as making coffee, being a treasurer, or taking care of the literature; even more important, we take calls from drunks trying to sober up, go to hospitals and prisons to lead meetings for those who can't get out, and other outreach activities. When people refer to "Twelve Step work," this is what they mean. This spirit of service has kept Twelve Step programs thriving since 1935. It's the cornerstone of the program, and it's the cornerstone of spiritual growth.

The commitment to "carry the message" is expressed in Buddhism by the Bodhisattva Vow to forestall personal enlightenment until you have helped all beings achieve liberation. "Beings are numberless, I vow to save them," it begins. In raising the stakes to such impossible heights, this vow places compassion as the central theme of the spiritual journey.

When the Buddha became enlightened, he thought at first that it would be useless trying to teach what he had come to understand because he thought that no one would get it. But soon he was driven by his own deep compassion to try to spread the knowledge he had attained. He saw that having this awakening for himself wasn't enough, that for it to have meaning it had to be shared. It's this same understanding that has inspired Twelve Step practitioners to show up for one another all these years.

BUDDHA MEANS *AWAKE*

After his enlightenment, someone asked the Buddha, "Are you a man?"

"No," he replied.

"Are you a god?"

"No," he repeated.

"Then what are you?"

"I am awake," he is said to have stated. This became the name that his followers called him: Mr. Awake—Buddha.

The Buddha is describing himself not as a thing—a god or human—but as a state, the mind state of clarity and alertness. There's a dynamic quality to this awakeness, being on the edge of what is happening right now, not lodged in a role or posture but paying sharp attention to everything as it unfolds, responding in the moment.

It's interesting to me that 2,500 years later, in a completely different context, the Twelve Steps say that the result of our spiritual development is "awakening." The implication is that previously we—and the Buddha—were in some sense asleep.

Certainly for the person in recovery, we can see our previous state as quite unconscious. When we are in denial about our disease and all its repercussions, it is as though we are asleep to the truth of our lives. In the insanity of our disease we were sleepwalking, reacting mindlessly to stimuli, following our addictive impulses with no awareness of their causes or their effects.

251

JANUARY 1972, STATE COLLEGE, PENNSYLVANIA

We finally get a gig in this town after almost two months of rehearsing and auditioning. We set up our equipment on a low stage in the corner of the bar, the smell of stale beer and cigarettes permeating the place. We're broke, but at least there will be free drinks tonight. I'm nervous, and I begin drinking even before the first set. I'm already asleep, asleep to the impulses that are driving me to drink, asleep to my own feelings. I start playing a little too loud, drowning out my own fears, cranking the adrenaline to override the feelings.

No one's familiar with our original music in this college town. The crowd just sits at first, staring, their bland gaze torturous. Between songs I pour another mug of Budweiser and guzzle. I try to play harder, faster, more intensely to make them like us, to get their approval. Finally a few people start to dance.

The next set, the bar starts to fill up and the dance floor begins to fill as the crowd gets their own buzz going. There's a woman who catches my eye dancing near the stage. During a break I try to talk to her, driven by other hungers, following them unthinkingly. When she shows no interest in me, I look around for someone else, anyone else.

The band plays on, the pitchers of beer perched on amplifiers. Finally the crowd catches up with us in the last set, the roiling mass of dancers flinging themselves around the dance floor—probably they're as drunk as we are now. The music gets sloppier and sloppier. My hands can't find the frets, my voice can't find the notes. I stumble around the stage. No one seems to notice. Finally, before the equipment is packed up, as we swill the last pitchers of beer, complete sleep takes over, and I go into a blackout. When I wake up the next day, the end of the previous evening is gone.

Recovery makes it possible to awaken from this deep sleep. From falling-down, blackout drinking to spiritual awakening is one of those "can't get there from here" journeys. With each of the Steps we rub a little more sleep from our eyes, and eventually we make that impossible transformation.

Each stage of our recovery then was at least a small awakening: seeing the truth of our disease in Step One; the stirrings of faith and making a commitment to our spiritual life in Steps Two and Three; awakening to our own role in our life's difficulties through inventory; seeing the pain we have caused others and trying to heal that; and, with Step Eleven, plunging deeper into our spiritual practice.

When I started to meditate, I didn't think of awakening in this way, as a process, as something that unfolded over time, perhaps a long time. Instead I expected something sudden. My greedy, thrill-seeking, escapist mind wanted a spiritual awakening to be mind-blowing, to bring perfect, permanent bliss. No doubt many people have experienced moments like this; every spiritual tradition has tales of sudden enlightenment, from Paul on the road to Damascus to Bill Wilson tumbling out of his bed and onto his knees in the hospital. The Buddha's tale of awakening is one of the greatest of all, mythic in its scope and implications; as he sat beneath the Bodhi Tree, the whole of the dharma revealing itself to him—all his past lives appearing to him, the Four Noble Truths and Dependent Origination coming clear.

At times I've tried to manufacture such experiences. On one retreat, late at night, as my mind became very still, an image arose, almost dreamlike. On a small stage, my personality acted out "Kevin," doing its little dance, imagining that this little performance represented the whole of who I was; behind the curtain was a vast ocean, the ocean of being, my true self. I saw how limiting my concepts of who I was were.

Was this an experience of No-Self? Was I verging on awakening?

The next day, in an interview, I told my teacher about my vision.

"That's not it," he said. "That's just a thought, an image." I realized that, once again, my mind was trying to create something dramatic. Enlightenment isn't a movie or a fireworks show, at least not for me.

The gradual process of the Steps, moving incrementally toward awakening, seems blasé in comparison to the inspiring stories we hear. Is there something lacking in those of us whose spiritual growth is gradual, no bells and whistles or burning bushes? Have we missed something? Are we less evolved, or does our spiritual awakening just take another form?

The topic of enlightenment has intrigued me ever since I heard of it as a teenager. Enlightenment was a great motivator for me in some of my early forays into meditation and spirituality. I thought it would solve my emotional problems, my financial problems, my career problems, my relationship problems, and my substance problems. The ultimate high, the ultimate cure, the source of all power and magic—that's what I thought enlightenment was. I don't see it that way anymore.

MEASURING UP

In my teacher training, when I was being given guidance about how to be a skillful meditation instructor and dharma teacher, Jack Kornfield brought up the question of enlightenment. He told us that in his travels in Asia he found many, sometimes contradictory definitions of enlightenment in Buddhist communities. In Burma you went through a structured training, attaining insights one by one as you worked toward "Stream Entry," or the first stage of enlightenment. Your teacher was supposed to be able to judge from your answers to certain questions whether you had attained each insight. Once you completed this process, you were "certified" and could be a teacher. Certain Zen traditions have a similar grading process, using koan, the paradoxical questions used to short-circuit discursive thought. A student moves up from one koan to the next, each answer presumably showing deepening insight.

In Thailand, on the other hand, enlightenment is seen by the Forest Monks as a moment-to-moment experience of awakeness. It's not something to attain through special practices and experiences, but something to be expressed in our daily living.

Some people use the contradictory descriptions of enlightenment as justification to dismiss the whole notion; others say that the experience itself is conditioned by the archetypal religious symbols we carry in our subconscious. One Zen saying is "What makes you think you will know when you are enlightened?"—as though the experience itself might be unrecognizable. There's a certain logic to this. Very often as we are transformed, we can't see it happening. The same could be true of enlightenment. Another saying is, "Now that I'm enlightened, I'm as miserable as ever," implying that enlightenment *doesn't* fix all our problems. Perhaps what we call enlightenment affects us only on a certain level, what we call spiritual, but doesn't necessarily have a direct effect on our "real" lives. This makes a certain amount of sense, too.

In his book *After the Ecstasy, the Laundry*, Jack Kornfield addresses this aspect of awakening. He talks with people who have had experiences of profound spiritual insight and asks them about how those insights became integrated into their lives. Many of the subjects describe long, painful periods of trying to make sense of their awakening, and of the awkwardness of trying to bring their new understandings into their mundane, daily lives. They put the lie to the idea of a magical transformation in which everything is fixed and we live "happily ever after" because we've achieved some special spiritual state.

I'm glad that the Twelve Step spiritual awakening appears in Step Twelve, not Step One. It comes out of a process, the difficult inner and outer work of the first eleven Steps. When my sponsor reads the Steps aloud in a meeting, he emphasizes the word *the* when he says "as *the* result of these Steps." I think this is to remind us of two things: one, that the Steps don't promise anything except spiritual awakening—not material, romantic, or emotional salvation; and that this awakening is in some sense inevitable, it *is* the result of working the first eleven Steps. We may not realize the ways we've changed ("What makes you think you'll know you're enlightened?"), and it may not take the form you expected or wanted ("I'm as miserable as ever"), but it's real, and if you examine yourself and your life objectively, you can see it.

One day I ran into one of my teachers on Telegraph Avenue in Berkeley. We started chatting, wandering up the hill into People's Park, the notorious site of sixties protests, and now a place where groups of homeless people sit on the grass drinking and watching pick-up basketball games. We sat on a bench in a corner of the park, away from the other people. This teacher had guided me in my own teaching somewhat, and I began to tell him about some of my insecurities about my role.

"I wonder if I should really be teaching," I said. "I'm not enlightened, and I know some people say you shouldn't be a teacher until you've at least attained Stream Entry."

"Do you see everything as impermanent?" he asked me.

"Sure," I said.

"And are you aware of suffering everywhere?"

"Yes," I said, gazing across the park at the desperate people gathered around shopping carts.

"Do you believe that you exist as a separate entity?"

Now I saw that he was going through the Three Characteristics—Impermanence, Suffering, and Not-Self—that the Buddha said marked all of existence. Insight into these qualities is the key to wisdom in the Buddhist tradition.

"No," I said. "I see that my sense of identity is created with thought. There's nothing solid about 'Kevin.'"

"Okay," he said. "That's Stream Entry."

I laughed. It couldn't be that simple. Or could it? Once again I was forced to look at my own conceptions of what awakening meant. I thought I'd given up ideas of magical transformation, but I saw that I hadn't completely. I still wanted to have at least one explosive moment to prove my mettle.

For me it can seem, day-to-day, that I'm just the same old person, stuck in my personality, my neuroses, my habit patterns. On the other hand, if I look at where I was when I got sober, the change is radical—almost unbelievable.

Going back to the Three Characteristics, I find it helpful to look at my relationship with Impermanence: I'm much less likely to get stuck in believing that the current situation will last forever, or that my current mind state isn't going to pass. This frees me from a lot of mental struggle and helps me be more accepting of things as they come and go. Awareness of Impermanence is a gift for me, one that helps me value this moment at the same time that I let go more gracefully. I see the natural cycles of life and I move through them with more ease. Aging—my own and that of those around me—feels natural. I'm not always happy about it, but neither am I confused; this is the way life is, and I accept that.

My relationship with the Characteristic of Suffering has changed immensely. For one, I recognize and accept much more my own pain. I see it as part of life that can't be avoided, and I don't see it as a sign of there being something "wrong" with me or with the world. It's just a natural part of things. I also have a strong desire to help others that didn't exist before I began my spiritual journey. Before I got sober—but after I learned Buddhist meditation—I made an effort to work with a hospice program, but it felt so unnatural and forced for me to help someone else that I dropped out. I didn't feel that I had anything to give—maybe I didn't. My own need for care and healing was so great that I really couldn't offer much to anyone else. Besides, self-centeredness was dominant in my personality. I'm still self-centered, but that quality is tempered with concern for those around me, which really only came when my own healing got to a point that there was something left over to give others. Before that, I needed to give myself everything I had.

Self-centeredness, of course, speaks to the third characteristic: Not-Self, sometimes called No-Self. Whatever you call it, as I have become more aware of this reality, of the insubstantiality of my own identity, it has become more natural to give. As this quality has grown, I've seen how incapable I used to be of simply listening to another person. Perhaps I was just socially inept, but only in sobriety did I learn to ask people questions during a conversation. If it wasn't about me, I didn't know what a conversation could be about. The concept of parenting was alien to me as well, since it involved taking care of another being. And even on trivial levels my selfishness showed: I would never offer someone one of my potato chips if I had a small bag. In fact, I remember at one point someone offering me one of their chips and thinking that it was sort of amazing that they could be so generous.

Self-centeredness is, of course, one of the qualities that the Big Book highlights as particularly alcoholic and destructive. And, while the concept of No-Self isn't addressed in Buddhist terms in the Twelve Step literature, the idea of anonymity as "the spiritual foundation" of the program shows the same insight. The Twelve Step founders needed to avoid personal exposure at the time because of social taboos regarding alcoholism; but, upon adopting this policy, they found that it had a more profound value than they had anticipated, creating a powerful basis for spiritual development: no leaders, no stars, no bosses, just partners in sobriety. This agreement to drop our social identity at the door of the meeting rooms results in a more honest, essential revelation of heart and spirit as members share their experience, strength, and hope.

No-Self can be understood on varying levels. On the simplest level, it's about not being self-centered or self-obsessed. For people getting sober, we take baby steps like accepting a service commitment at a meeting that teaches us the value—and joy—of helping others. The deeper insights around No-Self can happen as we begin to question the validity of identity itself. Buddhist practice encourages us to keep examining what we believe about "I" until we see through the construction of the ego. The St. Francis Prayer, which appears in Step Eleven of the *Twelve Steps and Twelve Traditions*, points to the deepest truth about No-Self when it says: "For it is by self-forgetting that one finds. . . . It is by dying that one awakens to Eternal Life." This death is not physical but psychological and spiritual—the death of the ego, of the belief in a separate, solid entity called "I." St. Francis is explaining that when we let go of the concept of self and our attachment to our own self-centered desires, we become aware of the richness of this very moment, which is the only reality and which is always here: Eternal Life. While this prayer may be construed as being about some afterlife or mystical experience, in fact I believe that it is simply speaking of awareness itself, living totally in the moment, that fully embodied presence which Vipassana meditation cultivates.

I've written this whole discussion of awakening so that you might explore what it means for you. The fact is, most of us are neither wholly asleep nor wholly awake; we're some mixture of the two. We need to see the ways in which we've woken up, and we need to cultivate those qualities; we also need to see the ways in which we are still asleep, and we need to abandon those. Alcoholic thinking is often extreme: I'm either perfectly enlightened or a complete spiritual washout. Seeing the ways that we've grown spiritually helps us to have more confidence and self-esteem. Sharing how we've grown helps others to see the possibilities for awakening in themselves. Seeing the ways we still need to grow keeps us from growing arrogant or complacent; it keeps the fire burning in our spiritual practice. Sharing our difficulties helps others to see that they aren't alone in their failings; clarifying in words how we are struggling helps us to know what the solutions are.

Ultimately spiritual awakening must be nurtured. The Steps give us tools for developing and maintaining a spiritual awakening, and as we live a life based on these principles, awakening keeps unfolding and deepening over time. The only real mistake we can make is to stop trying to grow.

OFFERING YOUR HEAD

I'm sitting in the front row of the Thursday-night meditation group in Berkeley. We've just finished the forty-five-minute sitting period, and James, the teacher, is getting ready to give his talk. He starts tapping the microphone but no sound comes out. He looks around, confused. I jump out of my seat.

"What's wrong?" I ask.

"This doesn't seem to be working," he says.

"Let me take a look," I say.

I follow the microphone cable back to the amplifier backstage. I find that it's come loose from the amp, so I plug it back in. Then I check the levels on the mixer and ask James to test the microphone again.

"Testing, one, two, three . . ."

A screech jumps out of the speakers, and I quickly turn the volume down. I look at the equalizer and see that the high frequencies are boosted, so I back them off and gradually bring the volume back up. Now when James speaks there's no feedback and the microphone is working fine.

"Thanks," says James. I've just gotten a new job. For the next two years I'm there virtually every Thursday to help with the sound.

When I jumped up to help, I knew exactly where that impulse came from: my training in Twelve Step meetings to be of service. There I had learned to set up chairs, make coffee, put out cups and ashtrays, sweep and mop floors, empty garbage, visit prisons and rehabs, sponsor other alcoholics and addicts, and of course, take the speaker's seat when asked.

The suggestion that we "tried to help other alcoholics" quickly spreads beyond the walls of the meetings and becomes a guide for living.

For several years the Thursday meditation group would go Christmas caroling at hospitals and old folks' homes. (Don't ask me why Buddhists are singing Christmas carols.) I remember James smiling as he played the guitar in front of an old woman who smiled back. Between songs I heard their exchange.

"You're happy," said the old woman.

"Yes," said James, smiling. "I love playing for you."

"That's the secret," she said. "Giving to people. Everybody thinks it's 'take, take, take,' but it's not."

"The secret," said James. "That's right. Hidden right before our eyes."

"Keep it up," said the woman.

James smiled and started singing the next carol. His natural generosity shone from his eyes.

One of Kabir's poems, translated by Robert Bly, says this perfectly. It uses the term *bhakti*, the Hindu word for spiritual devotion. In the poem, devotion is expressed for "him"—God, I suppose, but to me it's really about devotion to our spiritual path, whatever it is, and specifically to being awake in this moment and every moment, engaging fully in life:

The bhakti path winds in a delicate way.

On this path there is no asking and no not asking.

The ego simply disappears the moment you touch him.

The joy of looking for him is so immense that you just dive in,

and coast around like a fish in the water.

If anyone needs a head, the lover leaps up to offer his.

Kabir's poems touch on the secrets of this bhakti.

We could understand the poem to mean that we give away our ego—our "head," offering it up to God or the spirit. The poem expresses the deepest devotion: the willingness to give your life for another. The Metta Sutta, the Buddha's discourse on lovingkindness, talks about this love like this:

> *Even as a mother,*
>
> *Protects with her life*
>
> *Her child, her only child.*
>
> *So with a boundless heart*
>
> *Should one cherish all living beings.*

Step Twelve, with its simple suggestion to help, opens up the possibility of these powerful sentiments.

I told you about the person who asked me how to become a meditation teacher, and that I suggested that they focus on their own practice and let that possibility unfold if it was meant to. The other thing I told him, and I always tell people who want to teach, is that they should just be of service. This is how my own teaching career started.

It was another Thursday night. James announced that a local homeless services organization wanted to start a meditation group and that anyone who was interested in helping should come up afterward. I felt that he was looking at me as he made this announcement, and, although the idea of teaching meditation to homeless people sounded intimidating, after the class that night I volunteered.

"I was hoping you would," said James.

I felt as though I were offering my head—I had no idea what I was getting into, if I was qualified, or if I really wanted to do it. But my Twelve Step training compelled me to be of service, and so I instinctively responded.

Soon after, I gathered with a few others at the homeless center to organize the classes. The Berkeley Ecumenical Chaplaincy for the Homeless provided many services: clothing, job placement, housing placement, and spiritual counseling. The idea that homeless people would want to meditate seemed odd to me. "Shouldn't I be giving them food, clothes, and money?" I thought. "What good will meditation do for them?"

I soon found out. We met in a small carpeted lounge in a church near the university campus. The half dozen or so attendees sat in a circle, on chairs and couches or on the floor. I began by leading a guided meditation. Some of the attendees would fall asleep, but others would sit, backs straight, completely still. It turned out that many of the homeless people had done some kind of meditation before and were hungry for that spiritual connection. In their sharing, they didn't talk about their situations on the street, but rather their meditation practice, asking the same kinds of questions that practitioners often ask, about the pain in their knees or wandering thoughts. Surprise, surprise, they're just like me, I realized.

When I stood up that night and volunteered to teach the homeless meditation group, I began the path that led to this book. I did it because I knew by then that the secret to happiness is giving, not getting, and that freedom comes through openness and letting go. In the Twelve Step tradition we say, "You can't keep it if you don't give it away." Over the coming years I would learn more through teaching than I'd ever learned as a student.

SHOWING UP

When I was seventeen, I dropped out of high school for the second time. It had been a tough couple of years. Mononucleosis had wrecked my sophomore year, putting me back a year. My bouts with depression weren't alleviated by the weekly therapy sessions. My older brother dropped out of college and came home to deal with his own struggles. And I began to drink and take drugs. Right before the holidays, the band I'd been in since I was fourteen broke up.

At that age, Christmas and New Year's were times of hanging out with friends, going to parties, and having fun. Now that I was a full-fledged drinker and had discovered pot the previous summer, those weeks were even more wild. When January came, the idea of returning to school, pointless, boring high school, was impossible for me. Instead I lay on the couch. My parents didn't know what to do for me. I'm sure that by then they were questioning their own parenting skills, having seen their sons have so many difficulties. They'd tried different schools for me, and professional help. But still, I just lay there. One day I tried to write a song. It came out sounding like something by the Doors, completely unoriginal—and rather bleak.

My only escape from the pain I was feeling was sneaking out at night with my friends and getting high. At the end of the month my parents gave up and had me institutionalized. I was grateful.

There's no doubt I was suffering from depression at that time, but looking back, the one thing I know I didn't understand then was the idea of showing up, just doing something because it needed to be done, even if you didn't feel like doing it. I thought that if I felt this way, passive, depressed, despondent, that I had to act that way as well. I believed that my emotions were telling me who I was and how to be. "You're unhappy. Don't move." Only when I got sober did I begin to realize that it was possible to show up even when I didn't feel like it. What a concept.

Addicts and alcoholics have the habit of running from life. Running from their feelings, their problems, their responsibilities. As their disease progresses, their world becomes smaller and smaller, and what they are willing to deal with becomes more and more limited. Abusing substances itself is a way to hide out from life. This is why Twelve Step programs emphasize the idea of showing up.

Initially, this means, quite literally, coming to meetings, going to work, and appearing wherever you have made a commitment. If Woody Allen is right when he says, "Eighty percent of success is showing up," then simply following through in this way gives us a much better chance in life. In fact, it guarantees at least a B-minus.

When I began to follow this principle in sobriety, my life began to change. I showed up for work even though I didn't feel like it; I went back to school even though I was afraid; I kept my commitments at meetings even when I was tired or bored or had something else I'd rather do. The consistency of showing up allowed things to really get better in my life. I gained respect, experience, and security at work; I wound up with an advanced degree that opened up my career; and my sobriety became firmly established as I became part of the sober community. Most of all, my life started to feel integrated, not scattered and unfocused as it had before.

One story points to the profound importance of showing up. A single, sober Buddhist friend, Marietta, decided to adopt in her late thirties. She chose to take on a four-year-old child who had been abused in infancy and suffers from attachment disorder. Besides being an enormous act of compassion, this has required extensive education for Marietta. One of the things she learned about attachment disorder is that the children with this syndrome act as if they have no conscience. They apparently can't feel compassion or guilt. They don't show regret or shame when they hurt someone. Marietta learned that there's only one way for such children to develop these skills: to form a deep and abiding bond with an adult. This is Marietta's role: to show up for her daughter. So, the cure for this dangerous disorder is presence, commitment, showing up. To take it a step further, it becomes clear that every child who does *not* have this disorder has had a parent or parents who *did* show up in a continuous, reliable way. So, each of us who has had a normal upbringing has benefited from this quality that Step Twelve fosters.

Recovery from alcoholism or addiction is much like this process. In a sense, we have abused ourselves, and in order to recover our hearts—our compassion, our conscience—we must continually show up for ourselves until we begin to heal.

Meditation is another form of showing up. It's showing up for this moment, bringing our awareness into the present. People have the habit of spending most of their time thinking about the past and future. This is one of the first things you notice when you try to learn to meditate. Bringing your attention back to your breath, back to your present experience, means showing up in the most profound way. It's difficult because of the momentum of thinking that's present in the mind, but ultimately it's a question of living versus not living. Our drug addiction is a form of death, of turning off our life; in the same way, even the subtle movements of mind away from the present are attempts to escape from what is real. But when we do this, we miss our actual life. It's choosing to not live fully. Given how precious life is held to be, isn't it odd that we push it away?

Soon after she adopted, Marietta, a true bodhisattva, realized that it wasn't enough to show up just for her daughter and her own sobriety and awakening. She took the lead in forming a family sangha. Her commitment led to what today is a thriving community. Twice a month families gather and the kids get simple lessons on Buddhist principles and play games while the parents practice meditation and discuss mindful parenting.

It's said that when the Buddha awoke each morning, he looked out with his divine eye to see who needed his teachings that day. Then he would walk until he found that person, "carrying the message" of freedom. This spirit of infinite compassion is embodied in the Bodhisattva Vow and expressed by the spirit of service seen at every Buddhist event. Volunteers are the backbone of the Buddhist community, doing so much of the organizational work that makes the dharma available. Just as in the Twelve Step community, which is supported by people's desire to give something back, the bodhisattva volunteers are motivated by the great compassion and selflessness that their practice arouses, and find that the most natural way to respond to those feelings is to immerse themselves in giving, in making easily available the wisdom teachings that have so inspired them.

BREADTH OF PRACTICE: ALL OUR AFFAIRS

In Step Eleven I talked about depth of practice, the vital foundation for spiritual development. When I first began to practice Buddhist meditation, I thought that retreats were the only meaningful form of practice. As I talked about in Step Ten, I had the idea that if I could just do enough retreats, I'd be okay, and that otherwise I would inevitably lose my concentration and mindfulness. This was an addictive way to approach meditation—trying to sustain the high. Through daily mindfulness, and developing other qualities as well, I began to see that my growth was broader than just the development of deep states of meditation.

When Step Twelve says we should "practice these principles in all our affairs," it sends us off into the world with the ultimate task: Don't just do this stuff at special times, do it *all* the time. How can we manage this? Well, the Buddhist teaching on the Eightfold Path is a great guide—again.

The Path starts with Right View. Here we see the truth clearly, that there is suffering and the possibility of freedom from suffering. This inspires us to live our life in a way that will free us and others from suffering. This is Step One, and it is also Step Twelve. In Step One we see suffering in its most basic way, in our disease or dysfunction. In Step Twelve we see that we need to address suffering "in all our affairs." When we perfect Right View, this is enlightenment. We see the truth without the fog of delusion, of fantasy, of fear and resentment. This is where the moment-to-moment practice of returning to the breath, to mindfulness, guides us.

This vision and inspiration leads us to the second factor of the Path: Right Intention—willingness. Now that we see the possibility of freedom, we set our minds to it. Right Intention is difficult to carry through. Yes, we want happiness and freedom, but it's hard to make the sacrifices to attain it. In every step of the path we keep falling off, but Right Intention brings us back to starting over each time, coming back to the breath and coming back to our core values. Right Intention also means that we don't blame ourselves or beat ourselves up when we do fail; we just remember that the Law of Impermanence means that we can't stay permanently mindful and concentrated, that all we really need to do is "keep coming back" to the breath, to the moment, to our core values and intentions. The Steps point out the importance of intention at every stage. Knowing why we are doing this difficult work inspires us through the good times and the bad.

Once we've established this intention, the Eightfold Path guides us to live skillfully on the practical level. First this means Right Action, following the precepts. Here we commit ourselves not to kill, either physically, emotionally, or spiritually—a commitment to life is a commitment to being aware and accepting what life gives us, not shutting it out with drugs and alcohol or TV or sex or food. We commit ourselves not to take what isn't given; not to harm others or ourselves with our sexuality; not to harm others with harsh or untrue speech; not to harm others or ourselves with intoxicants. If we follow these Precepts, our lives will be transformed.

Right Livelihood guides us to find work that is meaningful, helpful, and inspiring for us. It also guides us to bring our spiritual life into our workplace, not to bring a different set of values to work than those we apply outside work.

Obviously, there are some professions that have more noble aims than others, but more important than the particular occupation is the intention we bring to it. When the person at the airline counter goes out of their way to help you make your flight; when the assembly-line worker carefully removes the defective tire; when the gas company repairman comes out in the driving rain to find a leak; these are all forms of Right Livelihood, bringing love and care to our work.

For many years I've worked as a technical writer for a software company, a pretty dry and mechanical job. The way I try to express Right Livelihood in this work is to realize that the person who is encountering the software for the first time is depending on my words to guide them. If I take real care, I will guide their learning process and make their life easier—not exactly heroic work, but service, nonetheless.

While we usually see work as something people do for strictly selfish ends, there's another way in which we can see that everyone in a society is contributing to the maintenance of that society, everyone's work serves everyone else. Of course there are exceptions—people who steal and kill or are just plain selfish, lazy, or greedy—but most people are contributing. Most people are part of the web of Right Livelihood that supports us all.

Right Speech appears again, showing the importance the Buddha put on how we communicate with others, as it is one of the precepts as well as one of the steps in the Eightfold Path.

The last three aspects of the Eightfold Path are typically associated with meditation, but in our daily lives they are equally important. Right Effort guides us to use our energy skillfully—to not waste energy and effort on useless activities—and to rouse the qualities needed for skillful action. Right Effort helps us avoid destructive behavior and cultivate positive habits. Right Effort is where we look at the "D" word: discipline. This quality, which has become somewhat demonized in our self-indulgent culture, is critical to a daily meditation practice. We need to find a way to apply it without creating aversion or resistance.

One of the suggestions my teacher James makes is to form a commitment to sit, to meditate, every day—even if it's only for a minute, literally. Some days I have plenty of time and energy and it's effortless and natural. At other times, it seems impossible to find a minute, much less twenty or more for meditation. Still, I go to my meditation cushion and plop down. Usually when I do this, a minute doesn't feel like enough. Especially when it's been a tough day, the relief of being still is too pleasant to give up so quickly. For me, and I'm sure for many others, this simple lesson about consistency and commitment is key. In early sobriety—and beyond—I have gone to meetings simply because of this teaching. And I never regret it. With meditation I find the same result. Many evenings I haven't felt like going to a meditation group, feeling that I was too tired to get anything out of it. But I'm always amazed to find that by the end of the evening, my energy is restored and my practice is invigorated again. Yes, we need discipline to show up, but once we do, most of the time our practice will carry us.

The last two parts of the Eightfold Path are Mindfulness and Concentration, the key components of meditation. In our instant culture, where speed and efficiency are core values, to approach tasks with care and attention goes against the stream. Just for fun, next time you go through a checkout line, see how many times the checker is distracted from attention to your purchases: the phone rings; the manager interrupts; another customer asks a question. Our interactions are so fragmented that we often don't see the person standing in front of us. Recently I bought a cell phone. I find it very convenient under certain circumstances. But, I've also noticed how it takes my attention away from the environment I'm in, so I don't see what's around me, and focuses it all on this communication with someone who isn't there. It's as though we were all floating around in little pods, separate worlds circumscribed by our self-interests, personal obsessions, fears, wants, and dreams. Mindfulness and concentration help us to reengage with the world.

For many Buddhists, this reengagement moves beyond the personal to the social and political. The Buddhist Peace Fellowship is the foremost organization in the movement called Engaged Buddhism. Here people use the insights and compassion developed in practice to address issues in the public sphere. While their opinions may be held very strongly, their way of expressing them is not confrontational or violent. In fact, the preferred means of protest for engaged Buddhists is silent meditation. I attended one such event in San Francisco, a peace rally.

As I came out of the subway, the streets were swarmed with protestors carrying signs. On a stage set up at the bottom of Market Street a speaker ranted through a PA system with numbing anger and self-righteousness. It was a scene of restlessness and chaos. I found my way behind the stage and down a grassy strip to where a group sat meditating. As I approached I felt the power of their silence. This was my destination, and I felt comforted as I found a place and joined them. Here amidst the anger and confusion we sat.

In this approach to political protest, we don't separate the ends from the means. If we want peace, we must be peaceful. We don't commit acts of violence in the service of ending the death penalty or eliminating nuclear weapons. Silent witnessing calls to our own conscience, our own inner voice to ask, "What is right?" Rather than shouting opinions and trying to coerce others into a viewpoint, this witnessing is an invitation to find our own answers, in a careful, thoughtful way.

As I sat on the grass, bringing my own meditative attention into the protest, I felt the power of our collective effort, our bodhisattva intention. Our silent voices seemed to speak more loudly, and certainly more clearly, than all the orators on the nearby stage. People milling about would stop and stare at us—the hundred of us doing nothing. If such observers asked themselves, "What are they doing?" as they gazed at us, or even, "Why are they sitting there like that?" then our work was successful. In fact, Engaged Buddhism doesn't so much seek to offer answers, but to encourage such questions.

BREADTH OF PRACTICE: DAILY MINDFULNESS

There are many ways we can apply mindfulness to our lives, and I'd like to share a couple that work for me. One of the great exponents and teachers on this subject is Thich Nhat Hanh. In his book *Present Moment, Wonderful Moment*, he even gives a whole set of verses to be repeated during every daily activity to focus the mind on the present action.

One of the easiest activities to do mindfully, I think, is walking. On meditation retreats we learn to walk mindfully, usually quite slowly. Being aware of the bottom of the feet, the movement of the legs, the whole motion and rhythm of walking is an easy, natural way to bring ourselves into the present moment. You can do this when you are walking down the street; when you are walking from your cubicle to the water cooler; when you are hiking, shopping, or rushing to make the train. Again, simply by placing our attention on the sensations happening in our body, the mind returns to the present, and our experience comes into focus.

Many people use certain cues to trigger daily mindfulness: whenever they walk through a door or grasp a doorknob, they remember to be mindful; if there are steps in your home or office, you can try to remember to come back to the present when you go up or down; whenever you step outside, you can simply look around at nature and feel and breathe the air.

All these forms of mindfulness, and many others, are based on awareness of the body: washing dishes, making your bed, taking a shower, exercising—all of these are ripe opportunities for awareness of the body. It helps that we aren't looking at a screen—either computer or TV—when we are doing them.

Another form of mindfulness is to pay attention to mental activities. This is what we do when we are being mindful of our reactions when listening to someone speak, noticing judgments or the desire to interrupt or change their words. It's also helpful to notice the tendency to want to change our experience. This is, of course, the root of the alcoholic/addict's dilemma—the desire to feel differently. First noticing that craving, then not reacting to it, strengthens our sobriety, and also begins to wear down our habitual escapist tendencies. And when we aren't escaping, we are, by definition, here and now, being present, with mindfulness for what is happening in our lives.

Begin to notice when you want to be distracted. Say you're in the car and you reach habitually to turn on the radio. What happens if you don't do that right away but ride in silence, at least for a little while? At one point, I began to notice how I would listen to the radio no matter what, even if I didn't like what was playing. So, I made the resolution that, if after checking all the radio presets I didn't find something I wanted to listen to, I'd turn it off. For an addict like me, this was radical. To do this with the TV can be even more difficult—it's much easier to turn a TV on than to turn it off.

We can apply this attention to food as well, even reading or using the telephone. As I walk around these days and see so many people in cars and on the street on cell phones, I can't help but think that they are just bored. I don't think they are all making critical calls. This craving for escape pulls us away from our life, away from engagement, and ultimately causes more stress and exhaustion. It doesn't mean we don't listen to the radio, watch TV, or use a cell phone, it just means that we pause before beginning and check what our motivation is. We also try to stop when we're done, not just keep making calls or flipping the remote out of boredom.

Again, this is about "progress, not perfection." Of course we'll have our moments when we'll just get sucked in—my favorite thing to zone out on is Sports Center on ESPN—but we do our best.

Another way to practice daily mindfulness is through the lovingkindness practice. We can do this practice in quick moments throughout the day. When we hug our children or our partner or friend, this *is* lovingkindness, but we can consciously add a silent word or just a moment of appreciation. With our children, we often are working so hard at taking care of them and trying to help them become better people that we forget to just look at them and appreciate them. Sometimes I'll see someone smile as I walk down the street hand-in-hand with my daughter and I'll remember how sweet and beautiful she is. I will look at her and try to see her—and us—through the eyes of a stranger, seeing a devoted father and daughter walking happily together, and a surge of lovingkindness, appreciation, and gratitude passes over me. I'm there, present for myself and my daughter.

Besides appreciating those we love, we can appreciate those we encounter. When I go through a toll booth or leave a parking lot and pay the attendant, I have a habit of consciously wishing the person happiness, this person who is sitting doing a drudge job on a smoggy highway or dank parking lot—and of course, it helps if I smile so they might actually feel the lovingkindness. There are so many people we encounter in our day who are helping us, and each of them can be someone to offer lovingkindness.

I can even offer lovingkindness to politicians—especially the ones I don't agree with. I see them every day in the newspaper, and when I do, a negative feeling often arises in me—anger, resentment, fear. When I take the time to remember that they, too, want to be happy and are doing the best they can, I let down my resentment and offer them some lovingkindness.

One practice I've found very interesting is offering lovingkindness to everyone I see on the street and then watching how my mind reacts. For a time when I was working in San Francisco, I did this practice every day from the time I got off the train until I reached my office. Each person I passed, I would say to myself, "May you be happy." What I found was that, even in these very brief moments, I had fairly strong reactions to every person: I didn't want to look at the dirty homeless person; I felt resentment toward the lawyer in the pinstripe suit; lovingkindness instantly turned into lust for the attractive woman; I felt completely neutral about the overweight, middle-aged woman. All my biases and judgments were laid bare in those few minutes, all the tendencies of my mind to grasp, to push away, or to shut down. This showed me the totally reactive qualities of the mind, and the fact that I really wasn't making a lot of the judgments myself—they were conditioned, automatic responses, and if I wanted to look at the world differently, be more open-minded and compassionate, I had to be careful that I didn't allow these instantaneous judgments to control my thinking. I need to be aware of those judgments as they come up, and then I need to let go if I want to engage authentically in the world. This is the ultimate lesson of daily mindfulness, noticing the habitual tendencies of mind, and replacing them with conscious thoughts and actions based on our best intention—"practicing these principles in all our affairs."

Back to Step One

After my first meditation retreat, I wrote a song called "Vipassana Blues," with the lines, "back to the breath and start all over again; when will it end?" Practice *doesn't* end. As the story goes, right before he died, the Buddha told his followers something like, "Everything's imperманent; keep practicing with diligence," then he went into meditation. He died while meditating. That's a pretty good clue as to how we should practice: right up to the end.

There is no end of the Steps, either. We don't get to Step Twelve and graduate. Instead, the Steps keep repeating—or we keep repeating them—in different configurations and patterns. Sometimes we go back to One, recognizing our powerlessness over alcohol or drugs; or we find ourselves powerless over something else, and use Step One to help us deal with that. At other times we find we need to do some inventory, a Tenth Step or full Fourth Step, then go through Five, Six, and Seven again. Or we realize there's an amends we haven't made. And of course, with prayer, meditation, and service, our lives are full of Step work. In fact, "work" doesn't seem like the right word for me. Maybe Step "joy." After all, it's this "work" that makes life worth living, that brings richness and meaning to our lives.

With all these words that I've written, my great, simple hope is that they bring some degree of that joy into people's lives. There's so much suffering in the world, and alcoholism, drug addiction, eating disorders, and all the other addictions and dysfunctions are their own, special hell realms. When someone who's trying to get sober calls me or talks to me in a meeting my heart practically breaks, I want so much for them to have what we have in sobriety, the possibility of living the life they deserve and which is their potential. Of course, I can't give them sobriety and I can't give them that life, none of us can. This is what the Buddha was saying; you have to do it for yourself. I only hope that this book will be a small piece of the rebuilding and ultimate redemption of people who do find the way to a clean and sober life.

In the Buddhist tradition of selflessness, our spiritual work is dedicated to others. In that spirit I close with these words:

I dedicate the merit of my work on this book to the awakening of all beings; may all beings be free from alcoholism and drug addiction and from the harm that addiction causes; may all beings be happy, joyous, and free from suffering.

GRATITUDE AND APPRECIATION

Without my wife, Rosemary Graham, this book might never have come into being. She helped me see the loss of a job as a "sabbatical," giving me the support I needed to write a proposal. Her editing was vital in helping me find my voice. Thank you, my love.

Three full prostrations to each of my teachers. In particular, Wes Nisker and James Baraz have guided and supported me for many years. I value each of you immensely as friends and teachers.

Ajahn Amaro has been a great inspiration to me over the past dozen years. His notes on the first draft and our conversations about the book were tremendously helpful. The other teachers who have been so important to me include Jack Kornfield, Joseph Goldstein, Leigh Brasington, Ayya Khema, Ruth Denison, Christopher Titmuss, Greg Kramer, Caitriona Reed, Annick Mahieu (Sunanda), Jacqueline Mandell, Stephen Levine, Stephen Batchelor, and Akasa Levi.

Noah Levine's belief in the project gave me the confidence to pursue it when I was still wondering if anyone would care. His thoughts on the first three Steps helped me form those chapters.

Many thanks to Santikaro Bhikkhu for sharing unpublished translations of material from his teacher, the great Thai master Buddhadasa Bhikkhu; Jeff Kitzes (Zen Master Bon Soeng) took my urgent call about the Heart Sutra. Reverend Heng Sure patiently discussed prayer from the Pure Land perspective. Rebecca Dixon and Barbara Newhall were discerning readers at important moments in the process.

Every person who has taught with me over the last few years has contributed directly to this book. Each of them helped me with pieces of the Buddhism/Twelve Step puzzle: Noah Levine, Ann Buck, Lloyd Burton, Sandra Weinberg, Dori Langevin, and Larry Yang. Thanks for the sweet teachings. Let's do it again soon.

Thanks also to all the Community Dharma Leaders with whom I was trained. Our sangha has been so rich and nurturing. I love you all.

I'm also grateful to the meditation centers that have supported these teachings: Spirit Rock Meditation Center, Insight Meditation Center of the Mid-Peninsula, Insight Meditation Community of Colorado, New York Insight Meditation Center, and Insight Meditation Center of Washington. Thanks to all the staff and volunteers whose grace and generosity allow these centers to thrive.

Stephanie Tade is the editor that an author dreams of. Her belief in the project and her faith in me surprised and inspired me from the start. Our friendship has been an amazing bonus. Chris Potash, who did the line edits and much of the heavy lifting, combines a no-nonsense professionalism with an easygoing attitude. Thanks for pulling me back from the cliff.

My agent, Candice Fuhrman, was the first publishing professional to back her belief in me with action. Her confidence in me as a writer makes me think I might try this again.

Many writing teachers have helped me with my craft over the years. Jim Krusoe, Judith Grossman, and Jane Anne Staw have had the most direct impact. Thanks to each of you for guiding me at a critical time in my writing life.

Thanks also to Leslie Berriman for well-timed advice and support.

Many Twelve Step members contributed their stories and experiences to this book. My immense gratitude to them.

The Monday Night Buddhism/Twelve Step group helped me develop many of the central ideas of the book and my Buddhism/Twelve Step workshop; my other Monday Night group helped me to learn to be a teacher. Thanks to the Berkeley Wednesday Night meditation group for your support, your presence, and your kindness. Thanks to the volunteers who keep the group going.

Thanks to Daniel Doane, my best dharma buddy for all the late-night conversations in the car in front of your house. I needed that.

Thanks to my sponsor for a thousand insights and all the years of love and kindness.

Both Buddhism and the Twelve Steps are kept alive, generation to generation, by sincere and deeply committed practitioners. To all of them I give my thanks for passing on these traditions. My deepest gratitude to the founders: Bill W., Bob S., and the Buddha.